M000275594

The Hum of the World

The publisher and the University of California Press Foundation gratefully acknowledge the generous support of the Constance and William Withey Endowment Fund in History and Music.

.   .   .   .   .

The publisher also gratefully acknowledges the generous support of the Director's Circle of the University of California Press Foundation, whose members are

Stephen and Melva Arditti
Nancy Boas
Gifford Combs
John Geiger
Gary and Cary Hart
R. Marilyn Lee and Harvey Schneider
Alejandro Portes
Rowena and Marc Singer
Thomas White

The Hum of the World

A PHILOSOPHY OF LISTENING

Lawrence Kramer

UNIVERSITY OF CALIFORNIA PRESS

University of California Press, one of the most distinguished university presses in the United States, enriches lives around the world by advancing scholarship in the humanities, social sciences, and natural sciences. Its activities are supported by the UC Press Foundation and by philanthropic contributions from individuals and institutions. For more information, visit www.ucpress.edu.

University of California Press
Oakland, California

© 2018 Lawrence Kramer

Cataloging-in-Publication Data is on file with the Library of Congress.

ISBN 978-0-520-30349-2 (cloth)
ISBN 978-0-520-97272-8 (e-edition)

27 26 25 24 23 22 21 20 19
10 9 8 7 6 5 4 3 2

Contents

Prelude   1

Sound and Knowledge   3

The Audiable: An Introduction   4

Some Leitmotifs   7

The Standard of Vision   8

A Philosophy of Listening?   11

Constructive Description   14

Sight, Sound, and Language   16

The Sound of Words   25

Seeing, Saying, and Hearing   27

The Audiable: Variations on a Theme   29

Music in the Air   40

"No Sound without Music"   50

Language and the Human   51

Lord Bacon's Echoes   53

Ripple Effects: Distant Voices   56

The Infinite Broadcast   60

Immanence   64

Reading Transfigured: St. Augustine   66

To the Life: The Image   69

Moving Pictures   71

Modern Times: The Cartoon   72

The Sound of Meaning   76

Music and the Audiable: A Suite in Three Movements   78

Plato's Singing School   81

Musical Synesthesia   83

The Music of Language   85

The Soundscape   86

Song   88

Noise and Silence   91

Fish, Flesh, or Fowl   92

Sensory Hybrids   96

"Waiting to Be the Music"   106

Circle Songs   109

Forty-Part Motets   110

The Ether   113

Elemental Media   115

Elemental Fluids   116

Writing the Soundscape   120

Haunting Melodies   123

The Lifelike: The Undead   130

Beyond Words?   133

The Audiable and the Audible   143

Into Silence   144

Enchantments of the Name   147

The Inaudible   152

On Saying "I am"   155

The Shriek   162

Metal   163

Here Comes That Song Again   165

The Mirror of Silence   172

Rhythmic Hearing   174

Media All the Way Down   175

The Auditory Window   178

Cacophony: Dispossession (Beckett)   181

Euphony: Repossession (Beckett)   183

Worldly Dissonance   185

Sounds of Battle: The Civil War   186

Sounds of Battle: World War I   188

Ulysses in Auschwitz   194

Intermezzo   197

Sounding Bodies   198

Pandemonium?   202

Songs of Entropy   204

By Hand   207

Past and Present   208

Consciousness   210

Acknowledgments   *221*

Index   *241*

Prelude

This is a book about the meaning of sound. The rise of sound studies across the humanities has drawn welcome attention to the material dimension of sound and to the technologies that shape auditory culture. These advances need to be complemented by a new examination of how sound is represented and imagined. *The Hum of the World* conducts such an examination across a wide range of sources, including artistic and conceptual sources from classical times to the present. Its purpose is to outline the fundamental character of auditory experience in the Western world as we describe or narrate or record or interpret it—generally speaking, as we apprehend it.

To that end, the book's segments gravitate around two core ideas. The first is that sound is the measure of life. Sound is the primary medium through which the presence and persistence of life assume tangible form. The sense of life spreads outward from sound, which conveys it as feeling and imparts it as meaning. This relationship is primary. The positive experience of aliveness is not merely in accord with sound, but inaccessible and perhaps inconceivable without it. The second idea is that this animating power of sound acts as a general background to sense perception. But it does not always remain in the background. The diffuse hum of the world can also become audible its own right. It has made itself heard in numerous venues from classical times to the present. When that happens, animation and the potentiality of sound fuse into a positive form capable of changing the apprehension of anyone who hears it.

These features of sound are both sensory and symbolic. They rank among the foremost means by which sound acquires a history. They also give listening the power to observe and reflect on itself—to become

1

self-aware. Recognizing them makes possible a philosophy of listening that greatly expands the scope of what sound, as sound, can tell us. The sense of hearing grounds the sense of being.

II.

In form, this book models itself after some of my favorite texts, each composed in the spirit of textual and conceptual adventure: Montaigne's *Essays*, Nietzsche's *The Gay Science*, Benjamin's *One-Way Street*, Adorno's *Minima Moralia*, Wittgenstein's *Philosophical Investigations*, Barthes's *A Lover's Discourse*, Derrida's *The Postcard*. In other words, *The Hum of the World* is an assembly of varied but interrelated reflections, set out in an intuitive sequence meant to suggest flow rather than structure. The flow also belongs to the auditory phenomenon that gives the book its subject and to the conceptual process that the book seeks to embody. The associative form deliberately avoids chronological or topical arrangement. It seeks to create a kind of soundscape in words, a loosely bounded multiplicity full of overlaps, cross-references, echoes, and intimations. Once past the first few sections, which introduce a number of key concepts, the vignettes and short essays that compose the book may equally well be read consecutively or piecemeal, in no particular order. Even segments that overlap may be read independently; cross-references are noted in the text. The freewheeling organization is meant to be reader-friendly, as is the writing, which aims to be evocative but is jargon-free.

To give sound its due, to recognize that experience is more essentially auditory than we may have supposed, is to listen widely. Both the topics to be addressed and the means to address them may belong, together or separately, to philosophy, aesthetics, music, media, literature, science, and history, on the understanding that the divisions between these fields of inquiry are more apparent than real, or at least thoroughly permeable. In recent years the boundaries between speculative and empirical thought have become the subject of renewed debate between those who want to harden them and those who want to break them down. It should already be obvious which side I'm on.[1]

What follows will divide, with inevitable overlaps, between speculative passages and passages of what would ordinarily be called readings, but here might be better identified as soundings. The rest is up to you. Treat, if you will, this book as a sounding board. Please scribble in the margins.

Sound and Knowledge

The world is alive with sound. The aim of this book is to gloss this deceptively simple sentence. The gloss is cumulative, a resonance produced by the series of segments conceived as an extended polyphony. The topics vary widely, but certain themes keep returning, as they might in a piece of music: what sound makes known, what listening reveals, what music conveys, what hearing promises, and one thing more, held by all these in common, which will take some explaining: a phenomenon I propose to call *the audiable*, or the hum of the world.

In recent years hearing has come to rival sight, even to equal it, among the principal means by which we make sense of things. To a large degree this change has been driven by technology. We live (at any rate in "advanced" societies) in a world saturated by recorded and transmitted sound, by ringtones and notifications and voices on mobile phones, by music and media everywhere. These sounds no longer seem to strike us as noisy; they have become the very sound of the ordinary. Our nineteenth-century forebears heard a similar change in the once-obtrusive sounds of modern mechanical technology. Our saturated sonic environment has, like those mechanical sounds, become second nature.

In this context, the development of a new academic field, sound studies, was inevitable. Cultural history is in part being rewritten as auditory history; our heightened awareness of the soundscape of modern life extends retrospectively to its predecessors. In one respect, however, this auditory turn is still incomplete. It has left unanswered, has perhaps barely even asked, a fundamental question. How does finally learning to listen change our conception of the world? In other words, what does sound, *as* sound, contribute to the production of human knowledge?

By "knowledge" here—and the point is essential—I mean neither sense experience nor empirical understanding. The knowledge in question is the extrapolation from experience that constitutes the work of the modern humanities, the knowledge produced by critical thought, interpretation, representation, narration, imagination, philosophical reasoning, and so on. The value of this knowledge has always been subject to debate. It has most recently been challenged by cognitive science on one hand and information processing on the other. The survival of humanistic knowledge can no longer be assumed. In asking its question about the work of sound, this book seeks simultaneously to practice, extend, and ratify the mode of knowledge that it examines.

To that end the book draws attention to a phenomenon that we know well from experience but have never named. The first step, then, is to name it. The name it will go by here is the *audiable*. That sounds like *audible*, and so it should, since sound is very much the issue. But the audible and the audiable are not the same, and the difference matters. What, then, is the audiable, and why does it matter? That question will require more than one answer, but one will have to be enough to start with.

The Audiable

AN INTRODUCTION

I.

The simplest way to characterize the audiable is as the material promise of sound. This definition comes with a proviso that enriches but also complicates it. The promise of sound is not made in silence. It is a threshold phenomenon with its own audibility. The audiable is the precursor of sound to come, yet it is also experienced through hearing, as if auditory sensation had a future tense. The audiable is the hum of the world. One has to listen for it. But how can that be done? How *has* it been done, and to what effect?

A host of instances will follow these introductory passages, but here, itself a kind of promise, is just one. *In Teaching a Stone to Talk*, Annie Dillard describes how she, and how anyone, can come to discern what I call the audiable.[1] It is not easy to do. It her case it requires a certain asceticism, mingled with a refusal, at long last, to be distracted:

> At a certain point you say to the woods, to the sea, to the mountains, the world, Now I am ready. Now I will stop and be wholly attentive. You empty yourself and wait, listening. After a time you hear it: there is nothing there. There is nothing but those things only, those created objects, discrete, growing or holding, being rained on or raining, held, flooding or ebbing, standing, or spread. You feel the world's word as a tension, a hum, a single chorused note everywhere the same. This is it: this hum is silence.

What Dillard hears is that silence is not the absence of sound. It is the sound one cannot yet hear, but which, paradoxically, can be heard in advance. This hum that is silence is the near-sound of life in motion, ebbing and flowing, or exposed to what ebbs and flows. It is also, and this is something we will return to often, apprehended as a kind of music, here a choral monotone (though in other testimonies it is something far more prismatic). The audiable is not always benign, but here it repays the emptying of the self that full attentiveness requires with the fullness of created objects, a rich immanence that is above all heard.

II.

The audiable is the undertone of auditory culture. That last phrase, like "visual culture," has become familiar. The concept of auditory culture emerges from the awareness, also familiar, that the kingdom of the text has been steadily shrinking since the Enlightenment, a process accelerated by the evolution of visual and digital media in the past hundred years and more. The rivalry of text and image is well known, and the role played by sound in modern cognition is becoming so. But the realm of the audiable remains to be fully explored, along with its repercussions for the realm of the auditory.

Chief among those repercussions is that the recognition of the audiable permits, and more than that, it mandates a broadening of the boundaries of auditory experience. The gamut runs from the almost impalpable vibrancy of that choral monotone, to the humming and thrumming heard through touch, to words or music echoing inside one's head. Sound is not quite borderless, but its edges are fluid. The heard world is a plenitude.

The audiable is the felt basis of audibility as such. It becomes perceptible on the fringes of meaningful sound, whether sensory, tonal, or verbal. It includes everything in sound that is outside and around language, including those aspects of language that hover behind the silence of writing and sometimes pierce it. Opening the audiable to the ear is a constant effort. For the audiable is incessantly being reduced to something ancillary, something distracting or subsidiary, despite its omnipresence and its frequent power. Why should this be? And should it be at all? Is sound shushed to preserve the opposition of the verbal and the visual as the basis of representation? Sound troubles representation, but is that a good reason to trouble sound? The auditory has in recent years wanted to become more audible. Some thinkers have listened to it. I want to ask what is lost when we don't hearken to the audiable, and what might be gained if we do.

III.

But lost or gained by whom? Just who, exactly, can hear that the world is alive with sound?

It has become imperative to ask this question because of the dawning recognition that even sensory experience is distributed unevenly both within and between cultures, that there are privileges involved in seeing, hearing, and feeling the world as a scene of knowledge and pleasure. There is a practical and an ideal answer to the question, and I would like to say that this book offers both. The practical answer is that the person for whom sound brings things to life is the one, whoever it may be, who has recorded the experience for others to grasp. The rest is a question of empathy. Not simple, not easy, and sometimes a question of forbearance. One reason for the very broad range of this book under the rubric of Western experience is that the experience of sound as sound does not, or should not, adhere to any norms. The very dissemination of this experience across cultures, times, and languages testifies to a certain inherent generosity in experience itself. The persons involved, the subjects who apprehend the world, are heterogeneous in principle, whatever historical inequities (not to say iniquities) may have confounded practice. In principle, there is no normative subject. And that principle supplies the ideal answer to the question. Anyone who wants to *should*—and I emphasize the word to bring out all its fraught meanings—*should* freely be able to share in the world of the audiable.

Some Leitmotifs

Although the topics in this book flow freely, three streams of thought run throughout: of sound as a source of engagement with life in what might be called the practices of sentience; of music as the original recording device for those practices, an art immanent in speech, and shared with the songs of birds and cetaceans, in which auditory knowledge and feeling become storable and retrievable; and of language as the means of reshaping auditory experience in the process of describing it. Each of these topical areas carries a thesis: that hearing (understood in its own right rather than as the other of sight) is the sensory form of promise and one capable of self-reference; that music is the means of giving auditory experience durable form, drawing pattern, shape, and movement from the whirligig of sound; and that when language, especially writing, addresses these sensory phenomena it not only records and describes them but also partly constitutes them, places them in historical time, and may change them.

And the links among these three? Sound, in the listening ear and the bodily interior, is in the first instance the medium of self-aware sentience, the mutual sensory opening of life and the world. Sound in this aspect makes imminence a sensory reality; it finds a means to preserve and extend that sense in music, both formal and informal; and it finds the means to interpret, develop, and recreate that sense in the language that constructively describes our experiences of sound.

Together with these theses, three parallel principles will govern much of what follows, which in turn aims to validate the principles.

First, the study of the audiable understands sound as a source of humanistic knowledge in a very strong sense: as primary, creative, constructive, and intelligible. In a trilogy on understanding music that immediately precedes this book I sought to show the same of music in particular.[1] Here the field of inquiry widens to include the experience of auditory sentience in all its forms. Some of those forms will be material, some conceptual, some musical, some verbal, but all, in some way, will be imagined—imagined necessarily, impossible to experience otherwise, not subject to measurement, and not reducible to anything else.

Second, mood and affect must be reconceived in terms that allow us to affirm the condition of "attunement"—the resonant mutuality of mental, material, and sensory states of being—without separating it from meaning and in particular without making the separation in order to produce a surrogate for transcendence. The surrogate is not needed because the experience of meaning as and in resonance is transcendence enough.

Third, it is necessary to distinguish between language as statement, "heard" without reference to its sound, and language as utterance, heard as fully sounded. The distinction does not establish an opposition—either term is rare in its pure state—but its historical practice has been marked by a bias in favor of statement that is long overdue for correction. The fluctuation between statement and utterance is as basic to language as words are.

The Standard of Vision

I.

Knowing and seeing, seeing and truth, have a long history together in the Western world; hearing has no place in their charmed circle. Appearances, we're told, can be deceiving, but this truism rests on the tacit assumption that under appearances there lies the truth, from which we can strip the appearances away until we see it, either with our own eyes or with the mind's eye. Othello knew enough not to listen to Iago until provided with ocular proof—provided, of course, in the form of a handkerchief, which is to say, just one more covering—but he did not know enough to hear the ring of truth in Desdemona's voice. Truth, we're told, meaning primary truth rather than mundane truths (*Who was she, really?* versus *Did she or didn't she?*), is ultimately unknowable, but when we think we know it anyway, if only for a moment, we speak of vision, the visionary.

Even if the visions speak, the source of their inspiration must show itself, if only by proxy: the legendary miasma rising to inspire the oracle's priestess at Delphi from a cleft in the rock, the voice of God issuing "in a flame of fire" from the burning bush on Mount Horeb (Exodus 3, KJV). In the Biblical story it is essential that God speak to Moses, but his word becomes efficacious only when graven in stone. Voice, as the word heard in speech, is a basic metaphor of presence, but it always seems to need someone to write it down. Voice lives in the word only when it ascends to the plateau of the dead letter. The coal on Isaiah's tongue produces a text.

When texts themselves carry a voice, they may still seem to address the mind's eye more than they do its ear. So, at least, said Joseph Conrad in a famous artistic credo. The statement is all the more memorable for "sounding" so much like its author:

> My task which I am trying to achieve is, by the power of the written word, to make you hear, to make you feel—it is, before all, to make you *see*. That— and no more, and it is everything.[1]

These sentences climb a rhetorical Jacob's ladder from the realization of alphabetic writing as virtual speech, to the deeper internalization of emotion (not touch, except in the sense that being moved emotionally is being "touched"), to the high point of understanding merged with visualization. Conrad goes on to reinforce the implied hierarchy of sense by leaping over the first rung of his ladder without a second thought:

> In a single-minded attempt of [this] kind . . . one may perchance attain to such clearness of sincerity that at last the presented vision of regret or pity, of terror or mirth, shall awaken in the hearts of the beholders that feeling of unavoidable solidarity . . . in uncertain fate, which binds men to each other and all mankind to the visible world.

Part of the work of this book, as of many other recent studies of sound, is to replace the ladder with a network of crossing paths, some diverging, some converging, on which the senses do not so much bind us to the world as release us into it. Along with the investigations made by sound studies into the materiality and technology of sound, it is essential to investigate the ways in which sound changes, and changes us, as we register it in symbolic forms: in recording our experiences of it, in taking it as an object of representation, in making music of it, in hearing ourselves know and feel. This process goes back to antiquity and no doubt long before, but it too changes once we grant hearing and listening the full epistemological value they have more often been denied.

II.

Speaking of that denial, it is worth noting that there is no auditory equivalent in English (or in the European languages familiar to me) of the word *gaze*. Neither of the word's primary meanings—as a verb, to direct the eye with the intent of close scrutiny; as a noun, the line of sight that can itself be seen as one observes what is looked at, painted, photographed, filmed, and so on—has a conceptual parallel that customarily applies to listening. Sound, indeed, is sometimes exonerated from the charge of seeking domination which has at times bedeviled the gaze, especially in the later twentieth century. (The exoneration is perhaps too hasty. We have also become aware that sound can be made an instrument of torture, and that escape from the noise of industrialized cities was an elite privilege in the later nineteenth century.) But it is certainly possible to direct the ear as well as the eye. We can listen for things. We can listen closely. We do both all the time. Music depends on them. So it may be time to think about the existence of an auditory parallel to the gaze and to observe its workings. We can, if we like, pilfer from the lexicon of vision and speak without apology of "the auditory gaze." Or we can simply observe the practices and records of listening more closely.

III.

Scholars sometimes speak of the preference for vision as "ocularcentrism." Aristotle spoke of it in more down-to-earth terms—in plain Greek—in the opening lines of his *Metaphysics:*

> All men by nature desire to know. An indication of this is the delight we take in our senses; for even apart from their usefulness they are loved for themselves; and above all others the sense of sight.... Even when we are not going to do anything, we prefer seeing (one might say) to everything else. The reason is that this, most of all the senses, makes us know.[2]

I plan to avoid learned parlance—this text allows itself only one invented word, and *ocularcentrism* isn't it—but the existence of the term is revealing. Seeing clearly is something we try to do, and should do. Ocularcentrism is a disorder, a bias, a bad habit or a covert ideology. The term is an attempt at gaining critical distance from what it names. The problem, as Conrad's statement shows, is that the preference for vision is so familiar, so much a part of the common sense of the world, that it passes virtually unnoticed—is that unseen? or unheard?—most of the time. We notice it mainly when it becomes excessive. That, however, is something which happens increasingly the more we treat the world as a global sponge for soaking up and squeezing out a flood tide of images.

This last, somewhat hyperbolic observation points to a key question: why the audiable now? What is this book really about and what does it hope to accomplish?

A Philosophy of Listening?

The early twenty-first century is facing a crisis of mediation that parallels the crisis of language of the early twentieth. "Crisis" is an easy term to use these days, which is part of what's wrong; say instead that in each case events have conspired to produce a loss of faith in the channels of communication on which we fundamentally depend. In the case of the last century, the problem arose from the widespread feeling that the language of science, then reaching unprecedented peaks of influence, had emptied out the language commonly used to express states of mind and spirit. The first made it difficult, if not impossible, to believe in the second. The case of the present century is perhaps worse. Although the languages of what C. P. Snow famously called the two cultures have learned to mix to their mutual benefit, other developments have widened and worsened the loss of faith that this mixing might otherwise help mend.

First, media saturation, critical suspicion, and political division have combined to foster a breakdown in the connection of language to truth. Philosophical tradition endowed language with both the power and the responsibility to be truthful. Both have seriously frayed. Language has almost become a species of rhetoric rather than the other way around. Its powers to conceal, deceive, evade, and mystify have come to seem primary. Catchphrases of all stripes regularly take the place of thought. In too much public discourse language has achieved its full Orwellian destiny and then some: War is peace, hate is love, tyranny is democracy, *and so what?* When the Hungarian State Opera stages *Porgy and Bess* with a nearly all-white cast and the national press trumpets the casting as a triumph over "racist restrictions" and "political correctness," something has definitely gone awry.[1] It would be entirely superfluous to give further examples: that's the problem. Of course acts of verbal good faith continue, but they are not a sufficient remedy. Too much abuse renders language itself suspect, not just its speakers.

The glut of media is impossible to miss, and so, especially in the America of Donald Trump, is the debasement of public discourse. As to critical suspicion, it has too often declined into the production of truisms. Bruno Latour argues the point in a widely cited essay:

> While we spent years trying to detect the real prejudices hidden behind the appearance of objective statements, do we now have to reveal the real objective and incontrovertible facts hidden behind the *illusion* of prejudices? And yet entire Ph.D. programs are still running to make sure that good American kids are learning the hard way that facts are made up, that there is no such thing as natural, unmediated, unbiased access to truth, that we are always prisoners of language, that we always speak from a particular standpoint, and so on, while dangerous extremists are using the very same argument of social construction to destroy hard-won evidence that could save our lives.[2]

One of the most striking recent developments in literary studies has been a concerted defense of taking writers at their word.[3] I don't think matters are that simple; language and its meanings resist every effort to contain them. We cannot restore trust in language by fiat. The only way to rehabilitate language is through language itself. This necessity will echo throughout what follows—as a matter of sound.

Second, the hollowing out of language coincides with an exponential rise in the power and number of images, to the point that the age-old quarrel between saying and picturing has in effect been settled: online, at least, and across media, text without imagery is nearly obsolete. Books remain the exception, some of them, but their eventual migration to non-paper formats is probably inevitable. The reign of the image is a problem not only, or even mainly, because images lend themselves even more readily than language to manipulative uses. The problem is that images are shorthand for depths of understanding that they also act to short-circuit; complex ideas condense to cliché in the immediacy of the image. They have a tendency to do so even when, as was (we like to say) the case in the past, words and images cooperate as well as quarrel, so that the images have a textual as well as an iconographic archive to draw on. With language in arrears, the image sheds its limits.

Third, the rise of digital technology has produced a large-scale shift in the uses and character of attention. This is not a matter of shrinking attention spans, which is just an urban legend. It is a change in the value, time, and power invested in different forms of attention that, like words and pictures, have an old rivalry that once depended on a countervailing cooperation that now seems to be unraveling. The rivals may briefly be characterized as close and diffuse attention, inclined respectively toward slow reflection and speedy scanning. This topic, however, needs more and more nuanced exposition, to which we will turn later.

Meanwhile, what can the introduction of the concept of the audiable do about any of this? What can we hope to gain from a reorientation of thought and expression that levels the powers of sight and hearing?

It would be folly to claim too much. The problems I have pointed to will be solved, if they are, by a combination of chance, change, and unintended consequences, perhaps with a little help from the many who have been thinking about them from humanistic motives. But no one can prescribe the solution, and anyone offering "the" solution is entranced by a fantasy—held captive, as Wittgenstein once said of himself, by an image.

Still, it may be reasonable to hope that reconnecting language with its auditory and audiable underpinnings will exert a pressure that pushes against the contemporary indifference of language toward truth. At the same time, angled differently, that pressure may open new possibilities of thinking and understanding. Some of these may have wider import, especially in relation to what I think of as the music of knowledge, the long-neglected play of sonority in the dance of words and images.[4] Such possibilities, should they arise, may also help re-inflect and chasten the image, in part by reclaiming lost ground for language and in part by recovering some of the conceptual archive from which the contemporary image has been severed.

At bottom I want simply to suggest that a certain auditory experience is basic to any sense of well-being and to any sense of confidence in what we think we know and what we feel we have experienced. If so, we should be more attentive than we traditionally have been to the role of listening in understanding.

But I do not want to exaggerate. No one can promise specific outcomes, or any outcomes, even if the words and ideas that imagine them are lucky enough to become part of a general conversation. Perhaps the most useful aspect of such a project is that it exists in the first place. One person's trying it may encourage others to do the same in their own terms. The audiable and its frame of reference are there if you want them.

Constructive Description

Basic to the project of discerning the audiable is a verbal practice, or, better, a verbal power, that I have elsewhere named constructive description.[1] The activity is not new, but its recognition is. A constructive description makes real the conditions it describes. Its language "sticks" to experience and elicits from it qualities that would have remained latent were it not for the description. Constructive description has some claim to be placed in the gallery of basic speech acts alongside the constative (those that assert), performative (those that do), and demonstrative (those that show). Constructive description is a speech act that forms, and in forming also transforms and ramifies. Once recognized as legitimate, and more, as indispensable, constructive description becomes one of the foundations of humanistic knowledge, both in retrospect and prospect. It becomes both an object of knowledge and a means of knowledge. Its role here means that the primary topic of this book is neither sound nor the phenomenology of sound, though both are inextricably involved. The topic is the formation of auditory experience in and through the accounts we give of it. The way of the telling is essential to the truth of the told.

Constructive descriptions may be eloquent or plainspoken, premeditated or spontaneous. We know them by their effect. They may also be either literal or figurative, though more often they tend to break down that already fragile distinction. For example, here is Christina Rossetti in "Up-Hill," a poem describing a wayfarer finding, as all do, that her journey ends in death:

> But is there for the night a resting-place?
> A roof for when the slow dark hours begin.
> May not the darkness hide it from my face?
> You cannot miss that inn.

You cannot miss the metaphor, either: the inn is the grave. But what if instead of explicating the metaphor one asks why it adheres to its object, why it becomes memorable, why it echoes other texts and echoes in them and beyond them? The answer, whatever form it takes, will be adequate only if it acknowledges that the description partly creates what it describes. To speak of the grave as an inn is not simply, perhaps not even primarily, to make a comparison. It is to make the grave exemplary of the peculiar human necessity to dwell, to compose a world of dwelling places, to inhabit spaces so that they becomes places endowed with meaning. The grave, runs the implication, is unthinkable except as a dwelling, the "long home" of *Ecclesiastes* 12:5: "The grasshopper shall be a burden, and desire shall fail: because man goeth to his long home, and the mourners go about the streets." The force of dwelling may even be written in stone: "Here lies . . ." and even, as in ancient Greek epitaphs, inscribed in the first person: "I, Gorgippus, without having looked on the bridal bed, descended to the chamber that none may escape of fair-haired Persephone." The echo of *Ecclesiastes* inflects Rossetti's text in alliance with the other, unmissable inn of the Nativity—but this inn has room for everyone.

The same echo reverberates in Emily Dickinson's "Because I could not stop for Death." The narrator, speaking posthumously, recalls coming upon her own grave in the course of her last journey:

> We paused before a House that seemed
> A Swelling of the Ground –
> The Roof was scarcely visible –
> The Cornice—in the Ground –

Dickinson's observation that the roof was scarcely visible adds an unsettling codicil: perhaps the grave defeats our conception even though it is a dwelling, or so we would like to think, or can't help thinking. In eluding our sight it eludes our grasp. There is nothing more to say about it. It is worth noting that Death in this poem says not a single word.

Among the many precedents for this equivocal form of homemaking, Wilhelm Müller's "The Inn" (Das Wirsthaus—literally host's house) is notable because of what Schubert did with it in his song cycle *Winterreise*. Here the weary wanderer visits a graveyard and wonders if he might find welcome in "the cool inn," only to discover that all the graves are full: "all the rooms occupied / In this house." Schubert extends this constructive description musically by ending the wanderer's surmise with a premature coming to rest: a perfect cadence in the tonic key. The music just goes on, and so must he. The description makes the wanderer's construction of the grave as a dwelling, and potentially any such construction, both inevitable and illusory.

Sight, Sound, and Language

I.

At one level the persistent favoring of vision (playing a favorite? expressing a taste? exempting a sense from stress as one favors a weak limb?) is just a philosophical prejudice that it should be possible to question or undo. A good many thinkers have been seeking to achieve that for some time, with mixed success.[1] The denigration of vision does not necessarily coincide with the elevation of hearing. We have learned to be critical of an overemphasis on vision without devising a credible alternative. But why not? What has stood in the way? Why sound now?

One answer comes from a level at which the preference for vision is *not* just a prejudice or, put more favorably, an inclination. At this level the favoring of vision is the material, like it or not, with which our shared sense of reality has been built up over time, a long time; it has the solidity of an edifice or a monument that it is possible to get around or deface but impossible to raze. Nowhere is this predicament more apparent or more strange than it is in spoken language, which continually leapfrogs over the sound on which it depends. Speech harbors a deaf spot. We "see" what it says—Conrad again—by using its sound as a lens. Hearing through the sound to its meaning comes easy; it takes some effort to hear the sound in its own right. Making the effort—such is the wager of this book—fundamentally alters the terms of understanding.

And then there is writing. Once writing systems arise, in all their historical plenitude, sounds that can be articulated can also be written. The sounds can therefore be seen, even by those who can't read them. The illiterate eye understands that sound is latent in graphic signs. This understanding seems built into the design of the modern metropolis, which developed in part as a cacophony of written sounds. William Wordsworth described the London of the 1790s in those terms, as befit its role as the center of enterprise and empire:

> Shop after shop, with symbols, blazoned names,
> And all the tradesman's honours overhead:
> Here, fronts of houses, like a title-page
> With letters huge inscribed from top to toe . . .
> Here files of ballads dangle from dead walls,
> Advertisements of giant size, from high
> Press forward in all colours on the sight . . .
>   In sailor's garb
> [A figure] lies at length beside a range
> Of written characters, with chalk inscribed
> Upon the smooth flat stones.
>   (VII, 1805: 165–77, 210–12, 221–24)

Nonetheless, the full resonance of the written-over city is available only to those who read. The power to read was for centuries a scarce resource and a social privilege; in the English law of the early modern era, literate persons accused of capital crimes could plead "benefit of clergy" and escape execution. The historical tendency has been to build up on that power: to ascend a scale of modes of seeing, each one more internalized than the last. At various moments in history, reading silently becomes more important, almost more resonant, than reading aloud; reading follows the movement of the eye, not of the mouth. St. Augustine's famous comments on this shift will concern us later on. Alphabetic writing systems first store articulate sounds as information (in Aristotle's long-authoritative account, the letters are symbols of the sounds), but what is written quickly becomes independent of any possible utterance, past or future. The silence of reading and writing becomes a cherished trait, as one can readily *see* in any number of paintings of these activities from Rembrandt to Chardin to Sargent. More exactly, what is cherished is the silence in which reading and writing take place. Sound does have its place in that silence, as we will discover later. Yet the *scene* of absorption in the letter retains a strong appeal.

In the one exceptional case—and it's a case to be considered in detail—in which sound itself becomes articulate independent of language, the category that covers the result has too often been either stigmatized or exalted for that very independence. The category is music. Unlike language, music cannot be understood without sound, or so the story goes. For Immanuel Kant this difference meant that music scarcely needed to be understood at all; it belonged to the pleasures of the senses, not to the free play of imagination afforded by high art.[2] Yet music has also been subjected to a history of analysis in which the score as written, not the sound as performed, is primary. To give sounding music its due, we need to forget about primacy altogether and ask what we apprehend when we encounter music in any form, be it sound or idea or text or memory. My own writing on music over a long career has sought to show that music (in particular, classical music) is rich in cognitive as well as expressive power. As this work has developed, its emphasis has shifted—without leaving anything behind—from what we can know about music to what music enables us to know. The role of music in this book extends that development. When we use it as an instrument of knowledge, music shows itself to be much more than one of the many things we hear, although with an unusual degree of pleasure. Music is one of the foundations of hearing.

II.

The default aim of injunctions to see (the model in English is "Behold!) is to compel wonder, recognition, admiration, and the like. The counterparts for hearing are warning, admonition, and command. Of course there is nothing exclusive about what Wittgenstein would call these language games, but their tendencies are strong. To make visible is to reveal; to direct someone to hear—even the phrase is telling; there is no parallel between making visible and making audible—is to instruct. Freud's idea that the superego originates in things heard finds its best confirmation here. This practice is not an index of the superego, not "proof" of it; it *is* the superego. One cardinal role of music is to free audibility of this yoke. Music makes sound revealing; it aims to make hearing a species of wonder. But it should be possible, and the point is the very argument of this book, to extend this enfranchisement of listening beyond music into the spheres of both ordinary life and extraordinary experience. Doing so should make available everything about knowledge that we cannot see.

III.

The preference for vision has been attacked on any number of grounds, now widely familiar: that it encourages detachment, objectification, subject-object thinking, inequality between the observer and the observed, voyeuristic pleasure. Yet it is hard to deny that the seen world is essential and that our engagements with it are not doomed to be exploitative. The deeper problem, perhaps, is that visual sense is so robust and immediate. As the cliché says, seeing is believing. The parallel for hearing is the inverse: I can't believe my ears. Listening seems always to involve layers of mediation that looking does not require. The problem, then, might come down to distraction. The seen world tends to block our perception of the rich, parallel, unpicturable world of hearing or, to revive a good old word, of hearkening. The world as seen does not blind us to alternatives; it makes us deaf. It sets up a standard of reasonable understanding some part of which rests on a foundation of absurdity—the absurd being (from the Latin) that which cannot sensibly be heard, be hearkened to.

What would it mean, what would the consequences be, if we started to think more in a hearkening mode? What would it mean to apportion the intellectual work of sight and hearing according to their distinctive powers and collaborative possibilities rather than to pit them against each other in what Jonathan Sterne has rightly decried as a mere litany?[3] What would be the consequences for thinking about knowledge, communication, art, ethics, history? Answering these questions, though only in part, and in part by sheer conjecture (not to speak of mirror play: speculation), is the project at hand.

Part of the answer is historical; it has changed with time and will change (is already changing) again. Prior to the Enlightenment, sound was primarily a material and bodily phenomenon. Afterwards, it became equally a manifestation of spirit, in particular one that took the place of the purely immaterial spirit that Enlightenment thought and experimental science had put in doubt. For Francis Bacon in *The Advancement of Learning*, sound was an affair of resonating bodies. For G. W. F. Hegel in his *Aesthetics*, it becomes an affair of the resonance of minds. Sensory matter in art, whatever its type, proves itself through "the power to call forth from all the depths of consciousness a sound and an echo in the spirit."[4]

Hegel's language is doubly symptomatic. On the one hand, it edges toward recognition of the audiable. The sound and echo called forth by art are supposed to be non-sensory (they are heard only in the spirit), but only a sensory metaphor, only an *auditory* metaphor, can convey what they are like, that is, give them a sense. On the other hand, the resonance between sensory and non-sensory sound anticipates a growing demand to find in sound a material replacement for the type of spirit lost to the Enlightenment while at the same time refusing to accept a purely material, empirically determined, morally vacuous world. Sound can either fill the void evacuated by immaterial spirit or hold the place once promised by it. As the product of vibration, sound leaves the body that produces it "uninjured." The ear apprehends "this ideal movement in which simple subjectivity, as it were the soul of the body, is expressed by its sound . . . and in this way the inner side of objects is made apprehensible by the inner life."[5] The sympathetic resonance between inner and outer dissolves the distinction between subject and object. In the process, spirit becomes an object of sense.

IV.

The nineteenth century took this kind of acoustic mirroring as an object of desire and a project of technology; those terms, too, became indistinguishable in ways still pertinent today. Although the world had always had an acoustic double, a globe of sound in which to mirror itself, the beginnings of our media- and device-saturated world also began to convert this mirroring, or rather this echoing, from a limit condition to a fundamental feature of the general soundscape.

This transformation is perhaps most evident in the continuity between early efforts at mechanical speech synthesis and the development of the phonograph. The quest for a talking machine begins in earnest in the eighteenth century, partly in association with the era's fascination with automatons. In 1804 Wolfgang von Kempelen exhibited a machine capable of producing sentences in English, French, Italian, and German through a simulated mouth. Operating the machine was something like playing an organ.[6] Joseph Faber's Euphonia, first exhibited in Philadelphia in 1845, actually used a keyboard and was said to be able to speak in any European language. It could also laugh and whisper. (The device was both a serious piece of science and a device for popular entertainment snapped up by P. T. Barnum.)

Faber covered the mechanical mouth, tongue, and jaws of the machine with a female mask so as to give the speech a face, and with it the dimension of subjectivity—"the inner life"—that would otherwise be missing from the assemblage. In short, Euphonia was the first talking head, though some images show her as a whole person with a body, or at least a dress, attached. (The additions made her head, with its dark ringlets, look less like the Medusa's.) Later in the century, after the advent of the phonograph, the Edison Company would produce the same effect in miniature in the form of talking dolls. More importantly, the speaking machine influenced the development of the telephone, the first step toward a world saturated with the possibility of voice transmission.

Voice was the primary concern of the early phonograph, too, which put recording in the place formerly held by synthesis. The best-known outcome was the series of public Tone Tests in which both the Victor Talking Machine Company and the Edison Company challenged audiences to tell the difference between live and recorded singing, the inner life and mechanical sound. But the phonograph also seemed able to capture spirit in a more literal sense. Edison had suggested that one of its uses would be to immortalize the speech of the dead, including their dying words. As Richard Leppert observes, the availability of "terrestrial eternity" figured heavily in the early promotion of early sound recordings.[7] Leppert particularly notes Victor's "necro-marketing" of Enrico Caruso, the first phonographic superstar. One advertisement from 1921 claims that the recordings have "bridged the oblivion into which both singer and musician passed. The voice of Jenny Lind is forever stilled, but that of Caruso will live through all the ages" (117).

That "live" seems to want to be more than (dead) metaphor. Leppert reprints a 1932 advertisement touting technical advances which carries the headline "CARUSO sings again" in large type. The text begins with "Caruso lives anew! A thing that cannot be—but is!" The accompanying image is of a smiling Caruso as Canio in *Pagliacci* straddling a big bass drum which he is poised to strike. One could hardly ask for a more perfect image of sending resonance into the distance. More generally, Victor would claim that recordings were the material form of subjectivity: "For the artist's personality no less than his voice is registered by the needle, and the aria he sings contains within itself all the subjective thought and effort he has put into the role" (111). The wording here is notable for its conjunction of interiority and technology, the personality and the needle.

Just how seriously to take this hyperbole is an open question. But the language was persistent, and Tone Tests were popular. The oddly Hegelian vocabulary seems to have spoken to a genuine desire to connect sound and spirit by means of resonant matter. By the time these ads appeared, radio was already a mass medium and talking pictures were about to become one. As late as the 1955 noir thriller *Kiss Me Deadly*, the exemplary way to shatter a person's spirit is to break a Caruso record, by then an heirloom. Changes in the soundscape had presumably always brought changes in the substance, not just the manner, of listening, but never before on this scale.

The audiable thus becomes—or rather might become, for this has happened so far only in fragmentary and marginal moments—the basis of a spiritual counterpart to what Jürgen Habermas described as the incomplete project of rational Enlightenment.[8] To listen through sound for the audiable is to make spirit apprehensible and (what is not the same thing) intelligible without abandoning the umbilical connection of sound to creaturely life. It is to render spirit itself a material-sensuous form independent of any particular system of belief or thought. Hearkening makes spirit audible without settling—perhaps not even raising, perhaps averting—the question of whether the sensory form has a beyond that is, as traditional culture would assume, spirit alone. The audiable is a resolutely secular phenomenon: a revelation of the *spiritual* primacy of the secular.

v.

There is an epistemic stake in the pursuit of the audiable, which I will describe next. But as I have just all but said, there is also the larger stake, which is the true wager of this line of thought: that by recognizing the audiable and learning how to hearken to it, we can take a critical step in formulating spirit for an Enlightened world without falling back on the fatal alternatives of blind faith or blind empiricism. In a sense, the subject to whom this project is addressed is the a-theological subject that Enlightenment cannot help but produce. This subject may also be irreligious, but need not be. It is possible, as Derrida said later in life, to "pass for an atheist" and still take a serious interest in spirit.

Without spirit, most would agree, and this indeed seems to be the judgment of history, life is without value. But why must spirit be immaterial? Why should it be? Anyone who wishes to reason along with Kant and Kierkegaard and to take the leap of faith can still do so within the framework set by the audiable. Nothing requires it but nothing prevents it. The brief here is not against belief but against dogma, the anxious rage of the true believer, which is also the mirror image of the soulless materialist. In the sphere of knowledge, the brief is against already knowing everything that matters and knowing only what you think you can prove. Underlying these speculations on the audiable, and sometimes surfacing in them, is the wish to make a contribution, however small, to a re-spiritualization of the world which is not a dematerialization of it, and thus to help create, or restore, the space where value matters, ethics matter, truth matters: the space of the value of value.

As to knowledge, the study of the audiable, of life as auditory, should form a contribution to the history and theory of thinking. This subject has very little in common with the old-fashioned disciplines of epistemology or the history of ideas. Nor does it coincide, exactly, with the more recent discipline of sound studies, although it stands to benefit greatly from the results of that more empirical, less speculative pursuit. It may even have something to contribute. The chief concern of auditory theory is not with the sources, behavior, or effects of sound but with what sound makes it possible to understand. What do we know, what can we know, in hearing? What does that knowledge feel like? When I say "I hear" and mean "I understand," just what *do* I mean? How do we imagine, represent, desire, remember, discover, and distort the experience of knowing by hearing, of knowing in hearing? What does sound make known?

VI.

These questions resonate with the recent development of expanded concepts of both sound and listening. Michel Chion's *Sound* (2010) argues for the detachment of listening from the visible sources of sound.[9] The "acousmatic" for Chion is no longer an outlier in auditory experience but part of its very basis. Nina Sun Eidsheim's *Sensing Sound* (2015) extends the sphere of sound and its perception from the acoustic to the vibratory and tactile.[10] My own aim is a yet further extension that incorporates language, the creation of symbolic forms, and temporality, all contributing to an evolving conception that fuses the ontology of sound with the aesthetics of sound.

That fusion draws sound away from its traditional attachment to, or perhaps we should say confinement by, the immediate present and reorients it toward the future. Sound is not only the notice of what happens now but also the notice of what happens next. The imminence of sound is the immanence of sound. The audiable is the sensed realization of this coalescence. Its vibrancy is a kind of tuning up. In its temporality, sound is latent music.

Concern with the audiable thus points beyond the content or structure of thought toward what it means to think in the heard world. How do the vicissitudes of hearing shape our forms of life? How do we hear what we know and know what we hear? The study of the audiable fosters the recognition that thinking occurs in an acoustic medium, that thinking is unthinkable without sound, and that the audiable, the audible, and the musical deserve recognition as features no less constitutive than language of human self-fashioning and self-knowing.

With this recognition in mind, the interpretation of the audiable should branch out into an examination of reflective acts of hearing. These are acts in which (perhaps listening for it, perhaps not) one hears something of import, something essential or even life-changing, and at the same time, in the same sounds, hears hearing itself. This doubling forms a parallel to the more familiar visual situation in which one can see the gaze by following lines of sight and patterns of mirroring. With sound, as with sight, the reflective doubling adds a further dimension of significance, literally a further resonance, to the experience. Many of these acts of auditory reflection are musical; the pages below will often return to music that seeks to listen to itself.

The Sound of Words

Language is the preeminent source of auditory knowledge. It fills the world not only with the sound of words and the voices that speak them, alone and in chorus, but also with all the sounds that go with speaking in bodies and spaces. Language overflows with sound and catches its own overflow. Its abundance of ways to name and evoke sounds teaches us how to hear. But in one respect language conceals what sound conveys. Its powers of meaning are so formidable that it is all too easy to abstract from the flow of rhythm and intonation and reduce meaning to statements and propositions. The result, a kind of backlash, is to encourage a futile quest for meaning beyond language. For human beings there is no beyond of language. I expect to be contradicted on this point, but it is one that needs to be upheld precisely *on behalf of* nonverbal experience, including the musical experience to which we will often return. Language, like sound, may seem to stop until one detects the underlying murmur of a return that has already begun, and was underway in the very moment of stoppage. Language often seems to make meaning *with* sound at the expense of the meaning *in* sound. We can ask the question of what sound itself means only in the very language that inhibits the question.

All right, then—but we can ask the question nonetheless, and perhaps make auditory knowledge more audible as a result. We can ask what sound makes known in sounding, and we can ask with resonance. The concept of the audiable is meant to give this question both a point of origin and—but never too quickly, and never for very long—a point of return.

One way to frame the question is to ask about the auditory form of silent reading, something that we will do several times in what follows. The way that reading has been pictured over the centuries offers a starting point. Painted reading typically seems suspended in a stillness produced by the reader's absorption in a book. The stillness is both bodily and auditory. It shows the motionless reader no longer listening or able to listen to worldly sounds because the mind is occupied with inner speech. Such paintings show the intensity of concentration by confronting us with the marks of what we can neither see nor hear.

But what does the reader hear? Real rather than painted reading makes sounds of its own, which intensity of concentration absorbs into the medium of inner speech. In such sounding silence, inner speech may be heard better than anywhere else. And what that speech is doing is not merely articulating the text but listening to it with an understanding that the speech itself expresses and extends. The voice in one's head has the same relationship to audible voice as the silence of painted reading has to the quiet in which a living reader may read. Silent reading is simultaneously an act of performance and an act of reception. The experience is auditory without being acoustic. It seems to offer greater pleasure and to make a deeper impression than reading without inner speech, which is perfectly possible. Its enunciation gives rise to an accumulating sense that permits the reading to continue and to know when to stop. The result is a condition of understanding that exceeds the text that has been read; that may be, and will be, paraphrased; and that could not exist otherwise.

What, then, if we were to say that speech, even inner speech, gives sensory form to what writing makes knowable? What if we were then to pose the question of what sound adds to knowledge? How sound transforms the knowledge to which it adds?

What is at stake in these questions is not simply a new topic or an expanded set of interests but a fundamental shift in the form and character of our collective self-perception, together with all its repercussions in the area of expression and worldly engagement.

Seeing, Saying, and Hearing

The instruments of knowledge in the seen world are primordially words and pictures, or more broadly what Gilles Deleuze called the sayable and the seeable.[1] These instruments or, more properly, these technologies of the visible are age-old antagonists, but they are also partners. Reflecting on their mutual entanglement, W.J.T. Mitchell coined the term *imagetext*, which facilitates thinking about the pair as forming a single epistemic field.[2]

But if the alternations of the pictorial and the linguistic do form the assumed and usually unspoken basis of communication, meaning, expression, and representation, what is this assumption leaving out or suppressing? What is it cutting out of the text or the picture? In other, less neutral words, what does the twinning of text and image arise to structure, regulate, and defend against? Any musician would know the answer even before the question is raised. The unruly element is the flow of inflection, vocalization, and vibratory sonority that is structured, or perhaps one should say channeled, as music. It is the becoming-audible that, in parallel with the terms "visible" and "readable," I have started here to call the *audiable*. The term stands to "audible" as "visual" does to "visible." I allow myself this one neologism (two, I suppose, if you count *imagetext*) to distinguish the audible from the auditory. The new term denotes not that which is perceivable by a sense, but a sphere of sense perception delegated to act as a primary medium of cognition, expression, and so on.

Thinking about the imagetext typically ignores the sphere of the audiable, perhaps because the default authority of the imagetext reduces hearing to the sensory channel leading from speech to writing. (Whatever can be spoken can be written, whether it is or not.) The opposition of the seeable and the sayable falls into the same trap; the sayable is really the readable; it is not *uttered*. This association persists despite, or rather because of, the "metaphysical" privilege so often awarded to speech as opposed to writing, the ascribed power to carry immediacy, meaning, or the sense of personal presence from speaker to listener, as if with no loss along the route of communication.

Jacques Derrida's famous but much misunderstood argument against a too-credulous attitude toward presence finds its real import here. The problem is that everyday language is not hard enough. Linguistic understanding commonly feels as if it passes straight through the linguistic signifier. In ordinary life we simply understand what is said without further reflection. Because of these things, we tend to forget that speech no less than writing exists in a material medium: sound. Even if we remember, we tend to identify understanding with the durability of the written or printed word rather than with the transitory embodiments of speech. We act as if the spoken utterance were written sub rosa on the mind—an old Platonic metaphor—whereas any fool can see that the text is written on parchment or paper. (Words on-screen require separate consideration, which would go together with the rise of the PDF as an intermediate form between the permanence of inscriptions and the heightened ephemerality of pixels.)

For these reasons, speech, no matter how valued it may be as a tangible conveyance of presence, is virtually never sufficient unto itself to secure understanding. Speech requires periodic supplementation by some visual form—if not by writing then by gesture or posture or ritualization, or, in modern media, by imaging itself. In any case, whether spoken or written, language tends toward the silence of comprehension. It is the nature and so to speak the mission of the audiable continually to chip away at that silence. It may act as a background to reading as a kind of ambient white space, the page of the air, or it may subjoin speech as a caption does an image, but in any case it occupies its own sphere just as the pictorial and the linguistic do, and just as nonsignifying marks or traces do in the visual field.

To feel (hear, and in this case also see, since these sense-modalities crisscross all the time, and not only figuratively) the thrum of the audiable, all one need do is momentarily leave open s paces in the text that introduce multiple meanings and an im possible problem in art iculation. If you read that sentence aloud without minding the gaps, you enact the covering that conceals but also proclaims the audiable, which opens outward and away from the textual surface like Alice's rabbit hole. If you read the sentence and perform the gaps, they assume the potential power to derail the utterance, not by intruding silence—they are no more really silent that the normal spaces between words—but by deforming the utterance with a purely phonetic quality that threatens to swirl out, obstruct, and decorate the surface.

The audiable cuts right across the visible-readable opposition, challenges the distinction between meaning and unmeaning, and does not itself form an oppositional structure with either text or image. It forms no structure at all; it is stubborn phenomenon through and through. But it supports no mystique, offers no warm soft alternative to the hard-edged world-picture; it is utterly contingent and endlessly mutable. The audiable arises in, emerges from, overflows, the space of a gap between noise and articulation whose edges may not be well defined if they are defined at all. Those edges form the frame of the world-picture, the lines of division between reason and feeling, concepts and their material signifiers, spirit and matter, all oppositions that have repeatedly been challenged within the world-picture itself, but that continually reinstall themselves there because of their indispensable practical and ideological uses. Within the world-picture, there is a continual movement from hearing (a perceptual process) to listening (a mental process); the results of listening become intelligible insofar as they can be depicted in words or images. The audiable arises in a recursive or redoubling movement, advancing from listening, or attending to what a sound conveys, to hearkening, or apprehending the process of conveyance. This happens in such a way that what is conveyed is not lost or obscured, but changed. Audiable sound strongly conveys both itself and something not itself, with definite, traceable consequences for both.

The Audiable

VARIATIONS ON A THEME

It is impossible to propose a mode of hearkening, a "philosophy" of the audiable, without drawing on the resources of philosophical and critical thought. But the language of that philosophy has no need to be esoteric, even though it can and should seek to be rich and strange. Part of the responsibility of the language to its topic is to explore the powers of invocation and evocation. This language of listening must imply a critique of empiricist and literalist approaches to communication by departing from them. Those who listen for the audiable must also try to speak it, that is, to speak, to write, so that its reverberations may be heard, or at least discerned.

Such language is addressed to anyone willing to listen with open ears. Its possible range of reference is nearly limitless: vocalization, bodily noises, speech, exclamation, the rustle and outburst of sexual intimacy, cries and whispers, transient sensation, music, singing, soundscape, voice, ceremony, birdsong, murmurs, animal sounds, pain, suffering, rhyme, rhythm, nonsense, nostalgia, water, imperatives, cacophony, the four winds, the grinding of machinery, echoes, ecstasy. This text means to catch as may be possible the resonance of these sounds, Hegel's soul of the body, and to release them again; to reach the edge of listening and pause there; to mimic the audiable in its own rhythm.

The audiable is a source of practical and material transcendence. It is established irrevocably as such by its apartness from the text-image system. It is made perceptible as such when the channeling of its substance and energy into texts or images is divined or interrupted or reversed. In worldly terms this always happens by chance. There is no way to plan for it and no way to be sure of hearing it when the opportunity occurs.

One fundamental consequence of this is that, insofar as the arts are matters of design, there is no art of the audiable. Only when the artwork eavesdrops on the conditions that make its own utterance possible does it, or rather may it, since the outcome is always contingent and uncertain, become a conveyance of the audiable. But when the audiable does appear, the register of hearing suddenly changes, becoming at once more intimate and more strange.

This outcome is not transcendent in the grand nineteenth-century sense, but something better. It is simply a condition of vibrancy, usually sudden, often fleeting, that we apprehend, in Wallace Stevens's constructive description,

> As if the air, the mid-day air, was swarming
> With the metaphysical changes that occur
> Merely in living as and where we live.[1]

There is no proof of the audiable. It is observable, but its existence cannot be verified by observation. It exists only in my recognition of it and expresses itself only in my report of it; it is always the product of a constructive description; it is not something "we," a "we," hear except in conditions of intimacy in which the words or gestures of one become the medium of the other's hearkening, so that the act of hearkening may be shared, which it always is with the inflection of a grateful or rueful incredulity. To speak of the audiable with you, I must also invoke it, and in such a way that it seems to you reasonable to listen to what I hear or say I have heard.

And yet the audiable is a constant companion, even when it goes unrecognized. The audiable is the perceptible potentiality of sound. It discloses itself when the condition of being about to hear assumes sensory form. Although it is not a natural fact it arises as if naturally as both cause and effect alongside auditory knowledge. When the ear is to the world, the audiable is also there. It makes itself known, has always made itself known, through the traces of itself that it scatters across the records of experience.

The audiable is utterly ordinary, the very basis of the ordinary—in the sense that the potentiality of sound, the ever-present hum or murmur of the acoustic envelope, is the indispensable background to the conduct of ordinary life—yet our actual encounters with it are and require the extraordinary. (Deafness is no impediment to this oscillation. The profoundly deaf cannot hear most sounds, but that does not mean they have no auditory experience. In hearing less, the deaf hear differently.[2]) In keeping with these observations, another way to understand the audiable is to take it as the material, positive form of the impossibility of silence in the living ear. We have no experience of the true, absolute cessation of all sound. We always encounter silence as the absence of specific sounds and acoustic textures, and when we imagine an absolute silence and fear (or desire) it, what we are imagining is the condition of our nonexistence: pensive death in fantasy, death itself in reality. Yet we cannot just listen to the audiable at will. If you sit quietly and alone in the depth of night and listen, the "silence" that you hear will still be a certain crepitation of faint sound. The audiable can manifest itself in that sound only when we are listening to something else or to nothing at all: only beneath or behind or above or within. We hear the audiable, so to speak, behind our backs. It is the thing that escapes us by turning every corner just the moment before we do.

The project of hearkening is the sounding, auscultation, sonar tracking, of the audiable in music, speech, writing, media, imaging, the body, and intimate and social relations, and this at two levels: that of describing the phenomenon and that of establishing its potential social-ethical value. The project is thus a kind of romance, in that, while the opposition of the see-able and the sayable always carries with it a contest of authorities—words are verified or falsified by the seen, the word explains or justifies what otherwise can merely be shown—the audiable seductively undoes the organizing and subordinating force of authority. It draws the listener into a zone of close proximities, literally of approximations, in which meaning is at once certain and indefinite, natural and more-than-natural, a zone that we inhabit against the "better judgment" of the epistemological skepticism of the realm of the image-text opposition. The audiable may be spoken, but it continually risks the disruption of voice by speechless but expressive sound, the cry, the gasp, the stammer, humming, sobbing, whimpering, sighing, and so on, as if voice were (but it is, isn't it?) a crystallization out of a steady indeterminate and preexisting background. I can describe the audiable only by imagining it. But this work of imagination, or so I want to suggest, although it cannot be rationalized, is eminently reasonable, inflected at every point by the very tone of reasonableness.

Hearkening to the audiable, I would like to say, is thus both a source of sustenance in itself and a resource against the seductions of absolutes and fundamentalisms. At its most acute, the auditory gaze offers a possible touchstone of humane life without the consolations of myth or faith. The offer could not be more timely, since the most urgent of needs today is precisely to sustain the idea of humanely reasonable identity against the lure of unbridled zeal. (Failing that, we will fail at everything else.) The audiable allows this identity without incurring its gravest failing, its distance from transcendence, rapture, exaltation, passionate intensity, even its hostility to these things. But the audiable must do all this, if it can, if anything can, without being—or precisely because it is not—revelatory, nor consoling, nor stable, nor subject to paraphrase as doctrine or principle, nor subject to appeal as a charismatic irrationalism. What it is, or can be, or always latently has been, is the shareable basis of an intimacy, communication, and mutual relation that goes above and beyond the text-image system without rejecting that system, and is therefore capable of both supporting the system at its best and containing the inevitable imperial ambitions that drive the system at, and to, its worst. The audiable is as confounding as it is transporting. I don't know, finally, what I hear in hearkening, but that I hearken at all supports and expands what I know.

No modern system of thought placed a greater emphasis on listening than psychoanalysis, which virtually began as an injunction to listen better. What survives of its legacy, recently much disputed or dismissed, in the emerging realm of auditory and audiable knowledge? The answer I would like to give is that although Freudian themes and theses may or may not still seem viable, they have proven to some degree expendable, whereas the underlying structure in which they are embedded is quite indispensable still: the situation in which the one person listens intently to another and prompts him or her to greater self-knowledge and self-command, often on the basis of recognizing desires and perspectives the speaker has avoided confronting. The specifics do not matter. What does matter is the relationship, which consists of a variation on Freud's formula that the therapist's unconscious is attuned to the patient's: it consists of a mutual hearkening in which each party listens for what becomes audiable in the other's speech.

This model of counsel applies far beyond the consulting room; it runs the gamut of sound. English has no positive terms in common use for sounds that operate beyond the bounds of language. Other than noise and its equivalents, such sounds may be inarticulate, preverbal, subvocal, non-linguistic, but they are nothing in themselves; they live in the limbo of prefixes. Although the specific sounds have names, they adhere to no general concepts. The concept of the audiable, together with associates such as vibrancy and resonance that recur throughout this book, represents an effort to right the balance.

Hegel says that only sight and hearing, the "theoretical senses," belong to the experience of art because only sight and hearing have no contact with what they sense. They are nonmaterial conductors of material forms. This idea may have a kernel of truth to it; the arts really do generally confine themselves to these two senses, and it is worth asking why. But the theoretical senses are not so aloof from the world as Hegel thinks. Sight has an intimate relation to touch, and, more importantly for present purposes, hearing is anything but immaterial. We feel sound as much as we hear it. Sound is a kind of body. Sight and hearing become aesthetic media not by standing apart from what they convey but by yielding to it, by growing dense and heavy with the matter that concerns them or, on the contrary, making all that matters shimmer and sing.

The traditional five senses differ among themselves in the degree to which their immediate effect is pleasure or knowledge. All five are capable of both, but each acts according to its own ratio. For humans, taste obviously stands at one extreme and sight and hearing at the other. What really sets the latter two apart, however, is not just the richness of what they communicate. Sight and hearing are the "theoretical" senses because they are also the *linguistic* senses. They are the necessary media of writing and speech, respectively. One might even say that, for humans, all sight is a kind of writing, all hearing a kind of speech. This reversal of what the senses make possible into that which makes the sensory intelligible, this reversal of that which the senses support into the support of sense, is more than merely speculative. It is the lived, practical, everyday means by which we experience ourselves as parts of a world.

Speech and music are contractions of the field of the auditory. All forms of articulation involve a certain loss, from the silence of writing to the muting of the hum of the world. Whereas sight works as a taking in, hearing tends to work as a drawing away, especially when distance is involved. We hear sounds from inside ourselves—we are always in the middle of the there and the here—but at the same time when we hearken to a sound we engage in a movement toward a beyond, an elsewhere, and one that can never be fully attained. This drift is our means of belonging to the world; the world is its anchor. Noise constricts or penetrates; it undoes belonging by interrupting the drift. But the drift returns the moment the noise stops. The auditory drift may be arrested only in the strange intimacy (internalized, sometimes, in forms of thinking and silent speech) of whispering into the ear. (Is this part of the erotic pleasure of putting the tongue into the ear? to kiss from within the motion of speech at no distance from the organ of hearing?)

The sensations of the audiable have no objective correlative. They are infectious endowments, transmissions in the form of a reception, the results of hearing as a prehensile, projective act, or, better, of hearing as an enveloping surface catching and magnifying the slight vibration that it encloses, which would otherwise be lost—or never found.

The concept of the audiable first suggested itself to me, perhaps, when I understood that the animation brought to song by the singing voice could survive on its own in instrumental music—a capability that I still regard as one of the great gifts of the classical music in which I heard it. That animation was not something I imagined; it was something I heard. But it was not quite sound, and the realization that I heard it nonetheless became the nucleus of the later concept.

The literal character of this act of hearing is fundamental. The audiable is not a metaphor. Nor is its value that of a metaphorical corrective to the favoring of vision. Metaphor is invaluable, but it is not inevitable, and in this case it needs to be ready to help make the audiable available without pretending to be its source. Even the most sweeping critique we have of visual bias and the world as world-picture, namely that of Heidegger, runs into a problem with metaphor. For Heidegger, "the world conceived and grasped as a picture" is the acme of a misguided modernity. It undermines the value of art, promotes the abuse of technology, and above all obstructs our primary participatory involvement with the world. Picturing empowers the observer at the price of separation from the observed.

Heidegger's alternative is auditory, but only in metaphor. Its medium is language, especially the language of a certain oracular poetry, Friedrich Hölderlin's in particular, which becomes the model for the language of Heidegger's own writing: musical, chantlike, and resonant, but only in metaphor. The language belongs not to speech but to writing. It seeks, by reflection, to "transport the man of the future into that 'between' in which he belongs to Being, yet remains a stranger amid that which is."[3] This language, by design, reaches neither the ear nor the world.

The takeaway from this impasse seems clear enough. It is one thing to chasten vision by invoking the ear. It is quite another to trace the relationship between hearing, listening, knowing, and feeling.

Likewise there is little point in arguing over sensory hierarchy, or, like Emanuel Levinas, investing ethical value in one sense over another—in his case touch and hearing, especially touch, in the caress, in preference to sight. Yet one dimension of the audiable does gain resonance from

Levinas's idea that there exists a condition of saying—a primordial pre-signifying bond forged through participation in speech—prior to the said.[4] It does make sense to identify a general condition of exposure to the speech of others independent of any particular speech act. This exposure would extend from the voice of the other to the enveloping soundscape and from there to the hum of the world. Hearing is the sense by which the world permeates the human.

Against Levinas, it makes no sense to idolize (as he does) the ontological condition of exposure as a morally necessary abjection before the Other. Nor does it make sense to understand the speech act (as he does) as an unavoidable concealment or distortion of the general necessity. With Levinas, it does make sense to understand speech as interacting with, rather than merely reflecting or ratifying, the general necessity of utterance and the exposure that goes with it. That necessity arises from what Walter Benjamin called the "verbal nature" of things, the inherent tendency of things in general to communicate themselves.[5] Some latter-day philosophers have revived this understanding of language as inherent in the order of things. They speak on behalf of "flat ontology" that takes the effect of any material thing on any others as a form of communication. Timothy Morton makes the point in writing (as I will later) about the wind harp:

> We don't hear the sound of the harp in some abstract sense. We hear the wind's "translation" of the strings. We hear the hollow sound box's translation of the string's vibration into amplified pressure waves. Entering our inner ear, these waves are translated by a pressure cell—the one plant cell in the entire body. This cell acts as a transducer, converting mechanical vibrations into electrochemical signals. And so on.[6]

Like the sound of the wind harp, the difference between what Levinas calls the saying and the said is neither abstract, nor empty, nor mute. It comes alive in the production of a space of apprehension, above all of a space in which the audiable may make itself heard. In this context the audiable emerges as the guarantee or (perhaps better) as the evincing, the evidencing, of the affirmative difference between things and our apprehension of them. It is the remainder left behind by every utterance, every symbolic act. It is the excess, in Raymond Williams's terms, of the lived over the articulated.[7] It is a positive presence, not a lack. It is not an indication of the inaccessibility of experience to language, image, or voice, but precisely the invitation that experience issues to these things. It is the whisper of a truth that is always still to be said, but that can to some degree (as Wittgenstein would say) be shown in saying. It can be shown, indeed, precisely in such reflective saying as includes the recognition of its own inability to capture everything by what it says.

> "In the beginning, understanding is a guess."
> Paul Ricoeur, *Interpretation Theory*
>
> "These are only hints and guesses,
> Hints followed by guesses, and the rest . . ."
> T. S. Eliot, "The Dry Salvages"

But there is no rest, and the guess never fully goes away. The line of thinking found in the preceding paragraph recognizes the audiable as the sensory underpinning of surmise: the conceptual and verbal leap without which understanding is impossible. Friedrich Schleiermacher, who gave the theory of interpretation—hermeneutics—its modern form in the early nineteenth century, took such "divination," as he called it, as foundational. "The general and the particular must penetrate each other," he wrote, "and this can happen only by divination."[8]

Modern theorists have been dismissive of this cognitive leap, but it remains a constant in experience and it has to be recognized and reckoned with. Divination belongs to the region of experience in which the empirical is transcended and the dogmatic is transgressed. In more everyday terms, we practice divination when we extrapolate from facts and suspend presuppositions. Matters of course do not end with that; divination always leaves much to be done, because it is by nature only a beginning, and often a false start. But only insofar as we move, by invention and interpretation, from divination to understanding, do we fulfill our actual mandate from the general condition of openness to speech.

Folk etymology has it that the term "hermeneutics" refers to the wing-footed Greek god Hermes (Latin Mercury), who is both a messenger and a mischief-maker. The middle, mercurial region between observation and prior belief, the hermeneutic, Hermes-inspired space of messages in motion into which divination ushers us, is the always sought-for space of insight, mutual obligation, secular transcendence, and human connection. Utterance in this region is to be understood and defended as far more than the expression of monadic or even dialogic points of view. And its audiable element is to be affirmed as the evidence (not the "sign") of the livability possible only in this space—nowhere else. But the livable is never merely given, here least of all. This middle region requires as much discipline, learning, invention, imagination, restraint, and critical intelligence as either of the regions from which it breaks, but without the poverty of the empirical or the violence of the dogmatic.

The audiable is the promise of voice. It is the condition of possibility of utterance even though its physical absence is no impediment to utterance. But the audiable is also the support of being. Absolute silence, the muting of the audiable, is, for a hearing person, de-realization. Nothingness is soundless; soundlessness is nothingness.

But must it be? A principle that will come up repeatedly here is that seeing without hearing is sensory breakdown, something unsettling, uncanny, only half realized. But of course this principle presupposes the universality of hearing, and that is only *almost* true. For the deaf, the envelope of silence (if one can call it "silence") would be perfectly ordinary. Is there a parallel to the audiable in a nonhearing world?

The answer is best left for those with direct experience. Suffice it to say here that deafness is not absolute; that the auditory, conceived as a hum, is vibratory as well as acoustic, gestural and tactile as well as sonorous; and that if one thinks of the auditory as a promise of spoken language, there may be a similar horizon of motion that is the promise of signing. Certainly there is a musical dimension to signing compounded of rhythm, expressive movement of the hands, and vibration. Signing songs are a flourishing genre.[9]

Silence is sometimes ineffable but the ineffable is rarely silent. Where speech is lacking, expression diverts itself into sound without words: sighs, gasps, cries, moans, sobs, croons, long vowels, intakes of breath, a ringing in the ears. Nothing keeps us from utterance. But the sounds we utter do more than take the place of speech. They also *hold* that place, until such time as language steps forth to continue the experience, to sound it out more acutely, to let it resonate from word to word, phrase to phrase, sentence to sentence, never fully found but very far from lost.

The aesthetic form of this resonance is known as song.

The past and the future are silent; the present is sonorous. From this simple, basic, but neglected fact we tend to infer the converse: the sonorous is present. But sound intends the future. Like melody, it embodies a principle of continuation in being perceived. Where melody seeks repetition, and shapes future hearings with each repetition it finds, sound in general is a sensory promise of more sound to come. The world is alive with sound because sound is the sensory form of continuation. Sounds cease; sound does not. The sensory form of that difference is the audiable.

So sound is the measure of life. I hope it is clear by now that in saying so I do not mean that sound received in its identity as sound signifies or transmits the feeling of life, as if the feeling existed elsewhere on its own. The sound and the feeling are different aspects of the same phenomenon. But the phenomenon is equivocal and elusive. One cannot take up the existence of vibrancy and the audiable, and the relatively rare occasions on which they become matters of sense, as bromides for making oneself feel good or wise. Listening in the sense I am seeking to speak of here is a source of knowledge and pleasure but it is also difficult. The philosophy of listening referred to in my title is neither a prescription nor a doctrine but a problem. The idea is to provide a stimulus, not to promote a shibboleth.

An ABC:

A: No animation without sound, no sound without music, no music without voice, no voice without the audiable.

B: In a secularized and rationalized world, a world thinkable only under the rubric of modernity, the proliferation of animated forms becomes the life force, immortality as semi-material semi-presence, the soul in things and of things.

C: These two conditions form a loop.

But as with the imagetext, sound is strangely—well, not so strangely—absent from recent efforts to raise material things to the level of significance traditionally occupied by concepts. Latour and others want us to *see* that things act in the world as much as we do, and that, in Jane Bennett's words, there is "a liveliness intrinsic to . . . the thing formerly known as an object."[10] Sound at best plays second fiddle and at worst fades into the pantomime of lively things. This must change. Things, the thing, and objects are not, are never, silent. They fall onto an acoustic map and project acoustic spaces about them; they offer textual spaces for inscription and reading-off; they invite acoustic response and vocal or vocalizing performance. Things sing. Things too sing. Thinging is singing.

The audiable is the sound of the wave before it breaks.

Music in the Air

Modern music in the air is an artifice of technology, born of the assembly line and the elevator and before that of the department store.[1] Commercial and industrial modernity coincide with its rise, and it has now handily survived their fall. But the idea of music in the air is much older. Floating music, music heard across space, is a pastoral idea and a cosmological idea, in both cases with antique roots. At its most sophisticated in the era before its technological possibility, such music marked the intersection of the pastoral and the cosmological. This idea can be found working with undiminished force early in Thomas Hardy's novel of 1874, *Far from the Madding Crowd:*

> The sky was clear ... and the twinkling of all the stars seemed to be but throbs of one body, timed by a common pulse. The North Star was directly in the wind's eye, and since evening the Bear had swung round it outwardly to the east, till he was now at a right angle to the meridian. .... Suddenly an unexpected series of sounds began to be heard in this place against the sky. They had a clearness which was to be found nowhere in the wind and a sequence which was to be found nowhere in nature. They were the notes of Farmer Oak's flute.[2]

The sounds of the flute address nature from outside, not as an opposite, but as a supplement: the clearness of the notes to the clearness of the sky, the sequence of the notes to the rotation of the constellations. The music and the stars move to the same common pulse, even if the human pulse is, in a trope typical of Hardy, almost lost amid the grand but indifferent pulse of the cosmic whole. Farmer Oak's flute is of a piece with, in effect plays the same piece as, the shepherd's pipe of Virgil and Theocritus.[3] Thus Virgil, Eclogue XIII:

> Rise, morning star, and bring the kindly day
> While I lament, deceived in love . . .
> Begin with me, my pipe, Maenalian airs.
> Mount Maenalus ever has melodious groves
> And vocal pines, and ever hears the loves
> Of shepherds, and of Pan, who was the first
> Who would not let the reed stand by unused.
> Begin with me, my pipe, Maenalian airs.[4]

It ought to be possible, therefore, to compose a genealogy of music in the air. Not a chronicle, although that is possible, too, but a genealogy in the sense developed by Michel Foucault, an indirect speculative history that reconceives the phenomenon by uncovering the antecedents to which it is linked, not by affiliation, but by detour. Such genealogy is a history of forking paths. What follows in this section is a fragment of one such genealogy: a series of moments beginning in the sixteenth century and ending in the twentieth. The moments occur to Shakespeare's Caliban, roaming an island home that is no longer his except for its aerial music; to Robert Browning's Caliban, an outraged, quasi-Darwinian reincarnation of his namesake; to Wagner's Siegfried, listening to the murmurs of a bewildering forest on the cusp of the audible; to James Agee, caught between the metropolis and the backwoods in the dark night of a dark time; and to Toni Morrison's Milkman Dead, bound on a quest for origins that leads him, too, to a speaking forest in the dark.

The Island

Early in *The Tempest*, Prospero accuses Caliban of ingratitude for having been civilized, which from Caliban's point of view means dispossessed and subjugated. (Prospero, in exile from Europe, has appropriated the island from Caliban's mother. He rules there with the help of a book whose "white magic" gives him power over the four traditional elements: water, air, earth, and fire. All but water are personified, by Ariel, Caliban, and Prospero himself, respectively.) The exchange between master and slave turns on the major instrument of civilization, namely language:

Prospero:

> Abhorred slave! . . . I pitied thee,
> Took pains to make thee speak, taught thee each hour
> One thing or other: when thou didst not, savage,
> Know thine own meaning, but wouldst gabble like
> A thing most brutish, I endow'd thy purposes
> With words that made them known: but thy vile race,
> Though thou didst learn, had that in't which good natures
> Could not abide to be with. . . .

Caliban:

> You taught me language: and my profit on't
> Is, I know how to curse.
>   (Act 1, scene 2, ll. 351–64)[5]

But Caliban has learned to do more than curse. His way with words may be one of the reasons that audiences, unlike Prospero (who nominally speaks for them), tend to find Caliban oddly endearing. (Perhaps another reason is that Caliban speaks for the audience's own resistance to docility in the name of virtue.) Nowhere is this more true than in the unique moment when Caliban speaks lyrically to convey his impression of the island's ambient music. His description even anticipates the masque of plenty that Prospero will later invoke with magic. But Caliban's magic lies entirely in his speech:

> The isle is full of noises,
> Sounds and sweet airs, that give delight and hurt not.
> Sometimes a thousand twangling instruments
> Will hum about mine ears, and sometime voices
> That, if I then had waked after long sleep,
> Will make me sleep again: and then, in dreaming,
> The clouds methought would open and show riches
> Ready to drop upon me that, when I waked,
> I cried to dream again.
>   (Act 3, scene 2, ll. 148–56)

The isle is indeed full of noises, in the form of songs, most of them sung by Ariel, the spirit of the air placing music in the air. The audience is supposed to imagine Ariel as invisible even as it sees him singing. Caliban's music alone is actually invisible, which imbues it with an inherent sense of distance and gives it a greater degree of wonder—a primary theme in the play—than can be found in Ariel's songs (for which some music survives). Caliban hears the hum of the world.

The music that Caliban hears is edged with magic and enchantment— and the magic is not metaphor, since Prospero is literally a thaumaturge, although knowing this fact does not render the music less mysterious or expose its source. Depending on the production we happen to be watching, do *we* hear anything in this scene? If so, is it Ariel we hear? Should the "airs" be vocal or instrumental? Should we surmise that the sounds come at Prospero's bidding or refer them to the island itself? And if we do hear something, whether voice or instrument, are we drawn more to the factual truth that the sound originates in the motions of an unseen body behind the apparatus of theatrical illusion, or to the phenomenological truth that the music is simply there, in the air, both if we hear it and (perhaps even more) if we do not?

Shelley later, and Auden much later, would refer the play's music solely to Ariel—and Auden would ironically have Caliban speak in long-winded prose.[6] But Robert Browning, in "Caliban upon Setebos" (ca. 1860, published 1864), heard things differently. Browning remembered Caliban's ear and, in an important if disenchanting move, reconceived it as the ear of a purely natural being—Caliban as natural man. But then, Browning's is a post-Darwinian Caliban, caught up in the religious controversies of the Victorian era and portrayed as making a god in his own atavistic image. Browning's version of the island's music is therefore cruel and ominous. But it is still ubiquitous.

Browning's Caliban hears less than Shakespeare's and surmises more. He inhabits a world where music as such has vanished but where music in nature has become metaphor; as we will shortly hear, this is the very metaphor that will be rendered literal in Agee's narrative. In the case of Browning's Caliban, the metaphorization is a material process: the cry of a bird becomes a kind of rough music as a result of its reproduction on a pipe—in effect a panpipe—that Caliban has devised for himself. The music appears as a cry of pain, because everything this Caliban sees and hears is measured by a private utilitarian calculus of pleasure and pain. Yet the same music, imagined as if the pipe were sentient and had vocalized the sound, also becomes a cry of Promethean defiance. Caliban's ear hears itself in Caliban's surrogate voice. The sound in the air becomes musical only after it has been mechanically reproduced, in a travesty of the pastoral sound of the shepherd's pipe:

> 'Hath cut a pipe of pithless elder-joint
> That, blown through, gives exact the scream o' the jay
> When from her wing you twitch the feathers blue:
> Sound this, and little birds that hate the jay
> Flock within stone's throw, glad their foe is hurt:
> Put case such pipe could prattle and boast forsooth
> "I catch the birds, I am the crafty thing,
> I make the cry my maker cannot make
> With his great round mouth; he must blow through mine!"[7]

The mystery here is no longer magical but purely natural: the mystery of animal sentience. Browning's great feat is to have his Caliban *speak* for animal sentience, the very thing that animal sentience as such is incapable of doing. In the speech also resides a certain musicality, a bodily-material music mimicked by the rough magic of Browning's style in this text.

The Forest

The potential for enchantment that nonetheless persists can best be gauged if we shift our attention to a different Caliban, the Caliban-like figure of Wagner's young Siegfried. The Wagnerian hero-to-be notoriously begins as a natural, all too natural man in the music drama named for him. He not only rivals Caliban for brutishness, but may even in part be modeled on Shakespeare's Caliban. Like Caliban, Siegfried is a solitary misfit in a remote, primitive natural world, raised by an exiled and disaffected "father" and distinguished by unruly urges partly qualified by intimations of a finer sensibility.

That sensibility first manifests itself in *Siegfried* in the "Forest Murmurs" scene of act 2, in which the musicalization of nature portends Siegfried's coming of age as a hero. Reflecting on the mystery of his parentage, Siegfried hears sounds and sweet airs and the song of a little bird amid the rustle of the forest, a locale of course pregnant with enchantment in the German tradition. Unlike Caliban, he does not hear music as such but the murmurs of the forest *as* music. Only we, in the audience, hear music literally, and the music we hear is itself metaphorical, a representation of natural sound in its becoming musical. The music in the air does not cross into nature from the sphere of magic, but instead possesses a natural magic, or more exactly renders nature itself both musical and magical.

Within the opera's narrative, there is no music except the song of the woodbird in a forest otherwise full of natural sounds. Within the opera's staging, the forest scene appears as a becoming-music, even, perhaps, insofar as it does so, as a becoming-invisible, a scene heard but not seen, less a place than a distance that becomes a proximity. (Music in the air reveals itself as sound, or song, that renders distance as nearness, perhaps too much.). The audience simultaneously listens to Wagner's music as performed for the occasion and hears the narrative's forest murmurs *as* a music that no one performs. Siegfried, at this point half in and half out of the narrative, hears the same murmurs as musicalized, and therefore encrypted, speech. His question is how to understand the woodbird's song.

In this context, given the skill of Browning's Caliban with a reed, it is interesting that Siegfried too crafts a reed and tries, but fails, to imitate the bird's song. The sound of the reed or the shepherd's pipe or "oaten flute" is a realization of the distance innate to music "in the air." When both Berlioz, in the "Scene aux champs" from *Symphonie fantastique,* and Wagner, in act 3 of *Tristan und Isolde,* want to invoke that sound, they place the piper offstage. But Siegfried is bewildered by distance; he experiences everything close up. He can make music only on his horn, which he uses only to announce and declare himself, to close rather than to open distance. It is the horn that, when the reed fails, shifts Siegfried's register from pastoral to heroic and summons forth his antagonist Fafner as an ambivalent "good companion."

In contrast to what technology would soon amply demonstrate, music in the air for Siegfried is precisely a music that cannot be made: not played, not manufactured. It can only be heard, and heard only on condition of not being understood. The enchantment here is, so to speak, a product of pure rather than material metaphor, inaccessible except to Caliban's ear. Or ears, since what the audience hears incorporates but also exceeds what Siegfried hears, the audience having a capacity for nostalgia, based on the idea of natural magic, that the naïve and uncouth Siegfried lacks. Siegfried hears the floating music as a riddle; the audience hears it as an idyll.

A similar effect famously arises with the offstage singing at the beginning of *Tristan*, where Caliban's ear has mutated to Isolde's wrath, a form of selective deafness nonetheless penetrated by the disembodied song of a lovesick offstage sailor. In this case the positions of audience and character as established in *Siegfried* are equalized or even reversed. Isolde, painfully self-aware and self-evasive, hears an enchantment that she repudiates precisely because she wants it too much, whereas the audience hears an old song. But enchantment is always in the air along with the music. For Wagner, one might speculate, with the covered orchestra pit at Bayreuth in mind, the musicalization of space, space becoming the emanation of music in the air, is the fundamental form of enchantment itself in a modern era that renders all ears Caliban's ears. To invoke a still later Wagnerism, it is not time that becomes space in *Parsifal*, but music.[8]

The Porch

This is the assumption inherited by James Agee. His version of Caliban's music is like Siegfried's except that it rings through a forest of the night in which mystery has become nostalgia. Technology has intervened; with Agee music in the air assumes the pathos of modernity. His forest is no longer the forest primeval; it is not even the forest that Siegfried shares with his counterparts in the Brothers Grimm. It is a listening post from which the singing of animals sounds like the music of classical composers, music as likely to be heard on radio or shellac disk as in the live space of a concert hall. The only way to retain any sense of enchantment is to displace the sound of this music back again into the sounds of nature, Bach to a fox, gradus *ex* Parnassum.

Let Us Now Praise Famous Men, with photographs by Walker Evans and text by James Agee, is an account of life in the sharecropper South during the Great Depression, strangely divided between Evans's stark photos and Agee's rhapsodic prose. The text is punctuated by three meditative segments entitled "On the Porch," each of which describes the sights and sounds that came to Agee and his hosts as they all lay on the porch at night. The third of these segments is an account of music in the air; it closes the book.

The music—and it is always treated as music, never as natural sound, never as cry—consists a duet between two animal calls, one near, one distant. Agee never verifies the identity of the singers, though he eventually decides to treat them as if they were foxes. Like the noises on Caliban's island, those in Agee's Southern woods are transporting; they create the space of a transient utopia in a world otherwise desperate and unforgiving. Agee and his companions are said to respond to the joining of these sounds with a silent laughter, a restorative joyousness, that Agee says he has "experienced only rarely: listening to the genius of Mozart at its angriest and cleanest, most masculine fire; . . . walking in streets or driving in country"; or in the early phases of tender sexual love.[9]

The source of this music's power is partly cosmological, as it is for Caliban and Farmer Oak, although the transport in this case is more chthonic than celestial—Agee is insistent on its corporeal and sexual qualities. But the power also derives from the ability of the ear and the word combined to hear, to have heard, these animal sounds as literal rather than merely figurative music, without even wasting a moment to deny the figurative hearing. So Agee will not only describe what has been heard simply as music—"[like a] low note on the clarinet. It ran eight identical times to a call or stanza, a little faster than allegretto" (464)—but he will even describe it as composed music, classical music: "The first entrance of this call was as perfect a piece of dramatic or musical structure as I know of: . . . the entrance of the mysterious principal completely unforeseen yet completely casual, with none of the quality of studiousness in its surprise which hurts for instance some of the music of Brahms" (467). As rivals of Brahms and Mozart, the foxes that make this music are anthropomorphic beasts, clever heirs to the fox of fable, the trickster Reynard who constantly escapes punishment and cheats death. Yet they remain wholly natural and animal, creatures of the forest whose voices carry through the night air in tune with the ambient sound of the forest's murmurs.

This strange yet spontaneous conflation of musical art and musical nature gives delight and hurts only a little. The effect of the "drizzling confabulation of pastoral-nocturnal music" (470) cannot be communicated except by the music itself in its own fleeting interlude (Agee says that it lasted twenty minutes). But the "grief" of this incommunicability pales before "the frightening joy of hearing the world talk to itself" (469). Agee clings for solace to the whisper of the audiable.

Another Forest

Agee's account goes awry in an unguarded moment. Hearing the music of animals in the air pleases him, he tells us, not only like listening to Mozart but also like "watching Negroes." This splotch of throwaway racism finds a corrective, and perhaps a part of its history, toward the end of Toni Morrison's novel *Song of Solomon*. The novel's hero, Milkman Dead, hears more than he would have thought possible in the barking of distant hounds—the heirs, perhaps, to Agee's mythical foxes. But before we can eavesdrop on Milkman, we need to go back a bit further.

In "The Sorrow Songs," the concluding chapter of *The Souls of Black Folk*, W. E. B. Dubois traces a loss of intelligibility that accompanied the preservation of African music among slaves in the plantation South. The songs maintain their power to sustain and comfort at the cost of memory and meaning:

> In these songs, I have said, the slave spoke to the world. Such a message is naturally veiled and half articulate. Words and music have lost each other and new and cant phrases of a dimly understood theology have displaced the older sentiment. Once in a while we catch a strange word of an unknown tongue, as the "Mighty Myo," which figures as a river of death; more often slight words or mere doggerel are joined to music of singular sweetness. . . . Of nearly all the songs, however, the music is distinctly sorrowful. The ten master songs I have mentioned tell in word and music of trouble and exile, of strife and hiding; they grope toward some unseen power and sigh for rest in the End.

The plot of Morrison's novel turns on a reversal of the effacement described by Dubois. Milkman hears a group of children singing a song "he had heard off and on all his life," an "old blues song" that his grandmother used to sing all the time. (302) The lyrics seem to alternate sense and nonsense, but Milkman is ultimately able to decrypt (in every sense of the term) the strange words of their unknown tongue. In doing so he recovers the previously unknown history of his own family, which is also a history of flight from slavery—literally of flight, of flying through the air, the act on which the novel ends. But the song is only the proximate source of this second freedom. Its ultimate source is music in the air that acts as a medium and peels itself back to reveal something more primary.

One intimation of this sound comes from a natural echo chamber, Ryna's Gulch, a ravine named for one of Milkman's ancestors who is said to have gone mad and "screamed out loud for days" when her husband, Solomon, flew away: "You know, like a bird. Just stood up in the fields one day . . . spun around a few times and was lifted up in the air." (323) Solomon's rise precipitates Ryna's fall, which becomes a musical cadence (from Latin *cadere*, to fall) in the nonsense verses of the children's song:

> *Black lady fell down on the ground*
> *Come booba yalle, come booba tambee*
> *Threw her body all around*
> *Come konka yalle, come konka tambee*

The sound from the ravine, carried from afar, strikes those who hear it as "a woman name Ryna crying. You could hear her when the wind was right." (302)

More elemental still is the sound of the hunting dogs. This music in the air makes its way into the text in italics, tongue-twisting scribbles of onomatopoeia that retard the narrative voice but also make it resonate: "The low *howm howm* that sounded like a string bass imitating a bassoon meant something the dogs understood . . . the long sustained yells, the tuba sounds, the drumbeat sounds, the low liquid *howm hown*, the reedy whistles, the thin *eeee's* of a cornet, the *unh unh unh* bass chords." (278)

At first this music sounds to the narrator or to Milkman (the two cannot be distinguished at this point) like a language, but only at first: "No, it was not language; it was what there was before language" (ibid.). It is the sound, in particular, of a mutual participation, a primary auditory medium that is also a primary joining. It is the sound that promises language and is its premise. Its form is the same kind of call and response that underpins its jazz-like rhythm and timbre. And underpinning that is a medium still more refined, audible only as a whisper, but a whisper that convokes an intelligible union of sound, sight, and touch: Calvin, Milkman's guide, "whispered to the trees, whispered to the ground, touched them, as a blind

man caresses a page of Braille, pulling meaning through his fingers"
(ibid.). The whisper is a metaphor, but the reader can nonetheless hear it,
caress it, the way a blind person reads.

Coda: Caliban's Ear

Music in the air originates, or so we used to imagine, as audible breakthrough, as something that literally airs, that is, reveals, uncovers itself.
But as it passes from myth to history and technology, such music merges
with the air itself: the airs become the air; the music becomes audible but
unheard. It becomes, we might say, *audited.* As Richard Middleton notes,
"Until relatively recently, music punctuated life; often the performed time
of the musical event stood in a dissociated, even liminal relationship to the
time of surrounding existence. The shift is not absolute . . . [M]usicalized
life and lived music interact. Nevertheless, the *specialness* of the musical
event that we can recognize in many traditional contexts—its capacity to
interrupt—has been attenuated."[10]

The history of this attenuation may be measured by such moments as
rub against the grain, those increasingly rare interludes or interruptions in
which music comes to be noticed, noted, and not merely audited. In order
to listen well, we need, like Caliban still, to have our hearing interrupted.

"No Sound without Music"

So I said earlier. But how can that be? Isn't music made of sound? Doesn't
it turn the natural material of sound into art?

Yes, and yes—and yet: Music is sound framed as a source of pleasure.
That framing changes the phenomenon it frames. Music stands apart
from sound as indication, communication, and warning. (It may even do
so for songbirds and dolphins.) The condition of music, hearing with
pleasure, hearing as a pleasure, fosters or excites a tendency to regard
music not simply as one possibility for sound but instead as a condition
immanent in sound. The sounds of music in the air just sampled all say as
much by the way their musicality echoes the ancient idea of cosmic har-

mony in contexts far removed from its origin. That will happen again in the course of this book. The pleasure consummated in music is the sound that attaches us to the heard world. When fully immersed in that world—alive with sound—we treat sound as if it were *destined* to music.

The attachment is hard to resist, even if one feels one ought to. St. Augustine struggled with music for theological reasons, and in reflecting on his ambivalence he discovered the reversal by which music comes to underlie sound:

> I confess that I find some pleasant restfulness in the sounds that [sacred] words animate when they are sung by a pleasant and well-trained voice. . . . They demand some place of honor in my heart, and I can scarcely give them a fitting one. For sometimes I seem to myself to give them more honor than is seemly. I feel that when the sacred words are chanted well, our souls are moved . . . with a warmer devotion than if they are not thus sung, and all the diverse affections of our spirit have their proper modes in voice and chant, stirred by I do not know what hidden kinship. But the pleasure of my flesh . . . often misleads me when sense does not accompany reason, to come patiently behind it, but only, having been admitted, strives to run ahead and lead. Thus in this I sin unknowingly and know it afterwards.[1]

Music pleases Augustine so much that he seems compelled to begin by understating its effect on him. His distrust of musical pleasure comes precisely from his understanding that it attaches him to the world; that it stirs up an obscure delight at being a creature of flesh, a being with ears. The music of a hymn does not merely distract the listener from the hymn's meaning, and hence from God, but it does so because it *attracts* the listener to the life embedded in sounding bodies. Stripped of its theological impropriety, this is a persuasive description: yes, that's what music does; that's what we ask it to do.

Language and the Human

If the world is alive with sound, it is presumably so for all sentient creatures, but not on quite the same terms. One key difference between the auditory worlds of human and nonhuman animals must come from language, taking the term in its strongest sense to include not just communication through sound but through fully elaborated systems that undergo historical changes and are capable of speculative and fictional elaboration, complex specifications of time, self-paraphrase and self-citation, and similar ramifications. For human animals (including the deaf) the heard world is a world steeped in language, a world in which sound is steeped in language. Like music, language, which is in first instance made of sound, has the power to reshape the thing it is made of. Where does that power come from?

The answer may lie in a dimension of language that modern thought about signification has tended to neglect, namely reference. Unlike signification, which depends on conventions, reference is genuinely mysterious. It does not feel conventional, but ontological, and it may be so because it feels so. We know perfectly well that the English *tree* has no more relation to its object than the German *Baum* or French *arbe*, but we also know that a tree is a tree. The force of reference appears most directly in the words called "shifters," which change their reference with every use. Words like the English *this, that, these,* and *those* echo the actions of pointing at things and handling them. Those actions form the link between reference and bodily presence. Their effect is to merge the names of things with the weight of the things themselves. The sound of language gives its reference body and animation, forming an auditory net in which all intelligible sound is at some point entangled.

Like music, reference acts as a medium of attachment to the world. St. Augustine, who discovered as much for music, did the same for reference in a famous account of language learning. The account is especially notable because Wittgenstein begins his *Philosophical Investigations* with a critique of it. Here is Augustine:

> When [others] called something by name and afterwards moved their bodies toward it, I saw it and realized that the thing they wanted to point to was called by the sound they uttered. And what they meant was made plain by the movement of their bodies, by a kind of natural language common to all peoples, which expresses itself through the face, nods of the eyes and other body parts, and tones of voice which indicate whether the mind's affections should be sought, possessed, rejected, or avoided. Thus by repeatedly hearing words in their places in different sentences, I came to identify the things

the words stood for and, having trained my mouth to pronounce these signs, I was able to express my will. In this way I communicated with those around me the signs by which we enunciate our wishes, and advanced deeper into the stormy fellowship of human life.[1]

Wittgenstein criticizes this passage for confining itself to the learning of nouns (ironically called *Hauptwörter*, primary words, in German). But he does not consider what form of life, as he might have called it, that such learning involves. Augustine stresses the effect of sound in relation to desire, the body, and action, which Wittgenstein ignores because his concerns lie elsewhere. Noun sounds, the sounds of primary words, replace the act of pointing or handling. But as Augustine emphasizes, this movement into utterance is not merely conceptual. The word forms the relay for expression, bearing-upon, seeking, caring, wanting, and so on, and it does so precisely insofar as its utterance establishes reference. Reference imports into language the force of behavior in and toward the world. Language thus directs and augments the force that connects the senses to their objects on behalf of need and desire. It absorbs gesture and appropriates intonation and facial expression. Routed through language, the sound of reference enables one to engage with the world, to join in the stormy fellowship of life.

Lord Bacon's Echoes

Sir Francis Bacon was fascinated by echoes. He wrote about them from the perspectives of both mythography and natural science. The two might seem hopelessly incongruous, but for Bacon they coalesce. Each leads to a perception of the world talking to itself. Someone speaks, explicitly or implicitly Bacon himself; the return speech, especially in the higher-order form of echoes of echoes, briefly transforms the speaker into a human "sound house" where sound can converse with sound. In the utopia Bacon describes in *The New Atlantis* (1627), sound houses display the marvels of a future technology. They contain "divers strange and artificial echoes, reflecting the voice many times, and as it were tossing it: and some that give back the voice louder than it came, some shriller, and some deeper; yea, some rendering the voice differing in the letters or articulate sound from that they receive."[1] For Bacon, who sought them out, the real-world places richest in echoes also have overtones of mystery or depth: a cavernous well "of twenty-five fathom," a cellar full of barrels, a chapel at Trinity College, Cambridge, a chapel a few miles outside of Paris.

As a naturalist, Bacon understands sound as immersive, self-replicating, and paradoxical. He often returns to the observation that sound, unlike sight, is circular and enveloping; he hears it flow around barriers and multiply itself almost to a receding infinity; and he puzzles over the observation that "one of the strangest secrets in sounds is that the whole sound is not in the whole air only; but the whole sound is also in every small part of the air. So that all the curious diversity of articulate sounds, of the voice of man or birds, will enter at a small cranny unconfused."[2] The experience of what we might call the self-similarity of sound in air compensates for its brief existence—"All sounds are suddenly made, and suddenly perish"—by swiftly drawing a circle centered on the observer: "If a man speak aloud in the middle of a field, he may be heard a furlong round him; and that in articulate sounds, entire, in every little portion of the air: and all this shall be done in less than a minute." Sound reaffirms the traditional form of the cosmos into which it vanishes.

Echoes defer the moment of vanishing. Echoes of the voice do so by literally forming an exchange of words, and one that rises to a chorus when the echoes echo each other. At the town of Pont-Charenton, near Paris on the Seine, Bacon stands at one end of a pillared chapel and multiplies his voice to create a disembodied but purely natural harmony, a kind of motet for multiple choirs (the image, which is mine, alludes to a real composition by Thomas Tallis that will concern us elsewhere). The echoes rebound on each other with an effect that requires an optical analogy to explain:

> [Upon my] speaking at the one end, [the chapel] returned the voice thirteen separate times. . . . [What I heard was] not different echoes from several places but a tossing of the voice, as a ball, different ways: like reflections in looking-glasses; where, if you place one glass before, and another behind, you shall see the glass behind, and the image within the glass before; and again, the glass before, in that; and many such super-reflections, till the images of the object fail, and die at last. . . . So the voice in that chapel makes succeeding super-reflections, melting by degrees, every reflection growing weaker than the former.[3]

The images die, and the sounds melt, into a shadowy afterworld which is also the potentiality of the repetitions that have led to them. Bacon never quite names, perhaps never quite recognizes, this mysterious substrate, but at one point he comes close. Pondering the brief life of sounds in air, he speculates that "either the air suffers some force by sound and then restores itself, as water does; or that the air readily imbibes the sound as grateful but cannot maintain it—for the air seems to have a secret appetite of receiving sound at first, but then other gross and more material qualities presently suffocate it, like flame, which is suddenly generated but instantly extinguished."[4] The language here edges toward the mythological; the air becomes a spirit thirsting for sound, always ready to grasp it but never able to keep it for long. The air might almost be said to want sound the way the inquiring mind wants knowledge—a possibility resonant with Bacon's mythographical account of sound as the internal monologue of the world.

The account comes at the end of a chapter on the god Pan, understood as a representation of nature in the large early-modern sense of the whole creation. Pan turns out to have a special relation to the nymph Echo:

> It is little wonder that no loves are attributed to Pan except his marriage with Echo. For the world delights in itself and, in itself, all things. Whoever loves desires something, but in plenitude there is no room for desire. Therefore the world can have neither loves nor desire (because it is content with itself) except perhaps the love of *discourse*. Such is the nymph Echo, a thing not substantial but vocal [*res non solida sed vocalis*]; or, when it should be more accurate, Syrinx, [namely writing] . . .[5] Among discourses or voices it is excellent to choose Echo alone as the world's wife. For the true philosophy is the one that echoes most faithfully the voice of the world itself and is written as if (*veluti*) from the world's own dictation; and is nothing other than its image and reflection, to which it adds nothing of its own, but only repeats and echoes it.[6]

A subtle gap opens here between the world and the discourse that describes it. Even when the discourse is as faithful as possible, perfection remains impossible; true philosophy must submit to the subtle qualification of the *as if*. Desire inhabits this intermediate space, specifically the desire for an ever-ramifying discourse that multiplies like the mirror images in Bacon's recollection of the chapel at Pont-Charenton. The two passages echo each other and—echo on echo—the thirteen-fold returns of Bacon's voice in the chapel as they melt by degrees into the auditory horizon. As the metaphor of marriage intimates, the space of desire is one with the space of potentiality. Sound, and sight too, become revelatory when love makes them hover between promise and fulfillment.

Ripple Effects

DISTANT VOICES

I. GOETHE

In 1786, Johann Wolfgang von Goethe took a sabbatical from both his literary fame and his duties at the ducal court in Weimar. He set off for Italy incognito on a journey that would last nearly two years. One of his first stops was Venice. He recorded his arrival there with something approaching reverence: "Now it stood written on my page in the Book of Fate, that on the evening of the 28th of September, by 5 o'clock, German time, I should see Venice for the first time."[1]

Goethe's initial impressions of the city were overwhelmingly visual, a tourist's phantasmagoria of gondolas, the Grand Canal, San Marco, the Rialto, and the crowded network of bridges and waterways:

> The large canal, winding like a serpent, yields to no street in the world, and nothing can be put by the side of the space in front of St. Mark's square—I mean that great mirror of water, which is encompassed by Venice. . . . The labyrinth of the city, everywhere intersected by larger or smaller canals, is connected by bridges. The narrow and crowded appearance of the whole cannot be conceived by one who has not seen it.[2]

But these sights were perhaps not the most striking sensory impression that the "strange island-city" made on Goethe. That was reserved for a reflection in that great mirror of water, not of the city's many sights, but of one of its sounds.

Goethe had heard that the gondoliers were supposed to be able to volley passages of classical Italian poetry across the water, singing in turn to melodies of their own making. He wanted to hear them and arranged for a demonstration. But he was not happy with the results; the singing struck him as "harsh and screeching" (*rauh und schreiend*). His Venetian companion assured him that the sound would be better if the distance between the singers were increased. He arranged for the adjustment, and it worked. The harsher sounds now seemed like a call for attention and "the passages which soon followed, and which, in accordance with their sense, had to be sung more softly, sounded like plaintive tones still resonating after a cry of sentiment or pain."[3] Only in the "sensation of the distant" did the singing "fulfill its purpose"; only coming from the distance did it sound "inexpressibly charming." Thus softened, the plaintive song sounded "like a lament without sadness" (*wie eine Klage ohne Trauer*). It induced tears in the listener, but tears of aesthetic pleasure rather than of grief.

The distance transforms the give and take of communication into a rhythm of empathy. The mutual call and response of the watermen turns the "still mirror" of the lagoon into a tide of echoes that seek each other from afar:

> Sometimes [the singer] lets his voice grow as loud as possible; it spreads far and wide over the still mirror. . . . In the distance another, perhaps a total stranger, hears him. Melody and Poem bind two strangers together; the second becomes the echo of the first, and he, too, also strives now to become audible to the one he first heard . . . The listener, who moves between both, takes part in it [all] while the two singers remain occupied with each other.

What binds the singers together is not the expression of their song but its material form crossing the distance: the carrying of the first voice over the water, the echo of the first voice in the second, and the auditory force of binding, of tying together, of connecting physically but without touch, produced by the mutuality of the voices. What becomes audible, at least for the listener, the third party, the eavesdropper, is the resonance of the primary act of communication between persons.

The boatmen, or so Goethe imagines, enjoy their connection without quite hearing it as transfigured sound. They hear only each other. But the listener hears what the singers cannot. The singers ride the swell of vibrancy, but the listener, shuttling between them, hears the resonance on which the singers depend: the sound of distance as a medium, and, as the undertone to that, the sound of audibility itself.

But the undertones do not end there. Goethe's description modulates subtly from recalling his auditory experiment to projecting a fictional scene. The passage I quoted earlier belongs to that fiction, or more exactly to the explicit fictionalization of the actual event. The language of the description changes as fiction takes over from memory. Twice in succession, first in relation to the experiment and then in relation to its fictional recreation, Goethe discards the logic of exposition for chains of detail, abandons narrative logic for lyrical evocation.

Here is the first passage: "The still canals, the tall buildings, the radiance of the moon, the deep shadows, the ghost-like drifting of a few black gondolas to and fro enhanced the peculiarity of this scene." The play of light and shadow and the ghost-like movement set up the transition to an event not witnessed but imagined. Here is the second passage: "This wonderful song . . . is perfectly suited to a lonely idle boatman stretched out on his boat, humming something to himself to pass the time . . . Around him all is still; in the middle of a great populous city he is as it were in solitude. There is no rattle of a coach, no noise of a pedestrian; a still gondala hovers near him and one can scarcely hear the plash of its oar."

These passages echo each other as the boatmen do, sharing the key details of stillness, distance, solitude, and the faint, almost nonphysical movement of a gondola. Furthermore, they share the lyrical rhetoric that moves from image to image without transition. The chant-like rhythm that results makes the writer's language a primary matter of sense and exposes its relationship to the medium of resonance that writing depends on no less than speech or song. These passages present their writer as a solitary figure seeking by his verbal music to win an empathetic response from a distant reader. At the same time, that music draws attention to the poetic process by which writing may reanimate the speech that, since classical times, it was supposed only to symbolize. Writing borne on the medium of vibrancy induces a type of perception that might be called the half-heard.

It is worth noting in passing that Goethe closes his account by adding yet another series of undertones. To the array of doubles he has already produced, he adds another, this time doubling the song of men with that of women, namely fishwives singing to each other across the water in their husbands' absence. The result is the same as with the gondoliers: the binding together of two strangers by "a call from a solitary person into the far and wide [*die Ferne und Weite*], so that another with a similar voice might answer." The meeting of the voices produces an aesthetic state that mirrors the gondoliers' lament without sadness. The women's singing "is the expression of a strong, heartfelt yearning [*Sehnsucht*], which in that moment is near to the bliss of assuagement."

II. BEETHOVEN

Some years later, in 1801–02, Beethoven, with his deafness rapidly advancing, remembered or imagined an auditory idyll much like Goethe's. He is unlikely to have known Goethe's description, which had only been published in a literary magazine in 1789. Nonetheless, the first movement of Beethoven's so-called "Tempest" Sonata for Piano, Op. 31, no. 2, recreates in musical form the privileged experience of Goethe's listener and the auditory substance of what that listener heard.

Most of the movement is highly agitated, but it begins with a mysterious slow passage that returns several times, in several guises, to interrupt the tumult. Toward the end, recollections of this passage usher in two longer interruptions. A slow, unaccompanied melody, in the manner of a recitative, twice rises out of an arpeggio and sounds very softly over an acoustic blur. The melody is marked "with expression and simple." The blur comes from holding the damper pedal down throughout the episode, so that lingering sounds accumulate under the melody and absorb the dissonances that the melody itself produces.[4] The expressive intensity rises with the second statement, which is a shade longer and several shades more dissonant than the first. The melody not only evokes the sound of a voice from afar but also, veiled by the blur, assumes a serenely plaintive quality well described by Goethe's "lament without sadness."

Beethoven narrates in music the same auditory experience that Goethe narrates in words. The recitatives in the sonata stand in softening contrast to the harsh sounds that precede them; they evoke the "inexpressibly charming" sound of distant song; and above all they make the medium of listening audible in the blur created by the pedal—the object of a fascinated auditory gaze that knows itself as both fascinated and auditory. The effect was probably stronger in Beethoven's day than in ours, when the quality of being-sounded produced by the pedal in these passages was fainter, more demanding on the ear, than its counterpart on a modern instrument. In a world where distance defined the absolute limit of live communication, the experience was paradigmatic in seeking to touch that limit and in finding magic there. Goethe again says verbally what Beethoven shows musically: this purely auditory play of call and response "is the expression of a strong, heartfelt yearning, which in that moment is near to the bliss of assuagement."[5]

The Infinite Broadcast

I. BABBAGE

The concept of the audiable is a ghostly presence throughout much of Western intellectual history. It is latent in the idea of cosmic harmony, the Pythagorean music of the spheres; in the material intersection of music, mathematics, and astronomy in the monochord, the one-stringed instrument that Robert Fludd, in a famous drawing of 1618, took as the spine of the Ptolemaic universe; and in the early nineteenth-century popularity of the Aeolian harp, a sound box usually laid in a window where its strings could be ruffled by the wind. The last instance marks a turning point.

In 1837, Charles Babbage, the originator, with Ada Lovelace, of the idea of the programmable computer, set out to defend the idea that the intelligence of God is discernible in nature. For Babbage, this intelligibility resides not in any supposed order in the natural world but instead in an information-based dynamics in which nature and the form of intelligence are identical. Divine intelligence saturates the world in the form of what we would recognize as data storage. The traditional elements of earth, air, and water become recording media in which everything that human beings have ever done and said is preserved, as if on a hard drive with infinite capacity.

Speech, or rather vocalization, takes pride of place in Babbage's description: "The air itself is one vast library, on whose pages are for ever written all that man has ever said or even whispered. . . . [And] if the air we breathe is the never-failing historian of the sentiments we have uttered, earth, air, and ocean, are the eternal witnesses of the acts we have done. . . . [W]hatever movement is communicated to any of their particles, is transmitted to all around it."[1] Babbage goes on to compare this universal communication to the ripples of water produced by throwing a stone into a pool, with the proviso that the ripples expand around the entire globe. Similar ripples traverse the seas: "The momentary waves raised by the passing breeze, apparently born but to die on the spot which saw their birth, leave behind them an endless progeny, which, reviving with diminished energy in other seas, visiting a thousand shores, reflected from each and perhaps again partially concentrated, will pursue their ceaseless course till ocean be itself annihilated." The image of concentric rings of receding sound or motion, diffused eternally throughout a spherical whole, gives the ancient music of the spheres a modern scientific form. At the same time, this image recasts the elements, with the air first among equals, as readable through what is written on it, audible through the sounds that it records. Or, more exactly, the air becomes quasi-audible, discernible as the inaudible substrate of the audible. The air, in short, in its rippling and trembling, assumes the vibratory hum of the audiable.

II. COLERIDGE

If one reverses the direction of Babbage's ripples, the result is the image of the world conveyed by the sound of the Aeolian harp. The wind harp, as it is also called, receives and transmits to the ear the rippling sounds that, for Babbage, the air transmits after receiving them from our mouths. The same image of acoustic cosmos emerges in each case. The image finds definitive expression in Samuel Taylor Coleridge's poem "The Aeolian Harp," composed in 1797. Like Babbage later, Coleridge formulates his image with religious intent. But where Babbage acts with confidence, Coleridge reacts with anxiety.

Speaking to his new wife (at the start of what would prove a bad marriage), Coleridge extends the image of the wind harp to encompass all of nature:

> O! the one Life within us and abroad,
> Which meets all motion and becomes its soul,
> A light in sound, a sound-like power in light,
> Rhythm in all thought, and joyance everywhere—
> Methinks, it should have been impossible
> Not to love all things in a world so filled;
> Where the breeze warbles, and the mute still air
> Is Music slumbering on her instrument. . . .
>   And what if all of animated nature
> Be but organic Harps diversely framed,
> That tremble into thought, as o'er them sweeps
> Plastic and vast, one intellectual breeze,
> At once the Soul of each, and God of all?[2]

The question carries the speculation too far for comfort, and Coleridge backs away from it abruptly. He credits his wife with darting a "mild reproof" from her eyes that restores him to conventional piety while the eloquence of his verse takes a nosedive. The result is a paradox, a text that exists to reject the majority of its own utterance, and the most eloquent and imaginative part of its utterance at that. It is probably safe to say that most readers have preferred the retracted passages to the retraction, as perhaps the poem secretly wishes them to do. In any case, the speculation, or auscultation, resonates with the traces of the universal hum. It discerns the audiable underneath the sounds that prompt it. The inaudible substrate of the audible makes itself present, as if heard, in the still air beneath the breeze. The muteness of that air (here to be understood in a double sense, because an air is also a melody) becomes a form of expression as the air fuses with the figure of music "slumbering on her instrument." Iconographic tradition suggests that the instrument is yet another harp, or perhaps a lyre, something that sounds through vibrating strings. The feminine figure of music may even form a rival to the reproving figure of Sara Coleridge. The personification fuses sight and sound: music slumbering is music not yet heard, but it is music nonetheless, and known to both the ear and the mind's eye as just that, music, the nexus of resonance and cosmic harmony, here rendered entirely immanent in nature until the retraction intervenes. The audiable assumes an essential form of its identity in this passage: nearness of cosmos, *sotto voce*.

III. THOREAU

Coleridge's conception, minus his retreat from it, finds a perhaps knowing echo in a celebrated passage from Thoreau's *Walden* that also has affinities with Babbage's thermodynamically impossible world of circulating sound and motion:

> Sometimes, on Sundays, I heard the bells, the Lincoln, Acton, Bedford, or Concord bell, when the wind was favorable, a faint, sweet, and, as it were, natural melody, worth importing into the wilderness. At a sufficient distance over the woods this sound acquires a certain vibratory hum, as if the pine needles in the horizon were the strings of a harp which it swept. All sound heard at the greatest possible distance produces one and the same effect, a vibration of the universal lyre. . . . There came to me in this case a melody which the air had strained, and which had conversed with every leaf and needle of the wood, that portion of the sound which the elements had taken up and modulated and echoed from vale to vale. The echo is, to some extent, an original sound, and therein is the magic and charm of it. It is not merely a repetition of what was worth repeating in the bell, but partly the voice of the wood; the same trivial words and notes sung by a wood-nymph.[3]

Thoreau explicitly identifies an acoustic surplus that rises to near audibility, or as-if audibility, when sound crosses the far distance. As a vibration or "vibratory hum" the surplus is more felt than heard, half-heard in being felt. It is an echo simultaneous with the sound it echoes, an "original sound" that does not repeat the sound of its source but instead gives voice to the wood under an additional as-if condition: as if the pine needles in the horizon were the strings of a harp. The sound of the bells remains distinct, each bell retaining its own tone, but changed by the undertone that bears it.

The sound of the universal lyre streams above or beyond the sounds that immediately occupy the ear. Distance is again its medium, as it was for Goethe and Beethoven (pp. 56–60). Subsidence, a lingering on the edge of audibility, is its form:

> There is always a kind of fine Aeolian music to be heard in the air. . . . a sound to make all men divinely insane that hear it, far away overhead, subsiding into my ear. To an expanded ear what a harp this world is! The occupied ear thinks that beyond the cricket no sound can be heard, but there is an immortal melody that may be heard morning, noon, and night, by ears that can attend, and from time to time this man or that hears it.[4]

Like Babbage's concentric rings, Thoreau's imagery of divine madness and immortal melody recalls the music of the spheres—a recovered music we will encounter again (and again). But for Thoreau the music of the spheres is the music of the earth. Literally so: he does not sharply distinguish between music played on an instrument and the "music" of nature. Each belongs fully to the diurnal round of morning noon, and night. The music even extends to technology; Thoreau hears its Aeolian vibrancy in telegraph wires. To hear it the ear expands, as if to become its own ear trumpet. When the sound of a piano reaches the listener from "beyond the gardens and through the elms," its melody fuses with, subsides into, the "thrumming" of the strings. The world stands as a vast reverberant body in which local bodies come alive with sound: "But let us hear a strain of music—We are at once advertised of a life which no man has told us of, which no preacher preaches."[5]

Coleridge, Babbage, and Thoreau all intimate recognition of the audiable in the form of a universal hum or resonance, and each in his own way suggests the reason for the emergence of this recognition in his era, broadly conceived: namely that the audiable (because nature abhors a vacuum) fills in a space once occupied by God.

Immanence

The audiable is unlike any and all auditory forms other than itself. It has no sound of its own, but takes on what one might call the cloak of audibility from the sounds it suffuses and surrounds. This interchange of vibrancy is what gives the audiable its worldly force. The perception of the audiable cuts across the distinctions between the animate and inanimate, subject and object, feeling and thinking, and helps to break them down. The audiable resonates amid the plenitude of intermediate forms—hybrids—with which, according to Bruno Latour, the world is full, and the fuller the better.[1] One facet of would-be modernity has been a hushing (a failed muting) of the audiable, a muffling of the harmony that (so it is said) rang (rings) out in premodern societies as if in sympathetic vibration with Fludd's cosmic monochord (p. 60; listen, too, to the polyphony of written sentences like these, which inscribe the audiable in their sounding typography.)

The audiable in modernity, then, is a hearkening back, a denial of disenchantment and even of the possibility of disenchantment. The persistence of the premodern is a key theme of modernity. But the modern audiable is also a hearkening forward. Modernity in one of its infinite guises consists in the effort to establish a durable cultural alternative to traditional cosmic and religious schemes of transcendence. Those schemes persist as sources of both nostalgia and real authority, but they are changed by their loss of an epistemic and spiritual monopoly. The secular alternatives, immersed in the sensory and corporeal density of life and its symbolic transmutations, aspire to an immanence with the force of transcendence without the credos: a transcendental immanence pure and simple.

Philosophers from Nietzsche to Heidegger to Deleuze and Guattari to Derrida, a raft of poets and novelists from Whitman to Stevens to Proust and Lawrence and Joyce, plus every celebrant of the cult of romantic sexuality in literature, drama, opera, and film, plus the series of idolized painters from Van Gogh and Monet to Matisse: the list of contributors to this project is endless. Some, especially on the philosophic side, but even many on the literary, find themselves caught in an unforeseeable dilemma. Their pursuit of a richly gratifying transcendental immanence leads either to a courting of transgression and debasement (Bataille, Joyce, Proust, Deleuze and Guattari, even Freud in a sense; Žižek's preoccupation with the "obscene," regularly characterized as viscous and slimy, is an emblematic point of culmination) or to a strange guilt-ridden austerity (Levinas, Derrida, the later Stevens). Ordinary sense experience cannot seem to hold the transcendental glow, and both the traditional schemes of spirit and the somewhat guilty departures from them pose dangers of being appropriative and reductionist. From these dangers the thinkers anxiously recoil. Only a handful of the painters seem free of this problem, as if they had found in the amorality of sheer looking a house of refuge. But note some of the disturbing features in the still-life paintings of Matisse during World War II: a jug posed at the very edge of a table, a cross-hatched black background that threatens to engulf the objects it sets off.

The audiable intervenes here as a means and medium of escaping both the hammer of anxious austerity and the anvil of cruelty and perversity. It holds out the promise, perhaps never quite fulfilled but never wholly cheated, either, of a transcendentalized immanence free of twists and terrors. Perhaps for this very reason we have not yet learned how to listen for it. The audiable speaks in whispers to which our ears are not yet attuned, for which our voices have not yet found the right responsive tones.

Reading Transfigured

ST. AUGUSTINE

Voice threatens to swallow up the listener it addresses at two contrary extremes: as the inner voice of self-accusation and self-punishment, remorse of conscience, always in excess of its charge, and as the voice from without that soothes and envelops, that laps the listener in a fantasy of immersion in pre-symbolic warmth. The one voice bites, as the etymology of "remorse," from the Latin, to bite back, suggests; the other dissolves the listening subject on its tongue. Each extreme, in its own way, prompts one to disown oneself on behalf of a supreme Other through whom the act of self-abnegation may become self-renewal. Against this, perhaps, stands only the elusive vibration of the audiable, in the guise of a proto-voice that can neither command nor seduce, but only—almost—be.

Two famous passages in the *Confessions* of St. Augustine lead to an intimation of that proto-voice in a narrative that touches on both extremes. In the first, Augustine describes his mentor, St. Ambrose, reading silently. The most noteworthy thing about what Ambrose is doing is that Augustine finds it noteworthy. The description has long been at the center of debates over the extent and even the existence of silent reading in antiquity.[1] Current opinion leans toward the position that both silent reading and reading aloud were common practices; the difference between the ancient and the modern is the modern readers read silently as the norm and aloud as the exception. In that respect they imitate Ambrose, who according to Augustine was unusual not because he read silently but because he never did otherwise. But the passage is equally interesting for other reasons, and the proto-modernity of Ambrose's practice is one of them.

Here is the passage:

But as he read, his eyes glanced over the pages and his heart explored the sense, yet his voice and tongue were silent. Often when we visited . . . we would see him thus reading silently and never otherwise. And after sitting in unbroken silence (for who would dare to interrupt someone so intent?) we would leave and conjecture that, in the little time he could snatch to refresh his mind, taking a break from the clamor of other people's affairs, he did not want to be distracted.[2]

Ambrose's originality was to make silent reading a wholly private act. It formed a buffer zone of silence between him and the many others he spent most of his time helping and giving counsel. Performed in view of anyone who happened by, Ambrose's silent reading was a way of affirming that his care for others required the leavening of the care (to echo Michel Foucault) of the self. The primary meaning of *feriatum*, which I have translated here in the phrase "taking a break," is vacation.

Augustine finds Ambrose's reading noteworthy not as a norm but as a special, particular practice: a means of taking meanings within oneself in order to refresh and repair one's mind. The silence of the reading is the antidote to the clamor (*strepitum:* din, crash, uproar, racket) of the world without. This silence is anything but a void. It is filled with the meaning that it permits the heart to explore. To those who know how to hear it, moreover, Ambrose's silence is something to be shared. Augustine and his companions observe the silence by imitating it and recognizing it as the perceptible form of the reader's intense concentration.

But what might they have perceived? What is the sensory substance of this communal suspension of voice? What comes between the eye and the heart, the page and the meaning? The answer emerges only later. It informs the turning point in the story of Augustine's conversion:

I was . . . weeping in the bitterest contrition of my heart, when suddenly I heard a voice from a nearby house as if from a boy or girl—I don't know which—speaking in chant and repeating over and over, "take up, read, take up, read" (*tolle lege, tolle lege*). Immediately my countenance changed. I began to think most intently whether it was usual for children in some sort of game to sing something like that, but I had never heard the like

anywhere. And curbing the attack of tears I rose, interpreting it as a command from God to me to open the [apostle's] book and read the first thing
I found there. . . . I snatched it up, opened, and read in silence . . . "Put on
the Lord Jesus Christ and make no provision for the desires of the flesh." I
did not want to read further nor was there any need to. Immediately afterward, with the end of this sentence, certainty was infused in my heart as if
by a light and the darkness of doubt was dispelled.[3]

The voice that Augustine hears—music in the air—enjoins him to turn
from external to internal hearing and heeding. The voice does not come
from a child, but *as if* (*quasi*) from a child. The as-if carries resonance at
several levels. For the Augustine in torment over his sexual appetite, the
childlikeness of the voice is presexual; it fulfills in material form St. Paul's
declaration that there is no male or female in Christ (Galatians 3:28). At
the same time it recalls Jesus's words in Matthew 18:3: "Except ye be con-
verted, and become as little children, ye shall not enter into the kingdom
of heaven." As voice, accordingly, the child's chant makes audible the
human being stripped of all extraneous attributes. It is pure subjectivity
pressed into sound.

Augustine's text retains the sound of the chant by repeating the chanted
phrase, itself rich in verbal music: the fluid *l*'s linking the parallel words
and the parallel final -*e*'s. The narrative explicates the chant as the chant
rings in the mind's ear. After Augustine does take up and read, the light of
truth arises in him immediately after the sentence he has been reading
ends. The transition confirms that the reading has a sensory form that
cannot quite be called silent. The interior intonation of the sentence opens
the quasi-acoustic space of the half-heard; the divine voice whose words
Augustine is reading fills the space to overflowing.

The resulting refreshment of spirit conforms to the private practice
Augustine had learned from Ambrose. He has been sitting with his friend
Alypius but goes off by himself to weep under a fig tree ("I don't know
how," he writes, nudging the reader to recall a pair of gospel passages in
which a barren fig tree symbolizes spiritual emptiness). When he hears
the child's song, he returns to the bench where Alypius is sitting, picks up
the book he had left there, and reads silently just as Ambrose had been
accustomed to do in the presence of the reciprocally silent Augustine.
Only then does he speak aloud to tell both his friend and his mother what

has happened. But the narrative ends, not with them, but with the reader of the *Confessions*, who is positioned to emulate Augustine as Augustine did Ambrose. The thread of spirit in this relay of readings, however rarefied it may become, is never other than auditory.

Perhaps, then, what we call silent reading should be called something else. The half-heard is a genuine sensory experience. It makes discernible the elemental medium of writing, the vibrancy of potential speech.

Before the invention of audio technology, the half-heard was the only available form of voice recording. It was the means by which writing preserved not only articulate utterance but also the tone, the music, of the utterance, so that reading to oneself could feel like a direct encounter with the writer's voice. Perhaps writing can no longer do that in a world where voice recording is pervasive, or perhaps it still can, but only as a kind of nostalgia, to be enjoyed in secret. Unlike the spoken voice in its transience, the half-heard voice was endlessly retrievable in the act of reading. It appeared, not as an imaginary sound that the reader subvocally ventriloquizes, but as reproduction that harmonizes with the vibrancy of speaking aloud.

Nietzsche bore reluctant witness to the intimate force of the half-heard in his intellectual autobiography *Ecce Homo*. He was reluctant because he wanted to avoid the contact that others were seeking: "When I am hard at work you will not find me surrounded by books: I'd beware of letting anyone near me talk, much less think. And that is what reading would mean."[4] Thinking in these circumstances is louder than speaking. Books, though mute, are noisy. Like Goethe's gondoliers and fishwives, they call for an empathetic response by sending the music of their voices across the distance.

To the Life

THE IMAGE

"That's my last Duchess painted on the wall," says the narrator of Robert Browning's famous poem, "Looking as if she were alive." How far can such a look go? Milly Theale, the doomed heroine of Henry James's novel *The*

Wings of the Dove, sees, through tears, a faint reflection of her fading life in a "mysterious portrait" by Bronzino:

> Perhaps it was her tears that made it just then so strange and fair—as wonderful as [her companion] had said: the face of a young woman, all splendidly drawn, down to the hands, and splendidly dressed; a face almost livid in hue, yet handsome in sadness and crowned with a mass of hair, rolled back and high, that must, before fading with time, have had a family resemblance to her own.[1]

Why is this portrait "to the life" so arresting—and troubling, with its livid hue? How close does what Milly sees come to the portrait of a young girl that the narrator of Edgar Allen Poe's "The Oval Portrait" admits he had at first mistaken for "a living person" and then, on reflection, adds, "I had found the spell of the picture in an absolute life-likeliness of expression, which, at first startling, finally confounded, subdued, and appalled me."

Can a picture be animate? J. W. T. Mitchell notwithstanding, the answer is No. An animate picture is no longer a picture. Those seemingly animate pictures in Browning, Poe, and James, like their later counterpart, the picture of Oscar Wilde's Dorian Gray, are so uncanny precisely because they *look* animate while obviously lacking animation. So the answer is not only No, but: On the contrary. Roland Barthes famously observed that all photographs are records of mortality; they all say, silently, *this was*. One reason why the invention of the moving image was sought after for so long, and valued so much when it succeeded, is that it relieves us of the stillness and, a little later but equally essentially, the silence of the picture. All pictured life is stilled life, still life, *nature morte*. Only moving images are animate. And to be fully animate they need the illusion of making sounds. The silence and stillness of the picture is alluring as a medium for contemplation, but only in physical spaces, little havens, reserved for the purpose. And there may not be safety even there, as Milly Theale discovers:

> The lady in question. . . . [with] her full lips, her long neck, her recorded jewels, her brocaded and wasted reds, was a very great personage—only unaccompanied by a joy. And she was dead, dead, dead.[2]

Moving Pictures

In a posthumously published note, Wittgenstein addressed the relationship of intention to perception by telling a little story about going to the movies:

> Only the intended picture reaches up to reality like a yardstick. Looked at from the outside, there it is, lifeless and isolated. It is as if at first we looked at a picture so as to enter into it and the objects in it surrounded us like real ones; and then we stepped back, and were now outside it; we saw the frame, and the picture was a painted surface. In this way, when we intend, we are surrounded by our intention's pictures and we are inside them. But when we step outside intention, they are mere patches on a canvas, without life and of no interest to us. When we intend, we exist among the pictures (shadows) of intention, as well as with real things. Let us imagine we are sitting in a darkened cinema and entering into the happenings of the film. Now the lights are turned on, though the film continues on the screen. But suddenly we see it "from outside" as movements of light and dark patches on a screen.[1]

Wittgenstein liked to sit in the front row of the movie theaters that he visited regularly; clearly he wanted to be as inside the picture as possible. That he takes the black and white character of the image as essential rather than as a limit imposed by technology is worth thinking about in relation to the idea of existing among shadows. Before the color image became the norm the projection of a film actually was a casting of shadows, a creation of the semblance of life from the traditional insubstantial stuff of death. But my interest here is in the *other* dark dimension: why is this movie so silent? Why is there no word here about the role of the acoustic envelope in bringing the world of intended objects to life?

Even the highly musical Wittgenstein seems to adopt, as a thinker, an unreflective form of the metaphysical tradition's pictorial bias, in which "I see" always exceeds "I hear." So what one has to add to these remarks is that if the processes Wittgenstein describes really did occur in silence, the silence of the audible, no amount of intention would succeed in getting us inside the picture, among living forms that, of course, include and indeed are the "shadows" of intention. Living forms are speaking shadows. What the audible does for us is precisely make sure that the world remains full of living forms, remains a world of meaning, by making sure that it is full of acoustic movement, of the endless background music, in several layers of articulateness, of the audiable. Turn that off, and the world goes dead, like a limb that has fallen asleep.

That is why real silent movies were never really silent. And that is why acoustic automata are so richly ambiguous: sources of dread in the implication that the animating force of sound may be a mechanical fiction, but sources of wonder in the implication that almost anything can become animate in a living world, and does so more often than not. (Mechanism has a resonance of its own; it troubles the mystery of animation, but only silence demystifies and mortifies. It's no accident that the fascination with automata begins in the era that casts irrevocable doubt on the immaterial reality of the soul.)

So we need to give a fuller account of the animating effects of auditory culture. And we also need to consider something more specific: what happens when particular living forms do go dead—not the world, not the wide receptacle of sound that appears to us preconceptually as the world, but particular objects and persons in it? What happens when they enter an acoustic dead spot? Or do they create such a dead spot by falling out of the picture regardless of audiable support? And what, then, do we do? What can we do? Or what should we do: since it's clear that we are never simply in or simply out of the picture, but live in a world in which living, dead, quickening, or stiffening forms endlessly circulate, addressing us and being addressed as we go about our ordinary and extraordinary business?

Modern Times

THE CARTOON

I.

The founding practices of auditory culture are formed around the conditions of listening, one set of them based on intimacy, another on distance. A primary institution of auditory culture in the intimate domain is the circle of narrative, formed by a group of auditors arrayed around the speaker or singer of tales. Walter Benjamin thought that this listening circle was the traditional sphere of the storyteller whose tales give "counsel" to the community.[1] Modernity replaces this orbital mode of listening with a branching one, the more so as visual media envelop and overarch textual ones. In a strange paradox, reading—silent, private reading, the surplus of which Benjamin is not wrong to take as a symptom of modernity—appropriates and reanimates the voice of the storyteller by distancing itself from the auditory source, real or fictitious, of that voice. The result is a continual dialectic between attempts to restore orbital communion and the experience of its sometimes pleasurable, sometimes hurtful undoing. In other words, modernity converts the source of narrative from the intimacy of shared speech to the transmission of information from a distance, and at the same time sparks the effort to reclaim narrative for intimacy, at least in symbolic form.

II.

The same effort found a place in Wittgenstein's darkened movie theaters at about the same time he wrote about frequenting them.

Sing-along animated cartoons have become a genre for children, but between the middle 1920s and the early 1950s they were a popular staple for adults in American movie theaters. Their drop in popularity coincides with the rise of television in the years when musical variety shows—vaudeville revisited—prominently filled the airwaves. But perhaps there is a deeper reason for their lapse.

Animation became popular when the energy of the modern machine age, its animation in a different sense, was still new enough to support an opposition between the human and the mechanical. Animated cartoons addressed the everyday anxiety associated with that opposition. They brought the contrary terms together in the lively but not lifelike figures on-screen and dissolved the incongruity in laughter. But sing-along cartoons went further. Singing along ratified the bargain between the human and the mechanical, between life and the mimicry of life. As long as the cartoon characters remained less than lifelike, the spectators could embrace the animation of modern life by contributing their own. Life came from the singing.

The cartoons thus anticipated the solution to a problem not identified until much later—the so-called uncanny valley. Computer-generated or robotic figures tend to provoke anxiety when they resemble human beings too closely. The live action filmed by a camera did precisely that in the very early days of cinema. The problem quickly disappeared as spectators learned to see film as depiction rather than illusion. But cartoons *are* illusions, transparently so; they can neither record nor depict life and action but only manufacture imitations of them. Cartoons implicitly ask the question that filmic images evade: what does it mean that we endow the figures on-screen with virtual life? And what, they add, do we want from music in the process?

Sing-along cartoons not only raised the question but also demanded an answer. Told to follow the famous bouncing ball atop the lyrics, the members of the audience had to make a decision: sing or not? Movie musicals, also at the height of their popularity during the heyday of the cartoons, presented singing for passive consumption. The cartoons changed the terms to active participation. As a spectator, one would not only have to raise one's voice but also to throw one's voice, lend one's voice. The cartoon became an extension of the lives that animated it past the point claimed by cinematic technology. The people in the theater may primarily have been there as an audience for the feature film, but when they sang along with the cartoon they became a transitory community.

Max Fleischer made the question of animated life the center of a series of short subjects issued under the rubric *Out of the Inkwell* from 1915 to 1929. The films were hybrids, combining footage of the cartoonist (Fleischer himself) with that of the animated characters, mainly Koko the Clown and his dog Fitz. An ad in *Moving Picture World* for September 1919 boasted that "the little clown who grows right before your eyes out of the pen point and then shrivels up and flows back—just drops of ink—is known from Coast to Coast."[2]

Koko and his creator are often antagonists. In *Bedtime* (1923), Max draws a barren peak and strands Koko there so that he, Max, can get some sleep. Koko, the cartoonist's alter ego, tries to sleep too, but his position makes that impossible and his attempts end with a fall from the heights. After a series of misadventures in which he escapes from a giant (a double for Max), Koko flees through a culvert. When he emerges, he turns into a giant himself. Koko becomes a kind of Golem, a lurching figure who dwarfs the skyscrapers of New York, through which he wends his way— shades of King Kong to come—searching for Max in order to take revenge. But when the clown's giant hands seem to reach through Max's window, the terrified Max rouses from what we now discover is only a dream. As always, Max literally has the upper hand. But the terror of his film persona is real enough, and so is the principle of uncontrolled animation that induces it. No wonder, then, that Max quickly runs to the drawing board and pours Koko back into the inkwell.

III.

Fleischer also pioneered sing-along cartoons. His studio created the bouncing ball, which sometimes bounced back in the form of self-observation. *In the Good Old Summer Time* (1926) presents Koko as an orchestra conductor who grabs Fitz and shakes him into the shape of a tuning fork. When the fork strikes the music stand, a note pops up visually and the fork morphs back into Fitz, who swallows the note. Animation, music, and synchrony all go together, just as the popularity of the sing-alongs suggested they should. Like Fitz, we come to life anew by swallowing the note, which is both a sight and a sound.

What motivates this peculiar harmony? One answer is suggested by the antagonism between Koko and his creator, which always ended with the clown back in the inkwell (but always ready to come out again). Animation by technological wizardry has a long history as an idea, to which cinema gives a belated material form. There is even an episode featuring animated figures in the *Iliad*. Hephaestus, the lame blacksmith of the gods, prepares to forge the shield of Achilles:

And in support of their master moved his attendants.
These are golden, and in appearance like living young women.
There is intelligence in their hearts, and there is speech in them
and strength, and from the immortal gods they have learned how to do things.
(Lattimore translation, 18: 417–20)[3]

Such creatures, however, can be dangerous. For every Galatea from Ovid there is a wooden doll Olympia from E. T. A. Hoffmann or Jacques

Offenbach; for every Pinocchio there is a Golem or Frankenstein's monster. Mickey Mouse may shake hands with Leopold Stokowski at the start of Disney's *Fantasia,* but when the conductor's baton becomes a magic wand in the "Sorcerer's Apprentice" episode, the latent terror of animated life breaks out in a flood. The story comes from a poem by Goethe that inspired a symphonic poem by Paul Dukas: the apprentice uses his absent master's power to make a broom fetch water, but he cannot make it stop. Suffice it to say that breaking the broom is no help. For Mickey the apprentice, the anarchic energy of Koko the clown becomes the mindless self-replication of the marching brooms—an assembly line of stick figures come to life and unwilling to die.

It follows that we need to control the creature we bring to life, to call the tune of its being. We call on music to do that because music exemplifies animation without anarchy. (At least it used to.) It even has that role in *Fantasia,* which choreographs the mechanical ballet of the brooms and its immediate sequel, the clash of dinosaurs who fight to the death to the strains of Stravinsky's *Rite of Spring.* As to Koko, the way to beat him is to beat time with him. In the sing-along features, the voices of the audience channel his unruliness into the inner dynamism and fluidity of music which makes one want to sing, or hum, or bounce along—a metaphoric pulsation that at one moment is life, at another just drops of ink, and never either one for very long.

The Sound of Meaning

Humanistic knowledge, the understanding of what we as human beings make and do in the world we inherit, is possible only under conditions of fundamental uncertainty. Discomfort with this hard fact has perennially led to attempts to overcome it, but nothing can do that—and nothing should, since the uncertainty is not only a risk the knowledge takes but the gift that allows it to flourish. Humanistic knowledge is indistinguishable from acts of understanding that are also acts of interpretation. It depends on expressive media—language, imagery, music, tone, soundscape, gesture, the look of faces—which invite understanding but cannot secure it.

THE HUM OF THE WORLD 77

My trilogy of books, *Interpreting Music, Expression and Truth,* and *The Thought of Music,* proposes that understanding music is the paradigm of humanistic knowledge, precisely because knowing what music expresses (what it conveys, what it does, what it sounds like, how it affects us, what it gives us to think—these and more) is so rich in uncertainty. But understanding music is a special case of understanding sound, and it therefore makes sense to ask whether perhaps there is a still more basic paradigm to be found in auditory understanding. Is the ancient idea of a music inherent in the order of things more than a pleasant fable?

I was mulling over these questions one pleasant summer night after reading an essay by N. Katherine Hayles suggesting that we should understand cognition apart from consciousness.[1] The knowledge produced by "cognitive nonconsciousness" far exceeds what we can know as thinkers. We should accordingly recognize ourselves as just one type of "cognizer" among a multitude that includes both all life forms and "smart" technologies, and with whom, or which, we have more in common than we have been accustomed to admit. Cognition, in this frame of reference, forms something resembling the inherent music on which I speculated a few sentences earlier. The resemblance extends to Babbage's imagined medium of all the sounds ever uttered or emitted (p. 60): that vast library of the air.

And the air was moving. At first not heeding it, my thoughts found a congenial medium in the faint sound of an oscillating fan. The white noise at first just seemed restful, an auditory cushion, but I gradually became aware, without knowing why or thinking about it, that the sound had a rhythm to it. As the fan moved back and forth, the sound of its motor rose and fell in pitch at or near the threshold of perception. The movement of my thoughts seemed to echo the ebb and flow of the sound, which in truth I only half heard, but sensed nonetheless. It then occurred to me that I was hearing a sensory image of my thought process—metaphorically, at least, the sound of thinking. I was eavesdropping on my own thoughts. That understanding prompted the further idea that what I was then experiencing was an audible form of the process by which sound becomes meaningful. Hearing the transition, which is more usually inaudible, almost instantaneous, I could also hear, or so I thought, that the meaning was not something added to the sound. Meaning was a dimension inherent to the sound, and one that I could observe directly with my senses. The

meaning was in the melody. The ubiquity of cognition, the classical harmony of the world, and Babbage's vibratory medium were all there in this
demonstration of what this book has named the audiable.

Need I say that this immediate blend of sensory and reflective understanding crested and dissolved like one pass of the fan's undulating song?
Like all such moments, this one was brief. But in its aftermath another
thought arose, this one having to do with noise. Could it be, asked this
thought (it is not clear that it was I doing the asking, and besides, the
night was quiet), that noise is so disturbing not because it is anarchic or
painful, harsh as those qualities might be, but because it, too, reveals an
inherent meaning to the senses: that of the violence to which any and all
material things, anything that can make a sound, is inherently subject?

Music and the Audiable

A SUITE IN THREE MOVEMENTS

I. OVERTURE

Music contributes to auditory culture by the way it is heard, used, distributed, talked about, reproduced, and so on. But it also contributes by the
way it is formed. Music in one of its dimensions is a reflection on auditory
culture, a lived theory of the auditory that becomes a lived practice. Many
musical utterances contain explicit moments of such animated and animating reflection, moments in which music philosophizes acoustic meaning, portrays the character of the audible, makes the audiable audible,
enters the audiable in sounding it out and transforms and transfigures it
before, as must happen, as we need to happen, the audiable sinks back
beneath the tones we hear. Take the two detached chords that famously
begin Beethoven's *Eroica* Symphony. "This is sound," they seem to say,
"not quite yet music. Consider where it comes from and what it can show.
For example, this . . ."

Speaking melody (melody written for words but sung or played without
them) is a more everyday conduit of the audiable—and it is always important to remember that the audiable is a primary support for the value,

really the privilege, of the ordinary. Speaking melody is the acoustic equivalent of reading through gap s in a text, but only—remember, there is no
art of the audiable; it cannot be conventionalized—in circumstances that
make the gap be tween voice and me lody aud(i)able. Similar considerations apply to the gaps between motivic and cantabile melody in general
and to overvocalizing, the technique by which the singing voice keeps on
uttering a word while stretching it beyond the bounds of intelligibility:
but again, only sometimes; the technique can be conventionalized but the
transformation can't be.

By bringing us to know the audiable in, so to speak, auditory glimpses,
music allows us to understand our usual unknowing reliance on it as a state,
not of deafness of ignorance, but of readiness to be caught unawares.

II. CHOPIN

When music makes the audiable audible, it is as if the music itself were
listening and thus giving us the opportunity to listen with its ears. Most of
the examples come from the so-called "classical" repertoire, and several of
them will get some attention here. But the most famous example is decid-
edly anticlassical, John Cage's famous or infamous 4' 33", the title of which
refers to the interval of four minutes, thirty-three seconds that an instru-
mentalist is instructed to divide into three movements while making no
noise on the instrument (originally that mainstay of classical composition,
the piano). But 4' 33" is directed less toward the audiable than toward
ambient sound. Although commonly regarded as a silent piece, 4' 33" is
actually a denial of silence, and in that respect it is a repetition of the
exemplary act of music-making. It just shifts the auditory focus from
music heard to music found. Writing of the first performance, Cage said of
his audience: "They missed the point. There's no such thing as silence.
What they thought was silence, because they didn't know how to listen,
was full of accidental sounds. You could hear the wind stirring outside
during the first movement. During the second, raindrops began pattering
the roof, and during the third the people themselves made all kinds of
interesting sounds as they talked or walked out."[1]

For a counterexample, consider Chopin's Prelude in F Minor. This is a
tiny piece, lasting only about a minute. It is also fragmentary, jagged,

agitated, and violent. It is aggressively noisy. It is willfully ugly. But after it reaches an inverted peak with a brutal series of deep-bass octaves, the music falls silent for a full five beats. Something has torn it apart, or it has torn itself apart. Five beats measured by the clock is not much, but given the miniature proportions, it feels long: longer than it is.

What are we supposed to hear in this empty space? It is a space that in some sense will never be filled, because the prelude ends with a brief formula that sounds, as it should sound, meaningless. So one thing we can hear is the impossibility of finding an adequate answer for the silence into which we have been plunged. It is unlikely that we will attend much to ambient sound, especially not with the kind of lyrical appreciation that Cage seems to have wished for. Unlike 4' 33', the Prelude in F Minor presents "real" silence in the form of a loss of sound—sound interrupted as opposed to Cage's visual composition of sound not produced but received. Cage's "silence" is a state of auditory fullness; Chopin's is an absence.

But the absence is not perfect. Those five beats without a sounded note bear the faint echo of the piano's resonance in the aftermath of the hammering octaves. The strings still tingle, like, or as, struck nerves. As the resonance fades toward inaudibility, we may catch for a moment, in a kind of auditory glimpse, the underlying promise of hearing something more, of hearing something to listen for. The Prelude pauses on the threshold of hearing the faint hum of the audiable, the half-sound that makes this music endurable. The music pushes its fury to the limit in order to reach the point from which to feel—maybe—that violence and incoherence are not absolute. Even if they are.

III. BEETHOVEN

A calmer search for the transparency that makes perceptible the condition of utterability is characteristic of music at its most thoughtful and most moving. Music comes close to this auditory transparency when it greatly increases either the intimacy or the distance of our listening to it. My own preferred examples are certain passages in the late quartets of Beethoven, short episodes replete with almost inexplicable difference. The Quartet no. 13 in B-flat, Op. 130, includes two such passages: for distance, the tiny, ethereal moment of concentration and withdrawal that stands in the place of a "development" section in the expansive first movement, and, for intimacy, the instrumental cry of anguish (so marked: *beklemmt:* oppressive, suffocating, weighed down) just before the close of the preternaturally serene instrumental song (so marked: *Cavatina:* a short, simple song) that forms the penultimate movement. But everyone will have individual examples, which can come from any kind of music and may come from acts of performance instead of acts of composition. The point is that music has the intrinsic potential to reflect on its own conditions of possibility as an auditory phenomenon. As the art of the audible, music brings us closer to the sensation and the perception of the audiable than any other cultural form or institution. That closeness accounts for the privileged place of music in my text.

But the audiable is a burden as well as a privilege. Music loses or denies it more often than not, not least by presenting—being allowed to present—the supposed absence of semantic depth in music itself as a cheap substitute for the audiable. Music as mere sound becomes the audiable in falsetto. Hence the candidly evocative language of description in the preceding paragraph, and throughout this book, and throughout my work. Unless we bring music into the realm of hearkening and realize that music, too, like all utterance, is destined to a meaning with which it maintains both intimacy and distance, music will not hold the audiable in keeping for us but rather will keep us from the audiable.

Plato's Singing School

In the dialogue *Timaeus* Plato imagines a *chora*—Greek for space, place, interval, receptacle, and womb—that forms the link between the sensible and intelligible worlds, an envelope through which all things pass but where nothing stays. The concept of the chora resembles one that it antedates by millennia, the concept of the medium, the material substrate needed for the communication of ideas or sensations or representations. Plato's chora is something like the medium of media, or, if you will, the Platonic form of the medium (though of course Plato would not have put it that way).

It is interesting that the two weightiest modern appropriations of the chora make no reference to its character as medium, though both assume it.[1] The better known of the two comes from Julia Kristeva, for whom the chora belongs to what she calls the "semiotic" realm of unarticulated impulse, drive, and utterance that precedes the acquisition of language. Kristeva's chora is noisy, filled with floating or surging bodily dissonance behind which the pliancy of the "choral" envelope hovers just out of reach. The audibility of the chora drowns out the audible that makes it possible.

Jacques Derrida does not hear the chora, or *khora* in his case, in the same way, or indeed at all. Derrida interprets the khora as the medium of being itself, as that which "makes space for being." Where Kristeva wants to recover a vital exuberance not confined by symbolic systems, Derrida wants to trace out the contours of the receding envelope.

What might the khora sound like? The answer seems to demand oxymoron: the khora would have to echo with things that remain unuttered; it would have to be filled with sound without tone. If the khora is apprehensible at all, it would have to be the speechless condition of possibility for speech, the a-musical condition of possibility for music. It would have to be very near, but just out of reach, and in that sense something very familiar, everyday life being haunted by the sensation of just that.

But no living being can experience such a sounding silence, if either word still applies. The khora wants to become the audible. At a bare minimum, no one can escape the audible undertone of the body itself, the body that is neither internal nor external, and is therefore already both world and sensibility. And as soon as there is sound, prior to the natural "music" of birdsong or moving wind or water, and certainly prior to melody, which already rises to the cusp of speech, there is a primary music filling the world, the acoustic current of the audible. Something in us needs to hear it on occasion and shrivels up if it does not. The sound it makes has no general form, but we can discern it in or as the overflow of the specific occasions of hearing that it invests.

Here is William Wordsworth on the subject, recalling a boy (widely assumed to be himself) who used to stand by night on the shore of Lake Winander to blow "mimic hootings to the silent owls":

and they would shout
Across the watery vale, and shout again,
Responsive to his call, with quivering peals,
And long halloos and screams, and echoes loud,
Redoubled and redoubled . . . and, when a lengthened pause
Of silence came and baffled his best skill,
Then sometimes, in that silence while he hung
Listening, a gentle shock of mild surprise
Has carried far into his heart the voice
Of mountain torrents; or the visible scene
Would enter unawares into his mind,
With all its solemn imagery, its rocks,
Its woods, and that uncertain heaven, received
Into the bosom of the steady lake.
    (*The Prelude*, text of 1805, IV.399–408)[2]

The reward of the hullaballoo is a moment in which silence becomes a voice. And the voice has never stopped echoing, as the change of tense at "has carried" reveals. It echoes beyond the boy's ken in the speaking silence of the reader who, like the boy, passes from the poetic mimicry of halloos and screams to the gentle shock of mild surprise that rewards the act of listening to an unheard voice.

Musical Synesthesia

Music constantly responds to the pull of mimicry, the partner and antagonist for its purely auditory expressiveness: beyond the mimicry of natural sounds, a topic that requires separate notice, to the mimicry of other sense modalities, especially vision and touch—and one modality more, which for reasons that will become apparent in a moment I cannot yet name. Why so? What desires and rewards are at stake in this?

In order to answer for music, we must first answer for synesthesia in general. One might surmise that crossing from one sense to another intimates the presence of a general sensorium, the parallel for the senses as a whole to the audible for the ear or the visible for the eye. This sensorium would be the principle of consistency or continuity that allows the sense-crossing and becomes indirectly manifest through it. It would be something like the sensory texture of corporeal existence as such.

Yet there is little record of this. It has rarely been signified or depicted. One might ascribe this lack to the general secondariness allotted to the "nonintellectual" senses in Western tradition, or one might find in it evidence that the sensory is very reluctant to abstract from itself, that sensing wishes to remain absorbed in its concrete material media. To do otherwise feels like a departure from sense itself, and in a vertiginous, a-conceptual direction far removed from the traditional sphere of the intelligible.

One corollary is that synesthesia, sense-crossing, is essentially additive. But it does not add one sense to another, because by definition it absorbs one sense into another; the sum total is always one. So what is added must be something else. And one candidate is the epistemic value entrusted especially to each of the three higher senses, sight, hearing, and touch. These values, too, cross constantly on their own, and no sense has an actual monopoly on them. But they do have primary affiliations: vision for mastery, hearing for truth, and touch for immediacy. What synesthesia does is add one affiliation, one function, to another by fusing their sensory-material media: the sum total at this level is always two. The combination of functions adds a reach, a suppleness, and a degree of power that the functions cannot attain on their own except in rare, self-transforming or -transcending conditions. And the combination need not be sustained to be effective. It is rather the more effective for being a point of origin, transition, or climax than for being a constant; its illusion, though powerful, breaks down quickly, like the crest of a wave.

To this music adds something distinctive, something that brings it close to the heart of the audiable and even, perhaps, to the sounding center of that hypothetical sensorium. Musical synesthesia goes beyond vision and touch to areas of sensing that do not involve the traditional five senses, areas to which the senses form only the portals, or line sketches of a rich, dense landscape: vibrations, resonances, the electricity of presence, body-organ sensations, body-without-organs sensations, and the feelings of position, inclination, and state of being (hot or cold, fatigued or energetic, alert or dull, agitated or calm, and so on and so forth). These are modes of immediacy more immediate than touch, which always involves a surface and therefore a barrier. They are modes of sentience that link the sensing body to the world without the mediation of a surface. In this they resemble only one sense, hearing, the only traditional sense that does the like and that therefore, if taken alone, especially in the suspension of vision and touch, itself in touch with things and forces without a name, forms a microcosmic image of the full sensory macrocosm.

From this we may surmise that music, as the art of suspended hearing, music insofar as it is the vortex that draws the ear in and down, finds in synesthesia the means to conjoin any and all of the epistemic functions to the confirmatory, absorbing, maximally dense immediacy of sentience itself. No wonder its foundation myth is the legend of Orpheus, whose song could bring stones to life and trees to dance, enhancing the sentience of all who could hear it, which was anyone and anything.

The Music of Language

The music of things, the music in things, is as common as light, but unlike light it has rarely been celebrated as a phenomenon unto itself. The partisans of images have tended to be blind to their own deafness, seemingly unaware that without the audiable vision is inanimate. The silence of pictures has sometimes been taken as an aesthetic or even a metaphysical problem, a muteness that instills every picture with an underlying pathos. But how often has it been realized that the problem of this silence pertains not just to pictures, images, or photographs, but to sight as such?

The same deafness affects the partisans of language. Giorgio Agamben, for one, says that the event of language (the potentiality of language apart from any particular language) is the precondition for any act of speech. The word from this point of view is only secondarily an acoustic phenomenon, even though all actual language is originally spoken. Agamben grounds the language that leads to speech in a higher-order speech for which sound is expendable: the speech of a Voice (the capitalization is his; the voice is no one's) that can be thought but not heard. The result is "no longer the experience of mere sound, and not yet the experience of meaning."[1] But for human beings, voice is never mere sound and never without meaning. All human voice intones. Intonation is a musical act. The act of music is the precondition for the event of language.

Without tonal expression, language has no ground. The tonal is the ground of utterance, even though it is itself groundless, a mere shimmer in the air—audible in its own right only as a potentiality within the audible. Insofar as tone is, as Hegel says, primordial music, already musical in its vibratory expressiveness (music, it might murmur, being at its core the inevitability of tonal ebb and flow), music is the medium in which the being-thus of things, the tangible condition of their being what they are, communicates itself to us as a quality. Language seeks to affirm or effect this being-thus; music connects us to it. Music, in the widest sense of the term, is the power by which being-thus, which (as Agamben says) is not a property of anything, becomes a trait of everything: a quality, or better, perhaps, *the* quality, of being as it befalls us.

The Soundscape

R. Murray Schafer's concept of the soundscape is something of a paradox.[1] It has become an essential part of our belatedly awakened perception of how fully sound participates in the framing of the sensory world. Sounds encircle us as sights confront us. But the term *soundscape* affirms the independence of the auditory with a visual metaphor. It cannot entirely escape the traditional tyranny of the eye. For that reason I generally prefer to speak of auditory worlds or the heard world, although it is tempting to hang on to the verbal and conceptual symmetry of soundscape / landscape.

Soundscape and landscape are not each other's echo or mirror image. The distribution in space of things heard is fundamentally different from that of things seen. A landscape, whether in nature or art, is never just a segment of the visible. It adheres to a structure of perception accorded to it by the gaze. That structure poses action, change, or motion in the foreground against a still, unchanging background. Figures may move in the landscape but the landscape itself does not move. (Nothing may move at all; the foreground activity may be merely potential.) The appearance of the landscape may change with the weather or the time of day but the landscape does not change.

Wordsworth attributed the moral and psychological value of landscape to this enfolding of change by permanence:

> The mountain's outline and its steady form
> Gives a pure grandeur, and its presence shapes
> The measure and the prospect of the soul
> To majesty: such virtue have the forms
> Perennial of the ancient hills—nor less
> The changeful language of their countenances
> Gives movement of the thoughts, and multitude,
> With order and relation.
> (*The Prelude*, text of 1805, VII.724–32)

Sound does not act this way. It fills space audibly with action, change, or motion but with nothing in the background except the promise of more sound, which is to say, nothing but the audiable. In another passage from *The Prelude*, nearby the one just quoted, Wordsworth represents soundscape as the inversion of landscape and detects the audiable in a sound that inverts natural law. The lines preface the description of a rustic festival held in a field at the foot of Mount Helvellyn:

> What sounds are those, Helvellyn, which are heard
> Up to thy summit, through the depth of air
> Ascending as if distance had the power
> To make the sounds more audible? What crowd
> Is yon, assembled in the gay green field?
> (VII.1–5)

The summit in the distance becomes something heard, not seen, while the sounds that should fade as they fall through the depth of air rise through that depth instead and become as if more audible the further they get from their source. Not until the changing sounds have reached the literal peak of their crescendo does the visible scene coalesce into a landscape.

Sound is always changing. Sound is change. The result is closest to a landscape when it is understood as typical of a time and place. The recurrence of typical soundscapes matches the persistence of recognized landscapes. But when a soundscape bears on a singular occasion, when it breaks with the typical as it did once under Mount Helvellyn, its landscape-like features disperse into the soundtrack of the event. The sound narrates itself, taking its course through the time that landscape arrests.

When we imagine looking into the future through a landscape, we usually imagine gazing into the far distance. But we do not have to imagine listening into the future. Listening into the future is just—listening. This inherent temporality forms one of the main links between sound and the sense of life. On occasion, it can also become an object of perception in its own right and assume meaning and affective weight. When that happens, it may draw the audible into the open, as it does in Wordsworth's question to Helvellyn. More often we just call the result music.

Song

I.

The experience of listening with heightened attention attaches most commonly to our need to hear what a voice is saying. When instrumental music attracts the same attention, the music finds its proximity to the audible insofar as we listen to instrumental sounds as we would to a voice, and so give the music a voice of its own, something between a metaphor and an acoustic quality.

Add a real human voice, a singing voice and thus a heightened one, and music permits the voice both to permeate or saturate language and to obscure or exceed language. The voice in song stands to language as, in the classic paradigm inherited from Aristotle, language stands to the primordial form of voice. Language elevates voice from the immediacy of sensation to the potentiality of values; song elevates the potentiality of values to the actuality of transport.

The ontology of voice might be imagined to develop from the top down, from heightened to "ordinary" voice, and not the other way around, almost as if voice in everyday life acted as a curb on its own exceptional potentialities, just so the everyday can be itself without too much interference from the sublime.

II.

Both as a scholar and a composer I have long been deeply interested in the art song, but of late I have been asking questions about song considered in its own right independent of genre and lyrics. One of those questions concerns the peculiarly personal character of song, or more precisely of singing, which is rooted in a paradox.

Song is transpersonal; in principle anyone can sing to anyone else. Yet sometimes song is as personal as can be; in the right circumstances, it seems to address the listener in the listener's most intimate core. The right circumstances do not involve the use of recorded song as acoustic wallpaper or manipulative underscore, however much these uses may depend on pretending the contrary. The question of recording will come up momentarily, as it should, given that recorded song is by far the dominant form in the modern era.

Latent in all song, and explicit in some, is a fluctuation between the dispersal and concentration of the sense of self. The paradox of song is that it intensifies the feeling of privacy by means of a public act. Song is always social. Even the maximally intimate space of a parent singing a baby to sleep depends on an extended network of cultural and textual traditions. At the other extreme, anthems create intense feelings of group solidarity, even in inappropriate circumstances. Nowadays British Rugby fans chant the spiritual "Swing Low, Sweet Chariot" to pump up their teams—and themselves—in complete indifference to, or ignorance of, the song's origin in the miseries of black slavery.

When a song does engage actively with meaning, as art songs, following the mandate of their genre, generally do, the paradox becomes a palpable part of the engagement. The music bends meaning and in doing so makes it personal to both itself and the listener. Yet the exchange depends on a primary social act, the address of one person, exemplified by the singer, to another, exemplified by the listener. Exemplified—but also uniquely incarnated. Song realized fully is voice in the flesh.

This description applies occasionally to recorded song, but inevitably to live song. Listened to attentively, recorded song can elicit a replica of the feeling of being addressed. But recorded singing can always be neutralized; live singing almost never.

Why? One possibility is that the singer is absent from recorded song, so that the listener is addressed by a device rather than by a person. The recording makes no claim on anyone. When the singer is present, even at a distance, the song necessarily incorporates a plea for recognition. The plea may be denied but it cannot be wholly ignored. Song in this context becomes a palpable form of the sharing that grounds all human relationships, the sharing out of sense and substance that Jean-Luc Nancy identifies with the experience of being. When the singer is a presence, the listener has a share in the song.

III.

This intensification of the element of sharing does not depend on outmoded distinctions between the human and the mechanical. It depends, instead, on the value of what John Durham Peters calls elemental media.[1] Peters suggests that a medium is precisely what the term indicates, a something between. Media form the condition of possibility for the passage of the known or the knowable from one location to another. The technology of communications media multiplies the channels for transmitting information across distances of time and space, but its core elements— channel and transmission—are equally present in nature.

For marine mammals, water is the elemental medium through which they communicate in what we rightly, and not metaphorically, call song. The water, which they are presumably aware of as a medium since, unlike most fish, they leave the water to breathe, becomes a resonant space full of signification and above all of their auditory links to their fellow creatures, often across great distances. Natural communication among whales and dolphins is not limited to the human scale of face-to-face encounter.

For humans, the elemental medium of speaking and singing, and for much else, is the circumambient air. But speaking and singing observe a difference for which nonhuman animals seem to have little use. Speech is an integral part of the auditory sphere, so much so that we generally share it without reflecting on or especially perceiving the sharing. Our sensory world is articulate as well as auditory, as full of speech as the whale's ocean is full of song. Human song, however, is exceptional, even in a world full of recorded music. The idea that song is heightened speech is plausible as far as it goes, but it fails to recognize explicitly that song is an independent activity that heightens speech only in the process of incorporating it—and therefore of transforming it in fundamental ways.

Unlike most speech, song makes its elemental medium palpable. Song is not only shared utterance but also shared resonance. Live song is an auscultation of its medium. It not only communicates through a medium but also communicates the medium itself as a source of conjoined pleasure and meaning. The presence of the sharer is essential to this experience, partly because recorded sound does not carry quite the same timbre as live sound, but even more because the experience expands the sense of the medium it vivifies. Live song, we might say, allows us to experience the air the way a whale or a dolphin experiences the water. What we hear is not merely the familiar stuff we breathe but the material potentiality of sharing, communicating, connecting one sentient creature with another of its kind. Live song has an undersong, and the undersong is the audiable.

Noise and Silence

Environmental sound and the sense of self may be more closely linked than we commonly suppose. Empirical studies suggest that people do better at creative tasks and problem solving when their environment includes an optimal level of sound, neither too noisy nor too quiet. One explanation for this result is that the right, moderate level of sound in the background makes processing information just difficult enough to foster a loose, flexible, multi-perspectival relationship to the task at hand.[1] I wonder, though, if something less mechanical and more fundamental might also be going on.

Unwanted sound, which is to say, genuine noise, breaks into the space around the body's surface, both inside and outside, where we feel our own presence. We recoil but cannot escape; the space shrinks, but to no avail. Unwanted silence does just the opposite: it fills too much space with self, often magnifying the sound of one's own thoughts. The cliché of a deafening silence has some genuine truth to it. At one extreme, the world hems us in; at the other, the world deserts us. In between these extremes, and in between the often desirable systole and diastole of the space of presence—liveliness on one end, peace and quiet on the other—the vitality of the auditory becomes the medium that connects the feeling of being oneself to the feeling of being one self among others, and among things other than selves. We buoy ourselves up on the hum of the world.

Most often, when things are going well, we do this without heeding; we depend on the sound we don't hear. Take this common experience up a notch, so to speak to the comparative degree, and we may relish that sense of being in the midst of things or worry that we might lose it. Go to the superlative degree, and there you will find the audiable.

Fish, Flesh, or Fowl

> ... Birds in the trees
> Those dying generations—at their song,
> The salmon-falls, the mackerel-crowded seas,
> Fish, flesh, or fowl commend all summer long
> Whatever is begotten, born, and dies.
>
> W. B. Yeats, "Sailing to Byzantium"

Henry Mayhew's *London Labour and the London Poor*, published in three volumes in 1851, is an exhaustive survey of the city's street life and a Dickensian record of its vernacular. It is also the revelation of a soundscape of unparalleled scope and intensity. The city reverberated with the cries of street vendors, wandering musicians, and beggars of all description. The streets acted like the strings of a gargantuan Aeolian harp thrumming to the sounds that filled them.

This soundscape was literally alive in several senses, but the source of its vitality was not primarily the playing and singing of street musicians, in whom Mayhew takes primarily a social and biographical interest. It is hard to draw a single impression from a cascade of two million words, but two segments of the text do seem especially reverberant. They are no more than moments in the soundtrack of a vast panorama, but they somehow stand out, not least for Mayhew himself. Perhaps surprisingly, he finds that the fullest feeling of life in the city arises from the trade in animals, specifically in birds and fish, the latter in the marketplace, the former across the metropolis.

The marketplace was infamous for foul language, to which it lent its name: Billingsgate.[1] Mayhew's account leaves out the obscenity to focus on the contrapuntal wealth of vendors' cries; presumably his Victorian audience could read between the lines. Moving from fish to fowl, the market's avian complement was the trade in songbirds, an astonishingly large enterprise involving canaries, thrushes, larks, nightingales, linnets, finches, and blackbirds by the thousands.

The sounds become significant in relation to labor. The two combine to fill the air with the sounds of life in excess of the labor required to sustain life. The excess is important because Mayhew, following Jeremy Bentham and John Stuart Mill, understood labor as "merely that which is irksome to perform" in order to gain subsistence. ("Aversion," wrote Bentham, "is the only emotion which labour, taken by itself, is qualified to produce." Only "*ease* . . . the *negative* or *absence* of labour" can form the object "of any such emotion as *love* or *desire*."[2]) According to Mayhew, the cultivation of birdsong acted as a substitute for leisure activity in a world where leisure was not a matter of time but of social class. Birdsong gave ease even during labor. Similarly, the fishmongers' cries served as a way of easing a little the life of immersion in the city's churning belly. The vendors shouted of necessity, but they did it musically.

Mayhew's account of Billingsgate is a verbal and sensory riot. It requires extended (but by no means full) quotation:

> The morning air is filled with a kind of seaweedy odour, reminding one of the sea-shore; and on entering the market, the smell of fish, of whelks, red herrings, sprats, and a hundred others, is almost overpowering.
>
> The wooden barn-looking square where the fish is sold, is soon after six o'clock crowded with shiny cord jackets and greasy caps. . . . Through the

bright opening at the end are seen the tangled rigging of the oyster-boats and the red worsted caps of the sailors. Over the hum of voices is heard the shouts of the salesmen, who . . . stand on their tables, roaring out their prices.

All are bawling together—salesmen and hucksters of provisions, capes, hardware, and newspapers—till the place is a perfect Babel of competition. "Ha-a-ansome cod! best in the market! All alive! alive! alive O!" "Ye-o-o! Ye-o-o! here's your fine Yarmouth bloaters! Who's the buyer?" "Here you are, governor, splendid whiting! some of the right sort!" "Turbot! turbot! all alive! turbot!" "Glass of nice peppermint! this cold morning a ha'penny a glass!" "Here you are at your own price! Fine soles, O!" "Oy! oy! oy! Now's your time! fine grizzling sprats! all large and no small!" "Hullo! hullo here! beautiful lobsters! good and cheap! fine cock crabs all alive O!" "Five brill and one turbot—have that lot for a pound! Come and look at 'em, governor; you wont see a better sample in the market." "Here, this way! this way for splendid skate! skate O! skate O!" "Had—had—had—had—haddick! all fresh and good!" "Currant and meat puddings! a ha'penny each!" "Now, you mussel-buyers, come along! come along! now's your time for fine fat mussels!" "Here's food for the belly, and clothes for the back, but I sell food for the mind" (shouts the newsvender). "Here's smelt O!" "Here ye are, fine Finney haddick!" "Hot soup! nice peas-soup! a-all hot! hot!" "Ahoy! ahoy here! live plaice! all alive O!" "Now or never! whelk! whelk! whelk!" "Who'll buy brill O! brill O!" "Capes! water-proof capes! sure to keep the wet out! a shilling a piece!" "Eels O! eels O! Alive! alive O!" "Fine flounders, a shilling a lot! Who'll have this prime lot of flounders?" "Shrimps! shrimps! fine shrimps!" "Wink! wink! wink!" "Hi! hi-i! here you are, just eight eels left, only eight!" "O ho! O ho! this way—this way—this way! Fish alive! alive! alive O!"

In the darkness of the shed, the white bellies of the turbots, strung up bow-fashion, shine like mother-of-pearl, while, the lobsters, lying upon them, look intensely scarlet. . . . Brown baskets [are] piled up on one another . . . with the herring-scales glittering like spangles all over them.[3]

The paragraph recounting the fishmonger's cries is a transcription of sound in excess. It is itself an instance of the thing it represents, a genial cacophony held together by its musicality. Mayhew hears the cries joined together as if in the form of a ballad, given a rhythmic life by the recurrence of the refrain "Alive, alive O." The phrase (best known today from the folk ballad "Cockles and Mussels") forms an epitome of the connection between life and chant. Its utterance consists in an exchange of inhalation and exhalation, which also makes itself felt in the heartbeat-like motion of the jaws, mouth, and lips. Its concluding "O" enacts a shift from a taut to an open throat, from a shout to the musical open vowel echoed on all sides by other cries. At the same time, as the English vocable of exclamation, the resounding "O" becomes, truthfully or not, an expression or promise of pleasure in the organic round of existence even in the smelly and crowded market. The "O" spills over to fill the soundscape in excess of the words or phrases that it follows ("Who'll buy brill O!" "smelt O!" "eels O!" "Fine soles, O!"). The liquid quality of the cry, perhaps "heard" better on the page than in the square, finds a visual echo in the descriptions of the pearlescent fish, scarlet lobsters, and spangled herring scales.

Where the trade in fish formed a genial chaos, the trade in birdsong created a civic order counter to the standard social hierarchy. It ran on a circuit from the working poor to the working poor:

> The buyers of singing-birds are eminently the working people, along with the class of tradesmen whose means and disposition are of the same character as those of the artisan. Grooms and coachmen are frequently fond of birds; many are kept in the several mews, and often the larger singing-birds, such as blackbirds and thrushes. The fondness of a whole body of artificers for any particular bird, animal, or flower, is remarkable.[4]

For Mayhew, buyers and sellers alike found in birds and their song a civilizing principle to counter the debasing harshness of urban life and the gross social inequality that imposed it:

> The humanising and even refining influence of such pursuits is very great, and as regards these pure pleasures it is not seldom that the refinement which can appreciate them has proceeded not to but from the artisans.... Many of the rich appear to remain mere savages in their tastes and sports. Battues, lion and hippopotamus hunting, &c.,—all are mere civilized barbarisms. When shall we learn, as Wordsworth says, Never to blend our pleasure or our pride With sorrow of the meanest thing that feels.[5]

Mayhew imagines the city as enveloped by a circle of sound in which the humanizing influence diffuses itself through a mixture of sympathy and pleasure—a very Wordsworthian combination. The trade in birds, and more particularly in their songs, seems to give urban form to the pastoral innocence celebrated in Western poetry from Theocritus and Virgil to Wordsworth himself:

> We find that there is round London a perfect belt of men, employed from the first blush of a summer's dawn, through the heats of noon, in many instances during the night, and in the chills of winter; and all laboring to give to city-pent men of humble means one of the peculiar pleasures of the country—the song of the birds.[6]

The bird-sellers join in a continuous band to form the amphitheater—a vast O!—that they fill with song. The commercial circle follows the diurnal and seasonal rhythms of nature, and with them restores the blessings of nature, or at least their distillation in sound, to the city that otherwise subdues the rhythms of life to the rhythms of labor.

Sensory Hybrids

I. CHAMBERS OF THE EAR (SAND AND REMBRANDT)

There is a sound of vision and a sight of listening. This statement does not refer to synesthesia, but to sensory crossings inherent within each sense. There are things that can be seen, or seen well, only under certain auditory conditions, as if sound were parting a curtain. There are things that can be heard, or heard well, only under certain visual conditions, as if a sight were striking a note on a tuning fork.

Some modern conceptual artists have sought to create visual objects that must be heard to be seen. In 1960 Harry Bertoia began creating a series of "sonambient" metal sculptures that are played by hand as if they were musical instruments—Aeolian harps for touching, brushing, or stroking. Even when at rest these tonal sculptures can be seen only as sources of imminent sound.[1] Since 2011 Jennie C. Jones has been making monochrome paintings on sound-absorbing panels. The position of the spectator alters the acoustic environment of the paintings even as their color remains fixed. Ambient noise dies down the closer one comes to these "acoustic paintings," but the quiet that results is still resonant:

"Resonance," Jones says, "can be low-voltage, too, a quiet hum . . . Come closer. If you listen closely, you'll hear what I mean."[2]

George Sand heard the same kind of resonance amid earlier technology. A long passage from her novel *Consuelo: A Romance of Venice* (1841–42) records the discovery of sensory crossings in the symbolically as well as practically resonant space of a theater. The description carries an extended footnote that also requires quotation. This is how the theater appears in the light of day, stripped of the illusions created at night by the artifices of lighting:

> Looking upward, one feels as if in some gothic church, ruined or unfinished, for all around is rough, shapeless, fantastic, and incoherent. Ladders in disorder . . . thrown against others half indistinct amid the confusion, masses of plank, roughly sawed, decorations turned wrong side out, without any meaning, cords mingled together like hieroglyphics. . . . We hear words from we know not where. They are eighty feet above, and the whimsical echoes filling all the corners of the strange dome, distinct or confused, as you pass to right or left, sound mysterious indeed. . . . Before you grow used to these objects and these noises you are afraid. . . . You understand nothing, and what neither the senses nor the mind comprehends . . . always alarms the logic of the senses.[3]

> This theatrical limbo has [a beauty] that strikes the imagination far more than all the mock glories of the lighted and ordered stage at the hour of performance. . . . "What!" you will say, "can external objects, without color, form, order, or light, put on an aspect that speaks to the eyes and the imagination?" Only a painter could reply: "Yes, I understand." He would remember Rembrandt's "Philosopher in Meditation": that great room lost in the shadows, those endless stairways which turn one knows not how . . . this disposition of light thrown adroitly upon the most insignificant objects—a chair, a jug, a copper pot—and how, suddenly, these objects, which did not deserve to be looked at, still less painted, become so interesting, so beautiful in their way, that one cannot turn his eyes away from them.[4]

Sand recalls Rembrandt's painting imperfectly; the canvas shows neither a jug nor a copper pot, the chair is invisible, and there is only one stairway. But the painting nonetheless throws light—literally—on the matter of cross-sensory perception. It uses light to make an argument about sound.

The painting shows a seated figure enveloped by a ring of golden light that extends partway into a room enveloped by shadow; the window that

Figure 1. Rembrandt. The Philosopher in Meditation [Interior with Tobit and Anna]. The Louvre. Wikimedia Commons.

admits the light on the left is countered on the right by a winding stair that begins in illumination but ascends into darkness. (Figure 1.) The painting bears a startling resemblance to a cinematic iris shot, as if to mirror the eye that contemplates it. Tradition regards the seated figure as a philosopher deep in thought; modern scholarship suggests that it is more likely to be the title character of the Biblical *Book of Tobit.* Tobit is blind. He is said to be awaiting the homecoming of his son, Tobias, who carries a cure for his father's blindness which, however, also portends his father's death.

If the figure is a thinker, then the light is both sensory and the light of reason; the proto-iris shot is a revelation of the medium of both vision and insight. Sand clearly saw the picture in those terms. But if the figure is Tobit, the sensory richness of the painted light is ironic. It illuminates nothing for the blind man who, when cured, will die. In that case the light serves only to reveal the empty space that, for lack of resonant objects, depicts absolute silence.

The silence is extreme, like the enveloping darkness. It persists in a state of expectancy suspended in time, forever unmet just as the action of the woman at right (perhaps Tobit's wife, Anna), bending over a half-seen fire, is forever incomplete. The scene turns the echo chamber of Sand's theater into a void. More than that, its extension of the iris at its center into an irregular circular darkness fuses the impression of an eye into an image that I cannot help but see as an ear, complete with labyrinth: the winding stairs leading to the unknown chambers of an interiority not yet available to discourse ca. 1632, when the painting was probably done, but very much so later. The picture is a lament over its own muteness, doubled by what it depicts. It is a picture of the need for sound, even the faintest or most obscure. The light streaming in and overflowing the window is almost the sight of the audiable that is yet to be heard.

II. THE POLYPHONY OF MEDIA (WHITMAN)

Music too can induce this kind of cross-sensory but nonsynesthetic perception. A late poem by Walt Whitman, "Italian Music in Dakota" (1881), testifies to the experience. The poem is in two parts, an extended lyric statement and a brief moralizing epilogue. My interest is in the lyric, which I will treat as complete in its own right, as if to compose an alternative epilogue.

The lyric describes the experience of hearing instrumental arrangements of arias and choruses from Italian operas played outdoors by a regimental band in the West. The outdoor setting and the absence of strings and voices might be expected to diminish or even travesty the music. But what happens is exactly the opposite:

> Through the soft evening air enwinding all,
> Rocks, woods, fort, cannon, pacing sentries, endless wilds,
> In dulcet streams, in flutes' and cornets' notes,
> Electric, pensive, turbulent, artificial,
> (Yet strangely fitting even here, meanings unknown before,
> Subtler than ever, more harmony, as if born here, related here,

Not to the city's fresco'd rooms, not to the audience of the opera house,
Sounds, echoes, wandering strains, as here really at home,
Somnambula's innocent love, trios with Norma's anguish,
And thy ecstatic chorus Poliuto;)
Ray'd in the limpid yellow slanting sundown,
Music, Italian music in Dakota.[5]
    (1–12)

Like Goethe's listener in Venice (p. 57), like Goethe himself, Whitman hears music softened and elevated by distance. The distance involved is not sensory, as it is for Goethe, but conceptual and imagistic. Nonetheless, it elicits the same series of perceptions that Goethe encountered in his gondoliers and fishwives, and that Beethoven voiced in his "Tempest" Sonata (pp. 59–60). The process is one we might nowadays call recursive or fractal. First the music makes its medium perceptible—a matter of sense—and invests it with aesthetic value. Then the same process overtakes this new matter to reveal a further, more vibrant, more elemental medium supporting the rest.

For Whitman the music seems to come from nowhere and everywhere. It is cut off from the sight of the instruments that play it and far removed from its usual venues, the city's frescoed rooms and the opera house. In this form, this distillation of itself to pure, migratory sound, the music intensifies its given identity. Its capacity to become "subtler than ever" in alien surroundings and to assume new meanings there surprises the opera-loving speaker—always, with Whitman, supposed to be the poet in person. The music moves him to name the arias and choruses he hears, to describe the feelings they evoke, and finally to address the music as if it were sentient.

At the same time the music makes audible in its hovering presence the distances that it has crossed. Its "wandering strains" literally wander through the landscape, or soundscape, until they find themselves "really at home." But the resonance does not stop there. As the music-from-a-distance palpably touches every matter of sense in the scene—"Through the soft evening air enwinding all"—the sound gradually becomes a kind of auditory transparency through which the air that it fills becomes a vibrant presence. The music becomes "subtler than ever" not only in its expressive quality but in the rarefication of its material presence. The sights recorded by the lyric condense into a richly satisfying and radiant sound wave: "Ray'd in the limpid yellow slanting sundown, / Music, Italian music in Dakota."

But the resonance does not stop there, either. Like Goethe's accounts of the gondoliers and fishwives, Whitman's lyric subjects itself to the same process as it describes. What the lyric says of the music it shows in itself. The text is an extended fragment, as enwinding as the music it speaks of. It is like a long single sentence but it has no predicate. Its verbs are all participles, signs of qualities rather than statements of completed actions or states of being. The poetry traces the passage of time but excludes the tenses that mark time. Like the music, the language of the lyric hovers and envelops. It touches on substantial forms: rocks, woods, the fort, and so on, to the "endless wilds" that extend its material horizon to infinity. In so doing the language becomes a substantial form itself. The last line names that form, "Music, Italian music in Dakota," which is also the title of the poem.

Everything prior to that act of naming forms a kind of enormous adjective, a constantly expanding medley of descriptive phrases. The movement from phrase to phrase tracks the auditory movement from music heard in medias res, "Through the soft evening air enwinding all," to music lingering in a moment when its sound becomes visual, even pictorial, without ceasing to resonate: "Ray'd in the limpid yellow slanting sundown." The lyric is simultaneously an evocation of the music it describes and a reflection on the quasi-musical form of its own composition. Its articulation becomes a disclosure of the power of language to transfix the reader by making the medium of language perceptible—a matter of sense—and at the same time pleasurable. And as with Goethe, that medium is understood to be, not writing, but the imaginary or potential form of utterance: the vibrancy of virtual sound.

Whitman too uses music to add the half-heard to the repertoire of the senses.

III. INCANTATION (POWERS)

Late in the next century, so does Richard Powers. Powers's 1988 novel *Prisoner's Dilemma* includes a scene of four-part singing that fuses the power of the heard with that of the half-heard and of both with the power of the audiable. The members of the contentious family whose fortunes the novel traces join in singing an old hymn tune, "Lo, how a Rose e'er Blooming." The result is that they discover the persistence of a bond "that each had tried so hard to evade."[6] Overcoming a false start in the first strophe, the singers become a "full chorale" in the second. They arrive at a quasi-metaphysical epiphany in the sound of a surprising harmony and the contrapuntal motion that shapes it. These details matter; the music's meaningfulness is fine-grained. Powers assumes that his readers are familiar with both the F-major tune and a particular seventeenth-century harmonization of it. This demand for musical recall has abundant precedent. Tolstoy, for example, in his novella "Family Happiness," assumes his readers' thorough familiarity with Beethoven's "Moonlight" Sonata. Two performances of the sonata by the same character determine the meaning of the title and form the turning points of the narrative. For the reader, the music in such texts must be half heard.

Powers's description freely mixes auditory and visual imagery, as if to suggest that the epiphany arises when the auditory gaze fixes on, and is transfixed by, a fundamental reality. The form of the revelation echoes the subject matter of the hymn, which is the Incarnation, figured as a rose. What singing this passage reveals both to the singers and to the readers who half overhear them is (like the rose) multifoliate in its significance. At the moment of "the deceptive modulation just before the last cadence," the music simultaneously incarnates the singers' mutual care, *caritas*, that is, the love binding them "despite their long gainsaying," the truth of "how hopelessly each cared what happened to the other"; their vulnerability to both fate and feeling (hard enough to acknowledge that the narrator feels constrained to mock it a little), that is, their shared proximity to "a place before irony, before wit, before anxiety, before evasion," a place where "surfaces dispersed," revealing "the still point underneath"; and a sound "well[ing] up in the ear" to which the singers "had no choice but to tune their chord." The tuning point is the still point of the audiable. The audiable is the true root of the "glorious chord."

This chord, which Powers calls the "surprise chord," depends for its glory on a passage of counterpoint that is equally rich in feeling and contrapuntal finesse: "a moment of tender visiting hovering over them as the tenors slid down that narrow half-step to the F-sharp." The F-sharp, sounding in lieu of the tonic's F-natural, is the point that transfixes. The singers' hold on the note and the chord that contains it is necessarily transient, washed away by the alto and tenor rising and falling respectively in response to the "incurable call back to tonic." But the "flash" of the chord unites the family circle around the "still point underneath." That still point is an echo of "the still point of the turning world," a phrase that runs like a leitmotif through T. S. Eliot's poem "Burnt Norton," the first of Eliot's *Four Quartets.* Where Powers finds the substance of connectedness in counterpoint, Eliot finds it in the parallel idea (ultimately drawn from the concluding cantos of Dante's *Paradiso,* where it also takes the form of a rose) of a cosmic dance:

> At the still point of the turning world. Neither flesh nor fleshless;
> Neither from nor towards; at the still point, there the dance is,
> But neither arrest nor movement . . . Except for the point, the still point,
> There would be no dance, and there is only the dance.[7]

IV. DURATION

The dance is as auditory as it is bodily. Sound in time moves between what has happened and what will happen. Auditory knowledge comes in the form of passage; what we know is what transpires. The Latin *transpirare* literally means to breathe across; sound becomes intelligible by breathing life into duration. Whitman's description in "Italian Music in Dakota" records that process as the knowable, the audible, and the eventful coalesce within the twilit landscape.

One aesthetic consequence of this immersion in passage is that music as an auditory phenomenon is a form of knowing as much as it is a mode of expression. In music, too, what we know is what transpires, commonly between definite boundaries that are lacking in everyday hearing. Music makes art of a constraint so familiar we rarely dwell on it. Auditory knowledge in general is constrained to occur in what is called, somewhat oddly, real time: not time as it passes but time as it presses, time over which the perceiver has no natural control. Visual observation may sometimes be time-sensitive and sometimes not; auditory observation is time-sensitive always. Sound is motion both materially and perceptually. Even recorded sound, which can be stopped and replayed at will, must be perceived as a duration in passage.

Listening as knowing affirms the fundamental temporality of human experience. It therefore requires a certain self-surrender, a certain patience, a certain openness to what comes, and, in coming, changes both what is and what has been. Music assumes its significance, its meaning for the listener, by what it reveals when listened to with this attitude. Such listening does not require self-abnegation, or what I once called "submissive listening"; on the contrary, mere submissiveness will hear nothing well. Listening as knowing is a creative act, a kind of retelling what one is hearing in the hearing of it. Auditory knowledge is the prototype of narrative, or better, of the act of storytelling that links parents and child or speaker and listeners. In the right circumstances it does what Walter Benjamin claims the storyteller does: it gives counsel.

Music sometimes reflects on its own immersion in passage. One way to do so is to create an additive pattern that must wait an appreciable interval for completion. Bartok does so memorably in his sixth and last string quartet, the first three movements of which begin with fragments of a slow movement marked *Mesto* (sad); the fragments grow progressively longer until the last movement reveals itself as the whole toward which the parts have been tending. The quartet as a whole reveals itself at the end to have been an act of what one might call defiant resignation: an effort to postpone the inevitable with no illusions of escaping it. The date of composition, August to November, 1939, suggests part of the reason why.

V. PULSATION (CHOPIN)

Another way is to make audible the sense of pressing forward that impels whatever transpires. Chopin's famous Prelude in D-flat, Op. 28, no. 15, known as "The Raindrop," does exactly that.

Before we can say how, we need a modest description of externals. The Prelude consists of three sections, the first of which is itself in three parts. The outer sections are in D-flat major, the middle section in C♯ minor. (The two keys use the same pitches, a relation known as enharmonic equivalence). The third section recapitulates the first six measures of the first and then segues into a brief epilogue.

This form is fairly ordinary; the music that fills it out is anything but. Repetitions of a single pitch occur in nearly every measure of the first and third parts of the first section, of the middle section, and of the final section. The pitch pulses and throbs under the melody in the outer sections, mostly as an inner voice, hovering just at the edge of obtrusiveness. In the middle section, as the mood darkens, the pitch goes over the edge and stays there for a long time. The middle voice becomes the upper voice; the melody sinks into the bass. The section will eventually undo this reversal, presumably to prepare for the restoration of the status quo in the third section—something that the audible pressure of passing time will not, not quite, let happen.

Something new happens to the incessant pitch when the middle section begins. The context for this pitch is continuous motion in eighth-notes, eight attacks per measure in common time. In the first section, the pitch occurs on five or six attacks per measure, and never on the down-beat. The middle section brings saturation: the pitch occurs on eight of eight attacks, downbeat obviously included, throughout the section, drumming its way through many consecutive measures. This heightened insistence, together with the reversal that puts the pulsation above the melody, makes the expressive force of the music secondary, or nearly so, to the exposure of the elemental medium on which the music depends, and all music depends. The impetus of time and the passage of sound become indistinguishable.

After hearing (or playing) the middle section, it is hard to perceive the final section innocently. The music makes only a halfhearted request that one do that. The epilogue begins by interrupting a restatement of the opening melody and continues with five measures in which, except on the downbeat of the first one, the pulsation again occurs on eight of eight attacks per measure. The ending is quiet, but it cannot unhear what has transpired before it, and it does not try. On the contrary: the recapitulation breaks off well before it would reach the middle part of the first section, the one extended stretch of music in which the pulsation departs from its solitary pitch. It is as if the music could not take its ears away from the sound of its own passage.

"Waiting to Be the Music"

Jazz musicians have often described what they do as a kind of storytelling. Unlike similar statements made about classical music, this does not mean that jazz improvisation tracks a definite literary or historical narrative or narrative genre. Instead, improvising becomes the means by which the musician inserts himself in a history that is both communal and personal with the aim of furthering it through expressive immediacy. Thus Sidney Bechet: "My story goes a long way back. It goes further back than I had anything to do with. My music is like that. . . . I got it from something inherited, just like the stories my father gave down to me." The stories, Bechet adds, contain "the part of me that was there before I was," and it is this part that is "waiting to be the music."[1]

That last phrase is pivotal. The music makes audible something otherwise inaccessible, something that resembles what can be told in oral narrative but can itself only be told in music. Waiting to be the music is its only mode of being until the music makes it known. But just how does that happen? And just what is thus made known?

Some potential answers emerge in the closing pages of James Baldwin's classic short story "Sonny's Blues" (1957). The story concerns two brothers: the narrator, a straight-laced and somewhat moralistic schoolteacher, and his brother, Sonny, who is everything the narrator is not: defiant, tormented, an outsider, a convicted criminal, a heroin addict—and a musician. The narrative is haunted by the Biblical question—Cain's question: "Am I my brother's keeper?" The question passes down from the fate of two other brothers a generation older, the narrator and Sonny's father and their uncle. As a young man, the father had to stand by helplessly as a group of drunken racists deliberately ran down his brother with their car, shattering the guitar he was carrying and killing him. The failure left the father a broken man. His legacy to his sons is a memory that cannot be borne, a story that cannot be told. These strictures are literal, not metaphorical; the narrator does not learn about his uncle's death, his uncle's existence, until his mother reveals the truth as she herself is dying. The trauma affects her sons like what the psychoanalyst and philosopher Nicolas Abraham called a phantom, a memory not one's own that becomes stuck in one's own unconscious as in a crypt.[2]

"Sonny's Blues" is about how to claim oneself by telling that story—not quelling it, but refusing to be quelled by it. The means to that end turns out to be what the title of the story points to, the symbolic restoration of that shattered guitar: Sonny's blues.

The narrator has gone to a Greenwich Village nightclub to hear Sonny at the piano with a jazz combo. The leader, Creole, understands the performance in Bechet-like terms as a process of painful self-examination: "He was listening to everything. . . . He wanted Sonny to leave the shoreline and strike out for deep water. He was Sonny's witness that deep water and drowning were not the same thing."[3]

Sonny comes to assent a little at a time, overcoming both his inner resistance and his rustiness as a pianist (he has not played for nearly a year). His playing is tentative at first, even clumsy, without a sense of direction. But when Creole starts playing "Am I Blue" Sonny becomes "part of the family again." He falls into the contagious rhythm of call and response, exchanging ideas with his fellow musicians: "Something began to happen. . . . The dry, low, black man said something awful on the drums. Creole answered, and the drums talked back. Then the horn insisted, sweet and high, slightly detached perhaps, and Creole listened, commenting now and then, dry and driving" (46). As the music continues, it moves beyond the plateau of aesthetic pleasure it has just achieved and carries the music back to its origins in experience: "Creole stepped forward to remind them that what they were playing was the blues. . . . the tale of how we suffer, and how we are delighted, and how we may triumph" (47). The reminder releases the phantom from the crypt. Sonny achieves a moment (perhaps only a moment) of breakthrough and enacts his story in his music. He goes back to the opening phrase of "Am I Blue" and makes it his own. The present becomes transparent to the past, and not just to Sonny's past alone: "He was giving [that tale] back, as everything must be given back, so that, passing through death, it can live forever." The narrator, in recognizing this act of restoration, becomes able to share it, at least this once: "I saw my mother's face again . . . [and] the moonlit road where my father's brother died. . . . [yet] aware that this was only a moment, that the world waited outside . . . and that trouble stretched above us, longer than the sky" (49).

The narrative arc of both "Sonny's Blues," the story, and Sonny's blues, the performance, follows an age-old literary pattern. The tale it tells is a quest romance: a search for truth or transformation that can be achieved only through a semi-ritual course of initiation demanding both courage and insight. Baldwin's musical version suggests that the search also demands listening, and in particular listening through what others hear. Such listening makes self-discovery possible through self-surrender. For Sonny and his brother alike, that means listening for what a passage of improvised music "says" and responding in kind. The response is not simply of music to music, but of music to what music can make known. The storytelling arc passes through a region of unheard or potential speech that precipitates itself into a musical gesture. This potentiality has no sound of its own but its presence is felt underneath every sound the occasion produces. Without it the music would be just note-spinning.

Just so, the role of "Am I Blue" in the story is musical as well as symbolic. Sonny's return to the song's opening phrase draws out its full import as a "speaking melody," a wordless rendition that carries the sense of the words.[4] As an opening, the phrase in the song casts "Am I Blue?" as the restatement of a question that the singer goes on to answer: "Am I blue? Yes, I'm blue. Here's why." The question sounds on an upward melodic leap. When the phrase returns at the close, it casts the same three words as a half-rueful, half-mocking declaration, sounding in the song on three falling steps: "Am I blue!" Sonny, so the narrator tells us, seizes on that declaration and turns it into something on which to linger, something that is no longer a lament.

"Sonny's Blues" also performs the kind of reciprocal listening that it describes. Although the hero of traditional quest romance is always a man, Creole has Sonny's combo improvise on a standard strongly associated with two women, Ethel Waters and Billie Holiday. (Waters sang it while appearing as herself in the 1929 film *On with the Show*; Holiday recorded it—with many melodic changes—in 1941. Recordings by Fats Domino and Ray Charles postdate "Sonny's Blues.") Since nothing is said on the matter, it is not clear whether this association was audible to Baldwin, but it nonetheless resonates through his text. The auditory history of the song creates a narrative counterpoint in which the musical past and the personal past sound together. The song is about abandonment by a lover; Sonny's blues is about abandonment by a world. The sound of the one blends into the sound of the other. Sonny escapes the fate of his social fathers by finding the voices of his musical mothers, as if to fulfill his own mother's role as the transmitter of a forbidden tale. The women's spectral voices—Waters' suggesting the storytelling power of the blues singer, Holiday's the need to succumb to the blues in order to surmount them—widen the circle of mutuality, of dependency, in which alone it is possible to find in one's story the saving element that was waiting to become music. The blend of agency and dependency finds its symbolic register in the bond between mother and son, concretized at the end of the story when Sonny sips from a drink his brother has sent him and sets it on the piano before beginning to play again. The drink of choice is scotch and milk.

Circle Songs

When the musicians in an ensemble listen closely to each other, no matter whether in a jazz group or a string quartet or just among people singing together, the sounds they make carry discernible traces of the sounds they hear. If the performance catches fire, the result is to make something audible that otherwise would have remained unknown, and perhaps unknowable.

In 1998, Bobby McFerrin led a group of improvising vocalists in what he called "circle songs"; the performance was broadcast in a public television series, *Sessions at West 54th*.[1] According to McFerrin, the circle song is a "search process" that requires the audience to show "a lot of patience" while the singers "meander a lot." Like James Baldwin's fictional session on "Am I Blue," discussed just above, the performance of the circle song takes the form of a quest for an emotional and social truth. But in this case there is no preexisting point of origin and the end remains unknown until the moment it arrives. The songs take off from a sound that McFerrin invents on the spot and they continue until it feels right to stop.

The improvisations ground themselves in ostinatos, which they often build up in layers. The singers call at will on melodic riffs, percussive effects, and drones. They observe no limits on the form of vocal utterance. They follow and discard the norms of "good singing" with equal freedom. They separate register from gender with abundant use of falsetto. They separate song from language by abundant use of vocalise and scatting. They separate their music from any single identity by mixing styles freely, a technique that extends to the multiracial makeup of the ensemble.

In one song, for example, the singers' meandering draws a circle around a man singing the phrase "I need you" in a voice that vacillates between tenor and falsetto. The sound has a gospel feel, but it is not clear, and remains uncertain, who "you" is: God, a beloved, the other singers, or the human community symbolized by the singing group. It could be any or all of them. After a while, the singer closes in on the word *need* and intones it in falsetto for a long moment. McFerrin responds with a falsetto of his own, even higher to my ears, which blossoms into a series of solo vocalises alternating with the group singing "hey, hey." The effect is more operatic than anything else, the sound of a genderless diva. The rising gleam of the high solo voices is ecstatic in itself and riveting for the ensemble. As the vocalises succeed each other, they may come to be heard as answering to the need expressed by the sound that called them forth. It is important that there is more than one; the need is great, and the answer must be ample. (Difficult, too, as McFerrin suggests at one or two points by dropping to the low end of his range in a harsh crackle.) Afterwards the music is free to settle on a new ostinato until it fades out with the ensemble's female voices vocalizing "oo-*wah*": a pulsation that leaves widening musical silences between successive cries.

In the course of their improvisation, McFerrin and his singers not only engage in reciprocal listening but also make the process itself audible as a source of knowledge and pleasure—and perhaps, here and there, of an opening to the hovering nimbus of the audiable.

Forty-Part Motets

In or near 1570 Thomas Tallis composed a motet in forty separate parts, a setting of the hymn "Spem in alium nunquam habui" (Hope in another I have never had). It was probably, though not certainly, designed for performance in an octagonal space with four balconies. In 2001 Janet Cardiff created a sound installation she called *Forty-Part Motet*, now on perma-

THE HUM OF THE WORLD

nent display in the National Gallery of Canada. It consists of forty head-high speakers through which Tallis's motet is piped on a loop, one voice per speaker. Visitors to the installation space (a reconstructed chapel in the permanent exhibit) can move from one location to another as the music circulates. The polyphony heard within these two works now resonates with a higher-order polyphony between them.

Tallis's motet begins by adding voice to voice to fill out a five-part choir, but the composition as a whole is not for forty individual voices but for eight such five-part choirs, which sing in various combinations in a complex pattern of accumulation, recession, and climactic accumulation. All forty voices sing together only rarely. The polyphony of the work is thus not primarily between voices but between choirs. Especially insofar as the latter sing from separate spaces, the course of the motet is not the kind of continuous combination of parts that one would expect from a normal choral work but instead a pulsation of massed voices swelling and subsiding and swelling again. Sound in its materiality assumes the force of spirit. The same might be said to happen in Cardiff's recreation, but in inverted form. Cardiff's piece really is for individual voices, and also for their silences, since many of the speakers will be silent at any given moment. The element of spirit lies less within the voices than in the spaces between them. And Cardiff's installation urges its mobile visitors to do what Tallis's music does for its immobile audience: to wander in space.

Tallis also takes pains to make sure that his text can be understood at least part of the time. And for good reason. On three occasions when all forty voices sing together, there is a general pause—a moment when no one sings. At least one of these unvoiced moments opens to the hum of the audiable, which appears, if it does, as the prelude to a moment of grace. Perhaps there is something of this in all three pauses, or so the music suggests by making a pattern, a kind of narrative, of their sequence.

The first pause occurs after the phrase "et omnia peccata hominum" (and all the sins of man) sung by two of the choirs (m. 73). The choirs fall silent in mid-sentence, opening a space of wonder, questioning, and vulnerability before the forty-voice ensemble completes the thought consolingly: "in tribulatione dimittis" (in distress you absolve). The harmony on either side of the pause is the same. Continuity upholds the promise of absolution.

The second pause comes after an extended series of antiphonal exchanges among the choirs. This time (m. 108–09) the mid-sentence break occurs between "Creator caeli et terrae" (Creator of heaven and earth) and the vocative "respice humilitatem nostram" (behold our lowliness). The situation here is more urgent than before. The completion of the sentence is now a plea or prayer rather than an affirmation; the words that complete the sentence pose the grandeur of God against the lowliness of humanity.

The harmony that follows with the entry of the full ensemble must somehow bridge the gap. It does so in a celebrated way. The chord that sets "respice" does not resume the harmony from the other side of the silence. Surprising in itself, it surprises further by an internal difference: the new chord should be in the minor mode but it sounds in major, as if to answer the prayer in the act of uttering it. This gift of unanticipated harmony picks up on a suggestion latent in the text. By placing the pause after recalling God's creation of heaven and earth, the motet perhaps calls for, and certainly receives, an echo of the harmony traditionally supposed to have accompanied the birth of the cosmos. The silent interval allows the ear to listen for traces of that undertone of creation, which were supposed to be inaudible except at moments of special grace. Shakespeare invokes this tradition at the end of his late romance *Pericles* when the title character is reunited with his long-lost daughter:

Pericles:

> O heavens bless my girl! But, hark, what music?
> Tell Helicanus, my Marina, tell him
> O'er, point by point, for yet he seems to doubt,
> How sure you are my daughter. But, what music?

Helicanus:

> My lord, I hear none.

Pericles:

> None!
> The music of the spheres! List, my Marina. (V, i: 225–31)

Pericles subsequently says of the "most heavenly music" that it "nips me unto list'ning" (ll. 234–35), which is a fair description of what this moment in the motet offers to do. Tallis has met the spiritual demands of his text by finding a way to compose the audiable into his music.

The full voicing lasts for only two measures. When it dissipates the harmony returns from the place of mystery to familiar ground. Precisely because its brevity makes it elusive, the union of this full cry with the silence that invokes it forms the spiritual and expressive pivot of the motet. In all likelihood, however, it cannot be heard that way in Cardiff's installation, which has no means of isolating the general pauses. Cardiff, so to speak, diffuses the miracle that Tallis concentrates. The resulting gain is the possibility of sustained wandering in the labyrinth of voice. The loss is the loss of the audiable—unless by chance one stumbles on it at just the right moment. The possibility is there.

The final pause (m. 121) reverses the order of "respice humilitatem," breaking after the latter and resuming on the former with a cadence. The cadence supplements miracle with rational understanding. It thus vindicates the hope (spem) that the reciter of the hymn has chosen to place in the Creator alone. This end, too, cannot quite be heard in Cardiff's installation except by chance; the looping of the music and the movement of the visitors deny finality to both. But Cardiff thus makes palpable a resonance that must remain latent in the motet. The meeting and parting of voices against a background of promissory silence forms a moving image of eternity—for a little time.

The Ether

In 1886, Charles H. Hinton proposed to understand the ether—the all-enveloping but next-to-immaterial medium in which light waves were supposed to be propagated—on the model of the recently invented Edison phonograph:

> Suppose the aether, instead of being perfectly smooth, to be corrugated, and to have all manner of definite marks and furrows. Then the earth, coming in

its course round the sun on this corrugated surface, would behave exactly like the phonograph behaves.

In the case of the phonograph the indented metal sheet is moved past the metal point attached to the membrane. In the case of the earth it is the indented aether which remains still while the material earth slips along it. Corresponding to each of the marks in the aether there would be a movement of matter, and the consistency and laws of the movements of matter would depend on the predetermined disposition of the furrows and indentations of the solid surface along which it slips.[1]

Its show of scientific reasoning aside, the rhetorical aim of this passage, congruent with *Scientific Romances*, the title of Hinton's book, is to merge the material wonders of modern science and technology with the transcendental wonders of ancient cosmology and religion. The cosmic phonograph recreates the Pythagorean music of the spheres, complete with the celestial motion that was thought to produce the tones of the harmonic series. Insofar as the Edison cylinder was most likely to record voices, whether singing or speaking, the cosmic phonograph also replicates the identification of cosmic harmony with the divine Word. And insofar as the ether is corrugated by marks and furrows, the model of sound-writing—phono-graphy—invoked is based not on alphabetic inscriptions but on pictographic glyphs incised in the recording medium, the language of ancient Eastern mysteries.

What is most striking about this series of images is the persistence of sound in the silence of space. The sound belongs entirely to the model, not what the model describes; there is no suggestion here that the earth actually elicits a sound from the grooves of the ether. Yet that is what it must do if it "behaves exactly as the phonograph behaves." What gives this description the status of romance, however "scientific," what allows it to identify the material universe of modern science with the enchanted cosmos of the traditional worldview, is the translation of light to sound, the conception of the ether less as a gauzy border between matter and spirit than as an enveloping murmur, song, or whisper, a continuous and permanent series of ambient sounds. In short, Hinton's phonographic ether is a figure for the audiable. And it is so all the more tellingly for what we know and he did not: that there is no ether, that the space it supposedly filled is empty and soundless.

In its own small way, this pseudo-scientific curiosity encapsulates the modern dilemma of the audiable, which we hear, and cannot help but hear, as a living presence, and know, and cannot help but know, as random background noise. A strange dilemma, perhaps, because there is no need to resolve it. At its root is a vibrancy that we can choose to let flourish in the cleft between what our senses say and what we say to make sense. The vibrancy is bodily; the romance comes from what it embodies.

And what is that?

Elemental Media

Light, it turned out, does not need the ether. It can go anywhere but a black hole. But sound needs resonating media, and if we think of its media collectively then something like the ether might come back into play as an elemental medium.[1]

In *The Marvelous Clouds,* John Durham Peters suggests that media are not merely bearers of messages nor even also messages in their own right but, further still, phenomena with a distinct sensory presence of their own. Media form part of the experience that they help to communicate. The concept of media thus expands to include the full infrastructure of experience where nature and culture meet. This expansion allows us to understand the primary elements of that infrastructure, especially the classical four elements of earth, air, fire, and water, as elemental media—exactly what the ancients understood them to be. One of my purposes in adopting this concept from Peters is to expand it further into elemental areas not commonly recognized because the older concepts of media have tended to keep them hidden.

The world, runs the sentence we began with, *is alive with sound.* Vibrancy penetrates every place we go, rhythmically rising above and dipping beneath the threshold of awareness. This immanent resonance, which I have proposed calling the audiable, is both a matter of sense and a matter of making sense. It shapes the quality of sentience and it transforms understanding. Thinking about this vibrancy is thinking *in* the vibrancy. The audiable is the elemental medium of the feeling of being alive.[2]

Elemental Fluids

And when being alive feels painful? If that pain finds expression in music, the music may seem to dissolve itself or its listener into an elemental medium heard as the rush of a fluid basic to life. Such, at least, is the testimony of three writers—two poets and a novelist—who heard the music of Chopin as a transmutation of piano to voice and of voice to such primary fluids: blood, water, tears, milk.

The writers, all American women, were working in an era when Chopin's music was widely regarded as a projection in sound of the frailty of his body and widely celebrated as an impassioned, often violent breaker of both social and bodily surfaces. In both respects the music was heard as the bearer of a more primary sound. Women were not alone in hearing the music in these terms, but those who did seemed to have used them to bind Chopin to themselves as a surrogate self. The vehemence of the composer imprisoned by his vulnerable body becomes an echo of the predicament faced by women seeking to break the bonds that limit their access to work, love, and cultural production. But this second self, an ironic appropriation of the idea of feminine "accomplishment" linked at the time to domestic keyboard performance, does not take the form of an alter ego. It takes the form of an elemental medium, a free-floating potential subjectivity, a diffuse object that saturates both internal and external space.

The three women are Emma Lazarus, the aptly named Kate Chopin, and Amy Lowell. Lazarus's best-known poem, "The New Colossus," is more familiar today than her name is; the poem's concluding lines are engraved on the base of the Statue of Liberty.[1] Kate Chopin is best known for a single novel, *The Awakening*. Amy Lowell was famous during her lifetime as a pioneering modernist poet, but her reputation sank rapidly after her death and has only just begun to recover.

Lazarus begins her sonnet sequence, "Chopin" (1879), by describing how Chopin's music breaks through the glittering surface of a salon:

> Of glancing gems, rich stuffs, the dazzling snow
> Of necks unkerchieft, and bare, clinging arms.
> Hark to the music! How beneath the strain
> Of reckless revelry, vibrates and sobs

One fundamental chord of constant pain,
The pulse-beat of the poet's heart that throbs.[2]

A simile follows: just as the underlying vibration and sobbing of the music breaks through the reckless revelry, "So yearns, though all the dancing waves rejoice, / The troubled sea's disconsolate, deep voice." Layers of sound spread out: here the music of the piano, pointedly left undescribed; there the primal sound of the sea fused with the heartbeat; and between them the voice that partakes of both.

For Lazarus, the voice belongs especially to outcasts of all sorts, those "who must perish by the way," those "set apart by Fate" who cannot speak for themselves. "A voice," she writes, "was needed," and Chopin, who filled that need, was also sacrificed to it. His "fragile frame, / Slowly consuming with its inward flame" has transmuted itself into a musical offering. The vehemence of the music is the sound of a self-immolation. This transmutation makes Chopin—makes Chopin heard as—a frail Odysseus, more heroic in failure than in success, one thrown "in the whirl / Of seething passions . . . scourged and stung / . . . in storm-vext seas." Like Charybdis, the whirlpool, his Muse is no "pensive nymph" but a fatal mother who nourishes him on another kind of fluid: "An amazon of thought with sovereign eyes, / Whose kiss was poison, man-brained, worldly-wise."

Kate Chopin's novel deals with the sexual awakening of a woman in a social world that has no place for it. One of the turning points in the narrative comes when Frederic Chopin's music, specifically the Fantaisie-Impromptu and some or all of the Preludes, breaks through the decorous surface of a salon with no less vehemence than its counterpart in Lazarus's poem. The pianist, like Lazarus's Amazonian Muse, is a formidable rather than a gracious figure: "She was a disagreeable little woman, no longer young, who had quarreled with everyone . . . [After finishing] she arose, and bowing her stiff, lofty brow, she went away, stopping neither for thanks nor applause." The pianist, Mme. Reisz, incarnates in feminine form the dissident voice in Chopin's sound. As one guest exclaims in response to her performance of the tumultuous D-minor Prelude that closes Chopin's cycle, "That last Prelude! Bon Dieu! It shakes a man!" Later, Mme. Reisz plays privately for the novel's heroine, Edna Pontellier, and the elements of voice and surging waters come fully into play:

Edna did not know when the Impromptu began or ended. . . . Mademoiselle
had glided from the Chopin into the quivering love notes of Isolde's song, and
back again to the Impromptu with its soulful and poignant longing. . . .

The music grew strange and fantastic—turbulent, insistent, plaintive and
soft with entreaty. The shadows grew deeper. The music filled the room. It
floated out upon the night, over the housetops, the crescent of the river, los-
ing itself in the silence of the upper air.

Edna was sobbing. . . .[3]

The transformation of the Fantaisie-Impromptu into Isolde's Transfiguration (which presumably replaces the placid middle section of the
piece) gives the kind of auditory layering invoked by Lazarus a singular
musical sound. It again transmutes the sound of the piano to the sound of
the voice, and not just any voice, but the already exemplary voice of
ecstatic song merging with a primal flow, the "billowing waves" of sound
and sea that Wagner's Isolde voices as they simultaneously give voice
to her. Edna's own transfiguration moves equivocally on the tide of her
sobs.

Amy Lowell's version of Chopin's transmutation is neither political, like
Lazarus's, nor erotic, like Kate Chopin's. Instead it is historical, the product of a thirst for something like spiritual nourishment in a modern era
that has made the very idea suspect. The surface that Lowell breaks with
Chopin's voice is a banality of her own making: a lightly self-mocking
address to her cat. The one-sided conversation occupies the first and third
of three sections; the second and longest section plunges abruptly into
memories of Chopin's life, presented in fragments and without explanation or transition, as if they were Lowell's own memories, or at least indistinguishable from them.

This central section is a kind of fantasy-impromptu on themes suggested by George Sand's account of the famously miserable journey to
Majorca that she and Chopin made in the winter of 1838–39. During their
stay Chopin composed several of the Preludes. These pieces made a strong
impression on Sand, who described them as highly evocative and "very
beautiful."[4] Lowell picks up the thread. She weaves together a collage of
images, quotations, and paraphrases that present the Preludes as the
musical sublimation of distressing sounds—driving wind, guttering rain,

chanting, screaming, "arpeggios confused by blood." Sand thought that this was literally true of the "Raindrop" Prelude and made it the subject of a famous anecdote. She and her son had left Chopin alone while they did some shopping, but a bad storm delayed their return by many hours. When they finally arrived, according to Sand, Chopin cried out, "Ah, I knew that you were dead!" In the meantime he had composed the prelude, unconsciously incorporating the rhythmic beating of the rain. Sand reports that Chopin rejected this idea, but while she acknowledges that the music was not merely imitative, she insists that it was nonetheless "certainly full of the rain resonating on the tiles" of the roof. The prelude simply translates non-signifying sound into an expressive signifier.

Lowell shifts Sand's literal account to the symbolic register. She quotes the exclamation ascribed to Chopin as if to capture his voice. She gives the quotation without attribution. She pairs it with the scream of an eagle (not found in Sand) and says that it comes from "some one in the house."[5] Even in the act of utterance, the voice has already separated from the person. It transforms the natural dissonances of wind and rain into protests, as if in that voice, against illness and mortality. Through Lowell's images, the music defies Sand's description of it as "very beautiful"; instead it comes with a stigma, "tangled with nets of blood" from the composer's mouth. The description includes the strange phrase "music quenched by blood," which turns on a double meaning. To quench is to extinguish, but the word is used only with reference to thirst and to fire. As fire, the music is extinguished by blood. But as thirst, it is inflamed by blood, quenched in reverse. The more the blood, the greater the thirst.

The section ends with a subdued statement of this idea. It is voiced by Chopin himself, ventriloquized a second time by Lowell from a letter the composer sent from Majorca to his friend and editor, Julian Fontana:

> "I cannot send you the manuscripts as they are not yet finished.
> I have been ill as a dog.
> My illness has had a pernicious effect on the Preludes
> Which you will receive God knows when."

Thus the real Chopin. The words less than eloquent, the attitude less than heroic. Yet Fontana did receive the Preludes, after all, and in their sound Chopin's illness transmutes itself yet once more by becoming, through the piano, the sound of a voice. Not his voice, but a floating voice that can become the listener's, here Lowell's, and impart to it a saving undertone. Lowell makes that undertone audible at the end of the poem in a series of almost-rhyming i-sounds as she advises her cat to quench her—whose?—thirst: "Therefore, Winky, drink some milk / And leave the mouse until to-morrow."

Writing the Soundscape

This music crept by me upon the waters.

Shakespeare, *The Tempest*
T.S. Eliot, *The Waste Land*

I. DOS PASSOS

It is 1930. John Dos Passos publishes *The 42nd Parallel,* the first novel in his epic trilogy *U.S.A.,* the same year that Hart Crane publishes his poetic epic, *The Bridge,* on the same continent-spanning topic. The *U.S.A.* trilogy begins where *The Bridge* ends, with sound. In a lyrical prologue, really a prose poem, also called "U.S.A.," Dos Passos describes "the young man," who is everyman, walking the streets of "the city," which is every city, in absolute solitude: "No job, no woman, no house, no city." Only one thing brings mitigation:

> Only the ears busy to catch the speech are not alone; the ears are caught tight, linked tight by the tendrils of phrased words, the turn of a joke, the singsong fade of a story, the gruff fall of a sentence; linking tendrils of speech twine through the city blocks, spread over pavements, grow out along broad parked avenues, speed with the trucks leaving on their long night runs over roaring highways, whisper down sandy byroads past wornout farms, joining up cities and fillingstations, roundhouses, steamboats, planes groping along airways; words call out on mountain pastures, drift slow down rivers widening to the sea and the hushed beaches.[1]

This paragraph performs what it describes. In depicting the way a living auditory body—"the tendrils of phrased words"—fills all of space,

THE HUM OF THE WORLD

crosses every distance, and links each thing it touches to itself and each other thing as a vine twines around a trellis, the words of the paragraph form linkages and cadences that show what at the same time they tell. Within this polyphony, which extends into the mind's ear, what the words show is primary, even though what they tell is essential. The linking power of the "phrased words" comes from the phrasing, the auditory reality of tone, rhythm, music: the gruff fall, the turn, the singsong fade.

This paragraph, more affirmative than anything in the more than a thousand pages that follow it, makes audible not only the lifelike proliferation of speech and the expressive resonances that go with it, but also the underlying readiness of these things to occur and to continue, their power not only as fact but also as potentiality and promise. The concluding phrases enunciate this readiness by making a rhythmic cadence on an image not of sound but of the place of silence to which sound tends as a river runs to the sea: the hushed beaches. In that hush the audiable becomes audible.

Crane seems to have sensed something of the same thing in his incantatory lyric "Repose of Rivers." The poem ends with a similar fusion of phrasing and imagery in sight (or maybe just the memory) of the sea:

> There, beyond the dykes
> I heard wind flaking sapphire, like this summer,
> And willows could not hold more steady sound.[2]

The penultimate line translates the sound of the summer wind into a shower of radiant particles. The final line shifts the locus of sensory apprehension first to imagined touch—the willows holding the sound in the swish of their leaves—and last to the "steady sound" itself, reproduced, half heard, in the resonance of the two closing iambs with the s-sound held by their strong beats.

II. CRANE

This, we're told, is how Hart Crane wrote his poetry: "Typically, after drinking copiously, he would put a 78 on a hand-cranked Victrola and play it 'a dozen, two dozen, three dozen times' while alternately banging away on a typewriter and loudly declaiming the same verse repeatedly."[3] The poetry thus came into being through, or as the trace of, a polyphonic chant among mechanical and organic instruments of expression, each of which served as a writing implement to transcribe the utterance of the other. This effort took the audible form of its own impossibility through the incessant repetitions by each instrument, in each medium: the turntable endlessly cranked to unreel its tunes, the clatter of the writing machine, and the outpouring of the poet's voice that seeks to subsume the other two and drown them out.

Music and machine fuse in much this way in "Atlantis," the last poem (but the first to be written) in Crane's magnum opus, the poetic sequence *The Bridge*, published in 1930. The title refers to the Brooklyn Bridge, which since its completion in 1883 has been celebrated as a masterpiece of both engineering and aesthetic design. For Crane, the bridge symbolizes the link between past and present and thus provides him with a point of departure for a wide-ranging examination of modernity and its impact on the history of the United States. "The very idea of a bridge," he wrote, "is an act of faith."[4] Music plays a fundamental role throughout the sequence, which Crane described as "symphonic in including all the strands"; the strands are both the elements of subject matter and "the bound cable strands" of the Brooklyn Bridge, which act like the strings of a musical instrument.

The fusion of music and machine frames "Atlantis," which both begins and ends with the image of the Brooklyn Bridge as a gigantic wind harp, a mechanical toy that is also a familiar Romantic image of the creative mind at work. The same is true of *The Bridge* as a whole, which introduces the image of the harp in its prologue: "O harp and altar, of the fury fused." The fury is both mechanical energy and poetic inspiration. The harp is both the Romantics' wind harp and the legendary harp of bardic singers. "Atlantis" begins with a sound in the act of emerging, "Through the bound cable strands, the arching path / Upward, veering with light, the flight of strings," and ends with a kind of angelic call and response: "Whispers antiphonal in azure swing."

Each half of this last line performs the antiphony it describes: in the i-sounds between "whispers" and "antiphonal" and the sibilance between "azure" and "swing," with the i-sound in "swing" extending the antiphony between the halves. The line almost dissolves into the resonance of the half-heard. Perhaps Crane's poetry has proven so memorable, despite its difficulty, because it so audibly writes the audiable.

III. NIPPER

Speaking of that Victrola, why did the image long associated with it, the Victor dog Nipper attending to his master's voice, become so famous? The answer, perhaps, has something to do with the history of media technology and its effect on the human senses.

Advances in visual technology have tended to precede advances in auditory technology: first the photograph, then the phonograph. But once the auditory device arrives, it exposes a void within the corresponding visual field, which thenceforth stands exposed as incomplete without the addition of sound. The photograph was always silent; the phonograph makes it seem mute. This principle (and I suspect it *is* a principle) is most obvious in the history of film. It also applies to the entertainments that anticipate film, the dioramas and panoramas of the nineteenth century. Most recently, it has attended the development of screens, from computer monitors to mobile phone surfaces, originally instances of visual technology that inexorably become audiovisual and would now seem quaint otherwise. Images may saturate the modern world, but not without acoustic help. The recording and diffusing of speech, music, and ambient sound arise as realizations of technological possibility. But the more possible sound reproduction becomes, the more necessary sound itself is revealed to be. The revelation is as bodily as it is conceptual. And it demands that we recalibrate our understanding of the senses as media of knowledge.

Haunting Melodies

Perhaps the second most famous element in Proust's *In Search of Lost Time,* just behind the *petite madeleine* whose taste releases the flood of involuntary memories from which the narrative arises, is the narrator's preoccupation with the "little theme" he hears in the violin sonata of the fictional composer Vinteuil. The fame of this nonexistent melody (or this melody lost to fiction that people go in search of anyway by proposing models: Franck? Debussy? Saint-Saens?) may come in part from the way it enshrines in literature a phenomenon in music so familiar that we forget how strange it is. The narrator hears something of himself in this theme. The theme becomes a precious fragment of himself that he would otherwise know nothing of. Probably everyone who loves music (and who doesn't?) has experienced something similar. But why? After all, music is something we make; it is not what we are. Why does music, and more particularly melody, because melody is the main thing involved, form an auditory image of the listener? Why does it so readily worm its way into our sense of self?

One possible answer—speaking of worms—may be suggested by another strange but familiar musical phenomenon, the sometimes maddening persistence of a tune stuck in one's head. Oliver Sacks called such unrelenting mental melodies "brainworms"; a half century or so earlier, Theodor Reik gave them the more Romantic name of "haunting melodies," a term he stole from a forgotten article published close to a half century before that. The different metaphors testify to a fundamental ambivalence.

Sacks, a neurologist, and Reik, a psychoanalyst, both think of music stuck in the head as an aberration, linked in some way to pathology. Yet both acknowledge that it is also linked to normality, or rather to the very foundations of the sense of normality. Sacks connects the persistence of the brainworm to our desire for the repetition of something that gives pleasure. The adult brain finds in the melody a relic of the child's insistence on hearing the same story, the same words, *again*. Reik thinks of the expressive quality of the melody as a residue of conflict, trauma, or intense emotion—something the self is not finished with. For Sacks the brainworm feeds on a lost sense of well-being that it tries too hard to recapture. For Reik the haunting melody returns us to a critical moment in our emotional lives. The moment is one we may keep secret even from ourselves, but it is one of the keys to who we are. The melody lures us back to it.[1]

Melody has this power because it is both immediately expressive and infinitely repeatable. Its expressiveness in the present incorporates a promise of its expressiveness in the future. A melody that could not be repeated would not be a melody at all, except insofar as it induced a desire to hear it again. But the repetition of melody is not an unmixed blessing.

A brainworm becomes oppressive when repetition overtakes the expressiveness of its melody and renders it meaningless. The melody becomes insidious; it drives us crazy—gaslights us; it becomes "sticky music," "stuck

in the head," an "earworm." The melody loses the power to haunt in a positive sense that comes from attaching the repetition to new expressive ends,
perhaps especially to those that tease us out of thought. Listeners absorb
themselves in the music they love precisely *as if* they were being haunted
by it. Melodic returns send shivers down the spine. But the line between
haunting as evocation and haunting as affliction is very thin.

Take these processes out of people's heads and they become harmless, if
sometimes annoying. They underwrite the familiar uses of melody in
advertising to give commodities a personality and in dramatic media to
give personalities a musical avatar. Theme songs are tamed haunting melodies. Put the same processes back in people's heads, and the haunting
melody becomes a kernel of self that is stuck in the wrong place: a talis-
man that should be external (and might be nice if it were) but that cannot
be expelled from the mind. The lucky charm turns into a splinter.

The brainworm becomes what Jacques Lacan called a *sinthome*, using a
homophonic spelling of the French *symptôme* ("symptom"; an English parallel would be to respell "symptom" as "symptim").[2] The sinthome / symptim is a thought or action repeated incessantly despite seeming to mean
nothing. The nothing somehow grows with each repetition. The problem
the sinthome poses is the possibility that the appearance of signifying
nothing may be a reality. The sinthome absorbs the sense of self at the same
time as it repels meaning. In that respect it bears a certain uncanny resemblance to something else. The sinthome exemplifies the condition long
widely taken, though we should know better by now, to be the essential
condition of music. The haunting melody gives expression to this likeness
in musical form. The melody becomes an ironic translation of music's puta-
tive status as sublime noise.

Make these processes part of a musical composition, and melody
becomes audible as an objectified form of self-negation, doomed to repeat
itself to excess. A haunting melody in real life is a mystery; a haunting
melody in a piece of music is a demonstration. The more such a melody
returns, the less it means. It becomes an automatism that exposes a fundamental flaw, an inherent vulnerability, within subjectivity itself. To feel
like ourselves, we must live among meaningful sound. Noise empties us
out. One reason why our pleasure in nonsense depends on heightened
rhyme, rhythm, assonance, alliteration, and the like is that those acoustic

phenomena, rhythm first among equals, take the place of the sense that we playfully cast off. But when sense is cast off *for* us, as if against our will, we begin to disappear.

Theodore Reik was flummoxed by this phenomenon courtesy of Gustav Mahler. For decades he was troubled by his failure to explain why a chorale melody from the finale of Mahler's Second Symphony had haunted him, hounded him, really, in connection with the death of a mentor. If he had only known, the answer comes elsewhere in the same work.

The scherzo movement of the Second Symphony is willfully grotesque: a wrong-footed dance based on the tune of a satirical song that Mahler composed at about the same time (1893). The song, "St. Anthony of Padua's Fish Sermon," recounts how St. Anthony, faced with an empty church, goes to the rivers and preaches to the fish. The fish enjoy the sermon well enough but it is meaningless to them, and after it is finished they go on with their fishy lives just as they did before.

The scherzo addresses a bigger loss of meaning. It is not funny at all. In a letter to a friend in 1896, Mahler described the music as resembling a moment of recoil from "[the] incessantly moving, never resting, never intelligible gear shaft (*Getriebe:* gear, mechanism) of life." He goes on to develop a metaphor for this recoil that immediately takes precedence over it. The music, he says, echoes the "gruesome" (*grauhaft:* gruesome, atrocious, bloodcurdling) experience of watching "the billowing of dancing figures in a brightly lit ballroom, into which you gaze from outside in the dark night— from so great a *distance* that you can *no* longer hear the *music!*" In another letter written at about the same time, he adds that the distant "turning and twisting of the couples," seen through a window, "seems senseless, because the rhythm, the key that unlocks it, is lacking. Just so you must suppose that to someone who has lost his identity and his happiness, the world looks like this—distorted and crazy, as in a concave mirror (*Hohlspiegel*)." The *Hohlspiegel*, literally "hollow mirror," forms a void that swallows rather than a surface that reflects. The result in both accounts, and the sound depicted at the climax of the movement, is a shriek: a sound that rivals the gears but cannot stop them, that resounds in the void but cannot fill it.

These imaginary scenes strongly emphasize the observer's being out of reach, at a distance from the dancing couples. They present love out of reach as the sight of unheard music. When Mahler published a program for the symphony in 1901, he watered down what he had said in his letters, confining himself to the safety of abstractions. But the program nonetheless retains sublimated forms of the earlier imagery of alienating distance. The music now sets the observer amid "the tumult that reigns around him"; it records his loss of childhood innocence and "the inner steadfastness that love alone can impart"; and it translates the spectral ballroom dances into a wider but nonspecific scene in which "the world and life turn into phantoms."[3]

The musical realization of Mahler's fantasy-parable translates the soundless whirling of the dancers into a rhythmic pulsation that will not quit. The dance rhythm we hear in the scherzo belongs to a haunting melody. More exactly, the nucleus of the music is a musical recreation of a haunting melody, with the odd twist that the melody is unheard: the music we hear makes audible in haunting form the missing rhythm and the mute twisting and turning of the bodies in Mahler's nocturnal scene. In other words, the music of the Scherzo gives sound to a sight from which sound has been amputated. The scene, as evidenced by Mahler's first two descriptions of it and even by the more abstract third, which still refers to phantoms, is a depiction of becoming haunted. It finds expression in an ungainly pairing of rhythm and melody that haunts the subject-hero of the symphony and defines the condition from which he must be redeemed.

As so often among those who hear, we encounter in this musical parable the trauma of sight without sound. But how do things look and sound when we shift our emphasis from the imaginary scene of the unheard music and its missing rhythm to the actual sound of the symphony? For Mahler's imaginary scene arises only in the music that we *do* hear. This is music that gives audibility to the inaudible by rhythmically imagining the effect of not hearing the dance rhythm. In so doing, it links both layers of rhythm to the rhythms of social and erotic life.

The music thus involves a rhythm that we can't catch and a rhythm we can't help being caught by. There is the rhythm of popular dance music and there is its distanced and alienated form in Mahler's scherzo. The effects of this doubling are vertiginous. The rhythm we hear is vivid in itself but it is supposedly only the trace of a rhythm that goes unheard. Its vividness, moreover, induces a kind of blindness to the scene placed at its source. For Mahler, at least, the music we hear does not portray or depict the scene of nocturnal observation, but only resembles the gruesome experience of the observer. The music sounds the way this gruesomeness feels. It recreates the experience of alienation proper to the absence of the dance rhythm, and perhaps to the absence of rhythm itself, which begins to disappear into a caricature of itself. The music is a rich sensory projection of sensory deprivation.

The "gruesome" lack of rhythm in Mahler's dance scene becomes a clumsy persistence of rhythm in the symphonic scherzo. The music makes the felt amputation of rhythm from the scene's dancing bodies into an audible process. In the text, the unheard music becomes palpable, and in a sense audible, because its missing rhythm controls the motion of the dancing bodies. The rhythm is the key that would unlock the door and let the observer into the community of the ballroom. It connects one person to another as it connects one performer to another. The lack of the key doubles the observer's isolation from the dancing couples, adding sensory to social breakdown. Perception takes the form of a coerced synesthesia. The observer hears the dance music by sight in the way a blind person sees a face by touch. The key that would make sense of the moving bodies elicits paralysis instead. The equivalent in the sounding symphonic music is the gradual loss of sense that overtakes the underlying dance rhythm (often only faintly audible, a phantasmal presence) in the way that too frequent or too emphatic repetition may drain the sense out of a word. The music becomes a parade of empty resonances. We might have known it would; otherwise why would the movement begin with a series of loud unaccompanied strokes on the timpani that seem to come from nowhere and to go there too?

The more general situation exemplified by this dance scene has to be understood with reference, not to music as such, but to the pair of sensory frameworks that Mahler's scherzo disrupts: the acoustic matrix that makes music possible and the field of vision.

Virtually any scene deprived of sound becomes the kind of ghastly pantomime that Mahler describes. Half the aesthetic of "silent" cinema turns on this problem, and so does the profound ambivalence typically produced by miming of any sort. This propensity reveals a fundamental asymmetry in the relations of hearing and seeing. To see without hearing, to witness a dumb show, is always disorienting, vertiginous, too near to an abyss. But to hear without seeing carries no inevitable sense of distress. It may, on the contrary, be transforming, ecstatic, revelatory: we close our eyes at both the musical and the sexual climax. There is no accounting for this difference except by the power of the audiable, the fundamental nexus of sentience, sound, and life. That nexus is precisely what Mahler's deafened scene suspends or rends.

A scene, any scene, includes an immanent soundscape. The principle that the visual entails the sonorous is effectively the founding principle and rationale of sound studies. Silence vexes the scene because the silence is invariably a subtraction, even from a scene that, like that of a painting, has never been heard and never can be heard. The basis of the visual is resonance. What allows a scene to become visually intelligible is the scene's sonority, and it is sonority that defines the general meaning of this intelligibility: that the scene is alive, that it is lived, living, animate, animating. The condition of lived visibility is—the audiable.

In Mahler's scene, the missing rhythm touches on the audiable through a kind of sensory rebound. The dancers are in the light, the watcher in darkness; the dancers are close to each other, the watcher distant from everyone. When these privations culminate in the default of rhythm, the silence imposed on the dance is imposed on the night as well, which assumes the silence of the thing seen. The night, the real night, is, like Caliban's island, full of noises, but the night evoked by Mahler is seized by a dead silence. The eeriness of the experience is not only that of the dancers' separation from the rhythm, but also of the watcher's separation from the audiable that would ordinarily penetrate the night and accompany the night wanderer. Rhythm is the movement of the audiable, the audiable in motion, the audiable as movement, as body, as life.

Lacking that, the watcher is as absolutely disconnected from himself as the dancers, unknown to themselves, are disconnected from each other. These rifts in sense and the sensible sound out most clearly, perhaps, in those passages of the symphonic movement where the dance rhythm sounds wooden, literally so, whether because the strings are playing *col legno* (that is, with the wood rather than the hair of the bow) or because a rute (basically a bundle of sticks) is answering timpani strokes on the downbeat to fill out the 3/8 measure. In general, the movement combines twisting, whirling figures in sixteenth notes—figures in the shape of worms—with a fractured dance rhythm in eighths, repeating each vertiginously in constantly changing colors until both lose their meaning and the dance rhythm disappears.

When it goes, as Mahler tells us, "the world and life turn into phantoms." Melodic motion ceases to be expressive and becomes the external form of an empty self. Hearing the depleted music is like watching those dancers through the distant window; the hollowing out of the rhythm exposes a rift between sound and sight that is fundamental to both and cannot be mended, so that even when they go together it is impossible to hear them as entirely one.[4]

Mahler's scherzo thus guarantees its own unintelligibility for its contemporaries, including Reik, who have no language to describe this music other than the language of emotion—certainly no language for a symptom without a subject, or an empty self as melodic motion. Reik does, however, grasp the element of depersonalization in the music even if he cannot identify it as such. He understands that the scherzo is the pivot of the symphony and that Mahler's two 1896 descriptions of it perform a shift from a first- to a third-person point of view. The shift marks the depersonalization at the core of the music: the disappearance of the self into the mechanism of its becoming haunted. The sense of self turns out to be expendable. One can suffer quite well without it.

It took, perhaps, another composer to provide a description in music to match Mahler's own. The third movement of Luciano Berio's *Sinfonia* (1968, 1970) consists of an extended quotation of Mahler's scherzo enveloped with a dense collage of other musical quotations. The melody, haunting as ever, sweeps up and discards the quotations around it like so much musical chaff. Berio described the result as "a kind of *Voyage to Cythera* made on board the Scherzo," referring to a poem by Baudelaire in which the quest for the fabled island of love discovers it to be a rock-strewn wasteland where carrion birds feast on the eyes and viscera of a hanged man and "castrate him completely."[5]

The Lifelike

THE UNDEAD

When Conrad, in the aesthetic credo discussed above (p. 9), writes that his task as a novelist is to make the reader *see* (the emphasis is his), he enacts a shift from word to image that anoints the image as the primary carrier of truth. Because the venue of Conrad's statement is reading, this shift coincides with a figurative turn from speech to silence. Both the speech and the silence are only virtual but the silence is also real, and its reality marks it as the proper medium of true perception.

This statement of Conrad's continues an ancient tradition of rhetoric in which the same shift proceeds not from virtual but from actual speech. The Roman rhetorical theorist Quintilian held that one of the orator's chief aims should be to give "lifelikeness" (*enargeia*) to speech by transcending its audibility. "Oratory," he wrote, "fails of its full effect . . . if its appeal is merely to the hearing . . . and not displayed in living truth to the eyes of the mind."[1] The aim of the orator is in effect to drown out his own voice with the silence of the seen. Truth comes from the imaginary equivalent of observation, not from the action of describing or testifying.

This alienation of truth to the image may be one reason why there is no auditory equivalent of iconoclasm. At least it is difficult to think of one. Catcalls aside, the impulse to direct destructive rage against music is rare in Western cultures. After all, the music is just sound. It dissipates in the air. Unlike an image it does not stand before one and insist on being believed. Unlike an image it does not pretend to be lifelike when it is actually inert. In this sense the only true images are imaginary.

Ironically, the dematerialization of truth in the image becomes more troubling when the images add to their lifelikeness by learning to move. At least in the early part of their history, moving images seemed both obviously illusory and uncannily real. They produced unease amid the effect of amazement. The iconic moments of early cinema—a gun pointed at the viewer and fired, a train bearing down on the observer, an eye filling the screen slashed with a razor—make this truth visible indeed. The dangerous emptiness of the moving image diminished with time and habituation but it has never disappeared. The primary antidote for it has, again from the earliest moments, been the combination of the moving image with sound: speech, ambient sound, and above all music, with its rhythmic drive and material, vibratory presence. The truth alienated into the image would fail of its full effect without the reality of sound. Lifelikeness without sound is less lively than it is undead.[2]

But undeadness is powerful. It even adds to the motives for iconoclasm by exchanging the diffuseness of sound for the concentration of sight. The silent material image takes life from the gaze that it rivets. The passage in Henry James's *The Wings of the Dove* that describes being riveted in this way (p. 69) also makes the experience audible, a touch more than half-heard. When the novel's fatally ill protagonist gazes with fascination at the centuries-old portrait of a richly dressed noblewoman, she clearly locks eyes with a momentary alter ego. But the fascination soon passes over into a return gaze by the pictured "lady in question." The painted gaze assumes the force of the evil eye: "[With] her eyes of other days, her full lips, her long neck, her recorded jewels, her brocaded and wasted reds, [she] was a great personage, but unaccompanied by a joy. And she was dead, dead, dead." The threefold "dead" is a classic case of protesting too much, as the reader can virtually hear in its spondaic thudding. The problem is that the lady in question is not dead *enough*. That rhetorical thud supplies the heartbeat that she lacks and in so doing seeks to diminish her undeadness. The exclamation is an act of symbolic iconoclasm.

The problem of iconoclasm is one concern of Caroline von Eck in an essay on the agency of images.[3] The essay cites the passage from Quintilian I quoted earlier. Von Eck discusses a sequence of images inspired by Velazquez's *Rokeby Venus*, which in 1914 suffered a slashing: a suffragette, Mary Richardson, "took a knife to her and caused severe damage to her neck, heart and torso—in fact the parts . . . attacked by real murderers when they really want to kill a living human being" (427). Von Eck's language also treats the image as if it were alive, thus deliberately exemplifying her point that the confusion of person and image is a primary aesthetic effect of the image. Richardson's gesture was feminist and political in its aim but its basis was *enargeia*.

More exactly, it was the uncanniness of *enargeia*, the deathlikeness in the lifelikeness, the perfectly accurate perception that there is something potentially haunting, even persecutory, in the image. This is especially so in the *Rokeby Venus*, which is not only lifelike in its portrayal of Venus's naked body but also in its display of the power of lifelike images to mesmerize the observer—in this case Venus herself, who is gazing at her face in a hand mirror.

Latent in this situation is the unremarked or disavowed ground of its uncanniness: absolute silence. The *Rokeby Venus*, like von Eck's other instances—Canova's statue of Pauline Borghese as Victorious Venus, Manet's *Olympia* and *Dejeuner sur l'herbe*—is a scene of silent repose. The *Dejeuner* is particularly revealing in this respect, because one of its two male figures does seem to be speaking, but only because he is visibly gesturing for emphasis. Meanwhile the figures to whom he is speaking do not seem to be listening, which we know from the direction of their gaze— toward us. The discomfiture immanent in these images aligns with their marked exclusion of sound. Their lifelikeness becomes queasy because their imitation of life is *visibly* inaudible. Silent life is false life. And in these cases the silence is extreme, because what the images exclude is not just the audible but the audiable. In these images the hum of the world goes mute.

Beyond Words?

I. MUSIC

Why does the celebration of music as expressive "beyond words" refuse to fade away? One can just as well claim that language is beyond music (Hegel claimed precisely that): musical expression is fuzzy, indefinite, inarticulate, more pleasure than thought (Kant said that last one); language is precise, capable of unlimited reference and assertion, the only instrument of reason, equally adept at pleasure and thought. Why, exactly, should one wish to be "beyond" all that? Of course there are things that words can't say, especially in their everyday usages, but language as art is as capable, some might say more capable than music, of intimating such things. Intimating them is one of the primary uses of language. And of course music has a striking bodily immediacy, but the rhythms of language are certainly not deficient in embodiment.

These questions as posed here may sound like a deprecation of music. They are not. They are a deprecation of the idea that the special value of music (and almost everyone loves some kind of music) is best understood by extrapolating from the difference between music and language. Perhaps that understanding is better sought by situating music in the continuous transformation of sound into meaning that forms the running background of experience. If we think of that transformation as immanently musical, from the intimation of the audiable on up, then music is its image and culmination. In ways both intelligible and pleasurable music links us to the auditory ground of our being—and not in some mystical sense but in and through the minute particulars of experience. Language is not part of this process until the time comes to interpret it, whether in music itself, as song, or in thought about music.

But I have given an alternative explanation, not answered my question. At one level, the trope of going beyond words is just an extension of the ancient "inexpressibility topos" that measures the significance of an event by its momentary power to disable adequate speech.[1] The experience is one of being shocked or surprised into silence, or mumbling, or a simple confession of being inarticulate. What can be said about such experiences usually comes afterward, upon reflection; as Wallace Stevens once wrote, "We reason about them with a later reason."[2] Music may be thought of as symbolically filling in the gap between immediate inarticulateness and a later utterance that may come or not as chance and skill will have it. To say that music is "beyond words" makes sense if that is what saying so means, but the very phrase "beyond words" implies a kind of lowest-common-denominator metaphysics that seems profound but halts further thought. To say that music is beyond words slips easily into saying that one is comfortable with being halted, which in a strange way feels like an accomplishment.

At another level, the value of placing music beyond words may stem from a fundamental asymmetry. Music has social and ritual uses, but for the past two-plus centuries, the period in which the trope of expression "beyond words" has flourished, the primary role of music has been to give pleasure. What we think of as music has no utilitarian value. The case is obviously the contrary for language. Language may give many kinds of pleasure, but its indispensable role is to be of use; language as language has maximum utilitarian value. Celebrating music as beyond words, therefore, may simply be a way of valuing a feeling of liberation from the world of use, work, and responsibility. Music, turning a classic Kantian paradigm on its head, becomes a medium that confers freedom on us by sublimely relieving us of duty.

II. RESENTMENT

These considerations raise an important question that has never, I believe, been asked seriously enough. Why are we so ungrateful to language? Why do we so often want to get "beyond" it? Does our resentment of language (expressed in the twin ideas of words failing us and our wish to get beyond words) stem from the discomfiting truth that the resentment disavows? For the claim that language is not powerful enough masks the recognition that, on the contrary, language is too powerful, that even when it is used poorly is it saturated with actual and potential meanings and actions.

Try a thought experiment: would you *really* want to be without language? To be incapable of it? What would that be like? Language is what gives us world, identity, imagination, connection. If we want to anthropomorphize something, what do we do? We make it talk. There is no personhood without language; the a-linguistic is the nonhuman.

(True, we share the world with the nonhuman, and recent thinking has asked us to chasten our sense of privilege and superiority to what also, temporarily, exists. But if anything, language is our best way to do that. We get close to what we are not by becoming more articulate, not by falling mute. The silences we may take, like the voices we may give, are each other's incubators.)

The same admonition that applies to musical works and performances applies more broadly to acoustic events and to utterance: language and nonlinguistic sound, including expressive and bodily sound, may come into opposition on occasion but they are *not* opposed in principle. Humans live in the place of language even when language is silent or silenced. Language and the nonlinguistic auditory have no single or dominant relationship but an endlessly reinvented matrix of relationships. All we can say is that neither can ignore the other without loss to itself; each is never out of earshot of the other.

Just as language cannot say everything (whoever thought it could?), the material and bodily dimension of the sounds we emit cannot serve as a surrogate for transcendental dreams we can no longer dream except through them. Language indeed, precisely in its receptivity to other expressive sounds up to and including the audiable, is our best hope to fulfill the challenge of living in a wholly secular, wholly material world—which in some sense we must all do regardless of our belief systems. At bottom, we speak to partici- pate meaningfully in being, both when we speak and when we do not, when we attend to utterance and when we attend to wordless expressivity. As I have said elsewhere, language can be deferred but it cannot be "transcended." The only available transcendence is radical immanence.

III. SEARCHING FOR THE WORDS

Resentment of language can even trouble those who depend on words the most and use them best. The virtuosos of language may quarrel with their instrument; no one can be as angry with words as a poet or novelist who lives for as well as by them. This intimate rage hovers in the background of an essay by Cormac McCarthy on language and the unconscious. The essay is not only revealing itself but also, unexpectedly, affords some insight into the relationship between language and the audiable.

McCarthy does not mean "the unconscious" in a psychological sense, Freudian or otherwise. He means it biologically. "To put it as pithily as possibly—and as accurately," he says, "the unconscious is a machine for operating an animal." But that makes matters all the more puzzling when we contemplate things like the imagery in dreams. McCarthy recalls the experience of the chemist August Kekulé (1829–1896), who discovered the molecular structure of benzene—the benzene ring—with the help of a dream "of a snake coiled in a hoop with its tail in its mouth—the ouroboros of mythology."[3] "Why," McCarthy asks, as if exasperated,

> since the unconscious understands language perfectly well or it would not understand the problem in the first place . . . doesn't it simply answer Kekulé's question with something like: "Kekulé, it's a bloody ring"? . . . Why the snake? . . . Why the images, metaphors, pictures? Why the dreams, for that matter?

One answer is that the unconscious *does* simply answer Kekulé's ques- tion; the ouroboros is nothing if not a ring. The question remains, why *this* ring, but that gets us back to the Freudian unconscious, which, contrary to popular opinion, is not a primordial morass but a system full of cultural resonances. (McCarthy's version of the unconscious would have to understand those too if it could come up with the ouroboros.)

But McCarthy's real issue is the gap he perceives between language and thought. Thought, he says, comes first; language is always trying to catch up. To make the point, he refers to the common experience of searching for the right way to put an idea into words. From the pause for reflection between the idea and the utterance, he infers that the idea must exist in the unconscious in some unknown form. We struggle to "resurrect an idea from this pool of we-know-not-what and give it a linguistic form so that it can be expressed. It is the *this* that one wishes to *put* that is representative of this pool of knowledge whose form is so amorphous."

Except it isn't. The inference does not follow. To make it is to confuse lack of consciousness with lack of language. The distinction goes back at least to Freud and Nietzsche. Nietzsche, though he uses the term "consciousness" to refer to the reflective knowledge that follows the use of language, strongly affirms the presence of immediate knowledge independent of language: "By far the greatest portion of our life takes place without [the] mirror-effect [of self-reflection mediated by language]; and this is true even of our thinking, feeling, and willing life."[4] Freud similarly contends that the unconscious coincides not with what remains unspoken at the moment, but with what *may* not be spoken.[5] In other words (and this is not an innocent formulation; there are always other words, and always must be), when I look for language, I know perfectly well what I think, but I have not articulated it yet. Or rather, I know it imperfectly well, because the articulation is also both discovery and creation: when I do articulate the thought I will also form it and, in forming it, change it.

The silence of thought is not an origin; it is just what McCarthy says it is: a pause. I do not come to it from nowhere. It is not as if, before that silence, I had never spoken or written. Language continues to resonate in its pauses and no human being can live in a world without it. (We pause; the world does not.) What I hear in that silence of thought is not absence but potentiality. And insofar as I sustain that potentiality between one act of language and another, what I hear is the resonance of the audiable. The silence of my thought is a form of vibrancy. McCarthy's suggestion that the far older and physically primal unconscious (in a combined biological, neurological, and psychological sense) is hostile to the latecomer, language, is right to spot the strain of resentment. But McCarthy misattributes the resentment to an innate atavism because he pays no attention to sound.

Resentment of language is culturally mediated. It depends on a conception of a higher or deeper order that language prevents us from reaching, but which only becomes thinkable with the help of language. McCarthy the novelist knows this, and sometimes writes passages in which an over-fullness of utterance posits a gap that no utterance can fill:

> He had weighed the woman's words, but he knew what she did not. . . .
> Those who by some sorcery or by some dream might come to pierce the veil
> that lies darkly over all that is before them may serve just by that vision to
> cause that God should wrench the world from its heading and set it upon
> another course altogether and then where stands the sorcerer? Where the
> dreamer and his dream? He paused that all might contemplate this. That he
> might contemplate it himself. Then he continued. He spoke of the cold in
> the mountains at that season. He populated the terrain for them with certain birds and animals. Parrots. Tigers. Men of another time living in the
> caves of that country so remote that the world had overlooked to kill them.[6]

Much more follows. McCarthy the essayist forgets the vibrancy of the pause he evokes here and the almost Promethean speech that follows it. His turn against language becomes an expression of the familiar modern feeling of being cheated of something primordial. The only trace he can find of that something is the silence of thought before language has broken it. But the silence of thought, like the silence that tends to prevail in dreams, even in speaking dreams, does not arise from the superior authenticity of speechlessness. It arises because the possibility of speech is in abeyance. But speech in abeyance is speech to come. Or, better, it is the *sound* of speech to come.

IV. SEARCHING FOR THE THOUGHT

Agree with him or not, McCarthy picks a good pivot point. Pausing to find the right verbal form for a thought is surely a universal experience. We know what it feels like. But what about the reverse: pausing to find the right thought for a verbal form? It turns out we know what that feels like, too. In particular, we know what it sounds like, for the knowledge involved is above all auditory.

When words are enigmatic, they impel us to find an understanding that will let the words themselves assume the peculiar qualitative character of making sense. The sense of an utterance has a sensory dimension. Part of that dimension is tonal; we give the utterance a different enunciation (whether actual or virtual) when we speak, write, or read it with understanding. The understanding that makes this possible, however, inevitably takes the form of more words. Where, if anywhere, do we find a sensory embodiment of thought making sense of a prior utterance?

When a vocal composition sets a preexisting poetic text, its instrumental part serves as that embodiment. ("Accompaniment" in this context is a misleading term.) The vocal part makes the enunciation; the instrumental part takes the place of the understanding. The relationship is not symbolic but perceptual. The flow of instrumental sound does not represent the understanding but simulates it.

When singing affects us powerfully, this transferred immediacy of thought is part of the reason why. In some instances, rare ones perhaps, the music also forms a reflection on the process of understanding the words it sets, a kind of parable of putting thought into sound. Both the vocal and instrumental parts may be summoned to participate. The sound may even include a touch of the audiable.

V. MAHLER

Such is the case at the beginning of the second movement of Mahler's Symphony no. 8. This ninety-minute two-movement work forms a symbolic history of Western spirituality. The first movement is a setting of the medieval hymn "Veni, Creator Spiritus" (Come, Creator Spirit; the second line is "Visit the mind of your people"). The vast second movement is a setting of the final act of Goethe's *Faust:* a mystical transfiguration scene that gives a positive answer to the question of whether Faust, despite his pact with the devil, can be saved.

The parable of putting thought to words comes in the first two vocal segments, a chorus of anchorites and a baritone solo by an ecstatic floating spirit. The chorus concludes by recognizing that the rocky mountainside it occupies is love's holy shrine (Heiligen Liebeshort); the solo concludes by bidding the enduring star at the core of eternal love to shine forth (Glänze der Dauerstern / Ewiger Liebe Kern). The parallel conclusions make parallel transitions, on an ascending scale, between one phase of thought and another. The instrumental ascent takes the form of a slowly evolving melodic efflorescence. The process is completely transparent. It starts with a single high tone in octaves and expands to detached instrumental phrases that are progressively knit together. The parable occurs to the voices: *to*, not *in*, because this layer of reflective understanding emerges not from what the voices sing but from the way they sing it.

For much of the chorus, the vocal line is crackled. Audible spaces open up between phrases and even between syllables. The singing is hushed and barely articulate. As time passes, however, vocal continuity emerges bit by bit. In the end it takes over. By the time the concluding recognition arrives, the voices are not only singing in continuous phrases but also singing for the first time in full multipart harmony. Fullness of understanding becomes fullness of sound.

Underlying this process is the octave mentioned above: a static E-flat on one desk of violins, maintained nearly without a break throughout the entire chorus. This octave sounds through every open space in the vocal part. It forms a vibratory hum to which all the other sounds cannot help but refer. As the vocal part progresses toward fuller enunciation, this vibrancy becomes less a distinct sound than a presence linking all the other sounds together. It forms the promise and potential of sounds gathered together in the act of singular insight with which the chorus ends. Its role culminates when it alone sounds for the equivalent of a full measure between the penultimate and final lines of the choral part; the sound of the origin centers the culmination to which it has led.

The baritone solo moves on from there. Enveloped by waves of melody, it echoes the earlier movement from broken to full speech by progressing from one type of text setting to another. Most of the vocal line is syllabic, meaning that each syllable of text is assigned a single note. (The preceding chorus has been entirely syllabic.) A little at a time, however, the line opens to melismatic touches, that is, to the assignment of more than one note to a syllable. An isolated syllable gets two notes; later on, two adjacent syllables get two notes apiece. Almost immediately thereafter the concluding epiphany breaks forth into extended, full-throated melismatic song; it leaps from enunciation to rapt intonation. Its intensity rises as the baritone peaks twice at the top of his range. This kind of melismatic climax is not unusual in itself, but here the forces that converge on it—the parallel to the preceding chorus, the pacing of the melismas, the breadth of the climactic leap, and the imagery of the text—combine to form an auditory form of heightened understanding that includes the act of understanding itself.

VI. BROKEN STRINGS

Sometimes such knowledge is unwelcome.

Two colossi stand next to each other in the desert west of the Egyptian city of Luxor, in antiquity known as Egyptian Thebes. Though they represent Pharaoh Amenhotep II (fourteenth century BCE), the colossi have long been identified with the mythological figure of Memnon, an Ethiopian hero of the Trojan War. Memnon was the son of Eos (Aurora), goddess of the dawn, and her once-mortal beloved Tithonus, for whom she procured eternal life but not eternal youth. (She forgot to ask.) Tithonus shriveled up and withered away and ultimately metamorphosed into a cicada. Originally a singer of epic verse, he dwindled into a chattering insect.

Between 27 BCE, when it was damaged by an earthquake, and roughly 196 CE, when it was repaired, the colossus of Memnon often emitted a "song" in the early morning, usually at dawn. It became a popular tourist attraction in the ancient world and the source of poetic metaphors in the modern one. As traditionally described, the statue's song resembled the sound of brass being struck or of a lute string breaking. In the mid-nineteenth century, Thomas De Quincey invoked these associations when recalling a sound that first occurred to him on a summer's day, in "gorgeous sunlight," by an open window, in the room where his sister, only a child, lay dead:

> I stood checked for a moment; awe, not fear, fell upon me; and, whilst I stood, a solemn wind began to blow, the most mournful that ear ever heard. Mournful! That is saying nothing. It was a wind that had swept the

fields of mortality for a hundred centuries. Many times since, upon a summer day, when the sun is about the hottest, I have remarked the same wind arising and uttering the same hollow, solemn, Memnonian, but saintly swell: it is in this world the one sole *audible* symbol of eternity. And three times in my life I have happened to hear the same sound in the same circumstances, namely, when standing between an open window and a dead body on a summer day.[7]

The sound is Memnonian because it comes in response to the light, but it also annexes a contrapuntal darkness, a Christian undertone to complement the ringing of the pagan statue. The "saintly swell" recalls, presumably, a long pedal tone on the organ. But the sound symbolizes eternity only in a negative sense, as befits Memnon's descent from Tithonus. The sound sweeping the fields of eternity is mournful because eternity is empty, like a vista that might be seen from an open window but that in this case is not seen at all, but instead covered up by the sound of the solemn wind, a kind of auditory cloak. De Quincey hears through the open window but he does not see through it. He sees only the means by which any of us enters into eternity: a dead body. And the chain of elements— wind, body, window, a summer day—three times repeated over the years, becomes a leitmotif in the story of his life.

The most salient point in this lapse of sight under sound is De Quincey's observation that the wind bearing the mortality of hundreds of centuries is, to reverse his emphasis, the *sole* audible symbol of eternity. What is that? And why only one? If the wind, this wind, is indeed the "one sole" symbol of eternity, perhaps that is because sound is inherently temporal. Vistas may extend into the infinite distance but sound simply fades and disappears. The auditory world is a world of sheer transience, and such presence as it offers it makes out of transience. For that reason, the sole audible symbol of eternity is, and must be, a long mournful note, a pedal tone under no melody, the echoing sound of a breaking string, the whoosh of a wind consisting of angry white noise. Listen for the infinite, and the audiable becomes a terror.

A century or so later, August Strindberg imagined a similar song near the conclusion of his lyrical drama *A Dream Play*. The play's heroine translates the mournful sound of the winds to reveal that their mournfulness derives from the winds' passage through the lungs of humanity. The sounds sweeping the fields of eternity, here echoing in the famous Fingal's Cave on the coast of Scotland—"the Ear of Eternity," according to Strindberg—become a common sigh on a global scale, as if every human breath were the last one.

The Audiable and the Audible

The audiable has no location; is it nothing more than a myth or a metaphor?

On the contrary: it reaches us in a dimension of bodily sense shared at least with sight and perhaps with touch, the dimension in which sense experience reflects on itself, just as consciousness does. This dimension is most familiar with respect to vision—no surprise there—although we do not have a name for it. There is a sight of sight, and it is pervasive. The condition of visibility becomes visible in the form of diffuse light: not the light of this or that, but just light. Wallace Stevens once said that the imagination, like light, adds nothing to the moment it perceives except itself.[1] The same might be said of light in this transcendental role—transcendental, let me emphasize, in the philosophical sense of being in excess of bodily sense, not of being metaphysically transcendent. I am reminded of this in particular because the night before writing this paragraph I stepped out of my house late in the dusk and found the entire landscape (I live in the country) bathed in a rich blue light, without apparent source, and perfectly continuous with the deepening blue of the cloudless sky. Later there would be a full moon but the moon was not yet up; the light came from nowhere because it came from everywhere. The effect was short-lived, and my dog, focused on smell, did not seem to understand why I was staring into space. But she clearly knew something else, and cocked her head to prove it: I was listening.

The audiable is the sound of sound. Its relationship to audible sound matches that of sourceless light to the visible scene. Like such light, the audiable fills space without definite limits. One cannot say what it sounds *like*, but one can hear it sounding. Like the sight of such light, the resonance of such sound is strangely reassuring in the absence of any felt need for reassurance. It offers the feeling of being deeply embedded in the world, of participating in existence just by being present. Ordinary sense experience relies on that experience but rarely conveys it. When I stepped outside last night my senses were caught by surprise. They turned over on themselves. Vision first: that seems hard to avoid no matter how sensitively one is attuned to sound. But sound caught up. And because there was no urban sound (or light) to distract me, and the roads were more or less deserted, I became acutely aware of how quiet it was for the moment. I could not hear a sound: just the sound that remains when all other sounds have gone away.

Into Silence

In his *Reveries of a Solitary Walker*, left unfinished at his death in 1778, Jean-Jacques Rousseau describes a state of bliss in which we are aware of nothing but our own existence. The experience fuses a heightening of sentience with a diminution of the senses. Rousseau says that it takes in nothing outside the self, but by his own account it depends on a tacit awareness of what it leaves out. This "feeling of existence stripped of all other affections" retains just enough of the sensory world to cushion rather than to penetrate the apprehension of being and nothing more. And what it retains is revealing:

> Such is the state in which I often found myself on the Isle of St. Pierre in my solitary reveries, whether stretched out in my boat which I let drift as the water willed, or seated by the banks of the unquiet lake, or elsewhere, by the side of a beautiful river or of a brook murmuring over the pebbles.[1]

The sensory sequence admits only motion and sound, first one, then the other. It passes from a lullaby-like rocking in a drifting boat, reminiscent of the near-motionlessness of Goethe's imaginary gondolier listening for distant songs across the water; to an awareness of being parted from agitation, even the modest unquiet of ruffled lake water; and, as culmination, to the reversal of that unquiet, the faint sound of a brook murmuring over the pebbles. The last image is familiar, a commonplace of pastoral idylls. But it takes on a second life here because of its isolation among the senses and because of its presentation as sheer sensory stuff, as oblivious to anything but its own existence as the walker is, or the stones over which it flows. Sound at or near the threshold of silence becomes the last, best avenue to the sense of sheer being.

At or near: but no farther. Reverie requires quiet, but it abhors silence. Break the thread of sound, and the absence of external sense becomes a void. Rousseau is plainspoken as to why. "An absolute silence," he writes, "leads to sadness. It offers the image of death."[2]

(Beethoven thought so, too. His *Coriolan* Overture, music filled with disquiet, begins and ends with acts of silence. The end, confirming what the beginning portends, marks the death of the titular hero in precisely measured silences interspersed with soft hollow octaves played by pizzicato strings. The silences pulse briefly like a negative heartbeat. When the music stops after the last of them, the ensuing silence assumes a gravity it would not have had otherwise. For an indeterminate moment it becomes absolute.)

Rousseau is careful to preserve the difference between the absolute silence a living being can know and the silence of death. The one is the image of the other, not its presence. The sadness of silence is an affliction of metaphor. But what if one were to go to an elsewhere less amicable than Rousseau's? What if one were to travel to the end of the earth and find that the difference between the image and the reality could not be sustained there?

This question is not fantastical; it is historical. The explorers who made expeditions to the Antarctic in the late nineteenth century found the silence that met them there to be literally deathly. It drove many of them mad, and some to suicide. Louis Bernacchi, who in 1899 was part of the first expedition to endure the Antarctic winter by choice, described the silence in terms that epitomize the common experience: "Enveloped in an atmosphere of universal death, wrapped in its closely-clinging cerements of ice and snow, the one expression of the Antarctica of today is lifeless silence."[3]

(Ralph Vaughan Williams thought so, too. In 1948 Vaughan Williams wrote the score for the film *Scott of the Antarctic;* he subsequently developed the film music into his seventh symphony, *Sinfonia Antartica* (1952).

The film depicts Robert Falcon Scott's ill-fated attempt to lead the first expedition to reach the South Pole. Upon arriving in mid-January, 1912, Scott and four companions found that the Norwegian explorer Roald Amundson had reached the Pole a little over a month earlier. All five men died on the return trek.

Vaughan Williams prefaced each movement of the symphony with an epigraph. His choice for the finale was an entry from Scott's final journal: "I do not regret this journey; we took risks, we knew we took them, things have come out against us, therefore we have no cause for complaint." The music is equally stoical. Its first half is a raucous death march increasingly punctuated by subdued passages suggestive of disorientation and ebbing energy. Its second half traces the lapsing away of music into sound and of sound into soundlessness.

The lapse is suffered in particular by the human voice, embodied in the wordless keening of a women's choir and solo soprano. The chorus enters briefly at midpoint together with the whoosh of a wind machine. Two minutes before the end, both the voices and the whoosh return and take over the instrumental texture. Silence descends by degrees. Already inarticulate because they have no text, the voices fade into the materiality of breath on a continental scale. First the solo soprano enters with a finely etched melodic line, only to subside into the indefinite vocalization of the chorus and the exhalations of the wind machine. This happens twice. After that the voices fade slowly into the sound of the wind machine until only the wind sound is left. Then it too dies away to nothingness. Yet again, but a world away, the final silence assumes a gravity it would not have had otherwise. For an indeterminate moment it too becomes absolute.)

P. S. This story has a sequel. In 1997 Peter Maxwell Davies received a commission to compose an Antarctic Symphony in commemoration of both *Scott of the Antarctic* and Vaughan Williams's music. One condition was that Maxwell Davies journey to Antarctica himself. In his program notes, he recalls an "extraordinary sound experience . . . at the edge of a heavy, but gentle, avalanche of snow from cliffs towering high on either side of the narrow channel through which the ship was passing—the chilling powder enveloped us all on the deck, with a whisper and hiss that paradoxically seemed to be more profoundly quiet than the previous silence; no-one could speak for minutes afterwards."[4]

Enchantments of the Name

What carries in the sound of a name? In English the use of a name is a call: one calls someone by name, summons or beckons, commands or entreats, in the naming. But the name may also come as conjuration, connected by irrational magic to those named. Names in this role are incantations. Shakespeare's Juliet famously says, "that which we call a rose / By any other name would smell as sweet." But the odds are that Juliet was wrong.

Humans alone can give as well as receive names, and the giving is thus a form of obligation. The giving of names is at the same time absolutely free, a primary assertion of the freedom immanent in the concept of the human, and hemmed in on all sides by constraints both visible and invisible. This ambiguity expresses itself in the two contrary dimensions of the (proper) name: the name as signification and the name as incantation; the name as bearer of meaning and the name as a conduit for the audiable.

Hart Crane's *The Bridge* is full of place names suspended between chanting and charting. The title of the prologue gives the first and foremost of these, but the name is one that never appears again. The title is "To Brooklyn Bridge." The rest of the sequence may from one perspective be thought of as an explication of this magical name on a continental scale. This explication is a cabbalistic labor that on certain occasions requires naming the continent. The labor ends with a return to the bridge and the disclosure of the mythical name that marks the span as both a recovered origin and a new destination: "Atlantis." This is the secret name, perhaps the name yet to come, of the continent itself, the "one name always" that Crane invokes in his short lyric "A Name for All": "I dreamed that all men dropped their names and sang / As only they can praise, who build their days / With fin and hoof, with wing and sweetened fang, / Struck free and holy in one Name always."[1]

Walt Whitman's name echoes through this celebration of animal consciousness, which recalls a famous passage from Whitman's *Song of Myself*—"I think I could turn and live with the animals"—also echoed in *The Bridge* at the beginning of "Quaker Hill." The "one Name" in which the animals build their day is the nucleus of the name to come that spans the continent.

Whitman's most focused acts of continental naming occur in his Civil War volume *Drum-Taps,* especially its original 1865 version—a work more ample than the "Drum-Taps" section of *Leaves of Grass* and more explicitly concerned with union, small u, and the Union, capital U, as a continent-spanning whole. Whitman centers this process, and the Union war effort, on Manhattan, to which he gives the incantatory Indian name "Mannahatta." From there the geography of the poem moves in circular sweeps to the west, as if in naming the continent the poem could secure its borders for the nation, which at the time of the text's composition the Civil War had not quite accomplished. Beneath the ritual acts, however, there runs an unspoken meaning, grounded in the historical significance of the names invoked. When Whitman calls up "The beach-waves combing over the beach on my eastern shore, and my western shore the same; / And all between those shores, and my ever running Mississippi, with bends and chutes; / And my Illinois fields, and my Kansas fields, and my fields of Missouri; /The CONTINENT," the place names, though incantatory in their immediate effect, subtly shift from verbal magic to signification. Illinois is Lincoln's birthplace, "bleeding Kansas" the scene of brutal guerrilla fighting over the western extension of slavery, Missouri the site of the 1820 Missouri Compromise limiting that extension until repeal by the Kansas-Nebraska Act of 1854. Incantation partly subsides into trope. Neither aspect of naming disappears, but their proportions alter.

Crane, who invokes *Drum-Taps* in "Cape Hatteras," follows Whitman's paradigm with one change, but a change that changes everything. Crane too centers his text on Manhattan; *The Bridge* incorporates a verbal map of the city that extends across the whole span of the poem, naming South Street, Wall Street, Avenue A, Bleecker Street, Broadway, and Columbus Circle. From there the geography of the sequence moves in circular sweeps from east to west, as if in naming the continent *The Bridge* could secure its borders from the Atlantic to the Pacific, not for the nation Crane knew at the time of writing, but for the mythical form of the nation to come that the writing prophesizes. This intent becomes explicit at the start of "Van Winkle," which compresses a transcontinental journey into just two lines: "Macadam, gun-grey as the tunney's belt, / Leaps from Far Rockaway to Golden Gate." The migration of names unfolds more enigmatically elsewhere: in the opaque local names of "The River"—Booneville, Siskiyou, Cairo, Kalamazoo—and in the intermittent use of neutral or puzzling place-names for several of the poem's sections: Why Cape Hatteras? Why Indiana? Where is Quaker Hill? These usages point to a general tendency in *The Bridge* to reverse Whitman's bias and shift from signification to verbal magic, from trope to incantation. Again neither aspect disappears, but their proportions alter—differently.

This shift is audible in the second of the two lines I just quoted. Far Rockaway and Golden Gate mark the eastern and western limits of the country's shores, and it is possible to read "far," "golden," and "gate" symbolically. But the thrust of the line is to subordinate these semantic implications to the sonorous leaping motion executed by the shift from the dactylic "rocking" of the line's first half ("Leaps from Far Rockaway") to the clipped iambics of its second half ("to Golden Gate"). The second half reinforces the shift with its alliterative phrasing and the slant rhyme between "belt" and "gate." The names leap from meaning to sound, as if the poem were not merely uttering the names but giving them. Crane slyly alludes to Adam's naming of the animals in the Garden of Eden by beginning the couplet with a homonym, "Macadam," which subordinates its primary meaning of "crushed stone" to the implications of its sound.

The incantatory tendency of *The Bridge* culminates, but also resolves, in the quasi-sacred final name of "Atlantis." Unlike "Brooklyn Bridge," "Atlantis" may be chanted in the text, but only at nearly the last moment, as the culmination of a long cable-strand of epithets: Anemone, Tall-Vision-of-the Voyage, Choir, Steeled Cognizance, and many more.

One of these epithets is simply "Bridge," which suggests that this one span is not simply *a* bridge, however exemplary, but, as the title gives it, *the* bridge, the material form of bridging in itself, the Platonic form of the bridge brought down to earth in New York Harbor. (Plato is cited in the epigraph to "Atlantis.") In this form the bridge is also a musical instrument, a gigantic wind harp of "bound cable strands" through which "Sibylline voices flicker." The "orphic strings" of the bridge harp channel cosmic harmony into incantation and incantation into the core of *poiesis,* the creation of something where before there was nothing:

> And through that cordage, threading with its call
> One arc synoptic of all tides below— . . .
> Tall Vision-of-the-Voyage, tensely spare—
> Bridge, lifting night to cycloramic crest
> Of deepest day—O Choir, translating time
> Into what multitudinous Verb the suns
> And synergy of waters ever fuse, recast
> In myriad syllables,—Psalm of Cathay!
>   (9–10, 42–47)[2]

The becoming-music of the name thus for a moment accomplishes the becoming-music of the world.

The dynamics of continental naming in *The Bridge* culminate with a passage in "Cape Hatteras" that fuses the arc of incantation with Crane's discovery of his vocation as Whitman's heir. Recalling the *Drum-Taps* poems "Vigil Strange I Kept on the Field One Night" and "The Wound-Dresser," Crane addresses Whitman as the witness to "fraternal massacre": "Thou . . . / Hast kept of wounds, O Mourner, all that sum / That then from Appomattox stretched to Somme." Signification outweighs incantation here with the names of Appomattox and the Somme, although the rhyme of "sum" and "Somme," with its multilingual punning, intimates a reversal. The reversal comes as Crane recalls the epiphany of first reading Whitman:

> Cowslip and shad-blow . . . bloomed that spring
> When first I read thy lines, rife as the loam
> Of prairies, yet like breakers cliffward leaping!
> O, early following thee, I searched the hill
> Blue-writ and odor-firm with violets, 'til
> With June the mountain laurel broke through green
> And filled the forest with what clustrous sheen!
> Potomac lilies,—then the Pontiac rose,
> And Klondike edelweiss of occult snows!
>   (166–75)[3]

The movement of Whitman's lines from prairies to oceans, presumably both east and west, fills out the continental span with images, the soil (loam) and breaking waves; the movement of Crane's lines in the heroic couplet that closes the passage fills out the same span with incantatory names. Potomac, Pontiac, and Klondike trace a kind of Northwest Passage across the continent toward a utopian goal, one that failed in reality (the Klondike Gold Rush of the 1890s) but that accomplishes itself in the "occult snows" of the poem's Klondike edelweiss. But the couplet leaps past these intimations. The closing couplet is almost pure incantation, a play of consonantal echoes and an age-old trope—lily and rose—stripped of its traditional meanings, all in a deliberately archaic verse form that ends by reeling off the names of flower varieties that do not exist except in Crane's text.

But existing is no bar to being dissolved in incantation. Sounding on the harp strings of the name is the burden (the air, the melody, the task, the meaning) of John Ashbery's poem "Into the Dusk-Charged Air." The poem is a catalogue of rivers, more than a hundred and fifty of them, and nothing else. One sentence follows another in no apparent order, and with nothing to link each to the next but the necessity of naming another river or two. These acts of naming occur in statements that seem to make sense but which lack all context and therefore strip the apparent sense of actual meaning. Only the names remain:

> The Rhône slogs along through whitish banks
> And the Rio Grande spins tales of the past.
> The Loir bursts its frozen shackles
> But the Moldau's wet mud ensnares it.
> The East catches the light.
> Near the Escaut the noise of factories echoes
> And the sinuous Humboldt gurgles wildly.
> The Po too flows, and the many-colored
> Thames.[4]

Ashbery's poem is a river made of names—a Heraclitean river in which one cannot step twice. The poem is a river made of sounds. If its East river catches the light (as it would, of course, being named for the source of sunrise), the glitter evaporates at once into the echoing noise of factories by the Escaut and the wild gurgling of the sinuous (sonorous) Humboldt. The poem takes incantation to the outer limit of Crane's

"Macadam": what flows there is not incantation of the names but the names as incantation. Read the text aloud, and what gradually begins to resonate through your voice and to fill the room with itself is the riverine flow of the audiable.

The Inaudible

The name as incantation emerges at the resonant end of the auditory spectrum. Does it have a counterpart at the hushed end?

The spectrum runs from the deafening to the silent, but along the way a series of hearing-types emerges, leading away from the audible without quite leaving it: the heard, the remotely heard, the half-heard, the audiable. We might think of these as the coordinates of the heard world. But what about the unheard? What about the inaudible? Does the inaudible have a positive form or is it merely privative? Is it entirely separated from the heard world or does it impinge on the world at certain junctures or even extend into otherwise unknown regions?

The category is complex. It includes, at a minimum, the familiar sounds I happen not to hear (the rustle of windblown leaves through a closed window), the sounds I cannot hear in principle (grass growing, the beating of a butterfly's wings, the whinny of a unicorn), and the sounds that no one has ever heard but that someone—who knows, even oneself—may hear at a later day. Insofar as sound gives the senses their future tense, insofar as the audiable is a form of promise, the inaudible is the lived potential of new sound, a touch of the future promised by sound as presence in action. The unsounded is a negative plenitude, like the dark matter that fills most of space.

Salome Vogelin suggests that the inaudible as the not yet heard is a reality in which composers and sound artists ground their vocation: the mandate to bring those sounds to life.[1] What kind of hearing act accomplishes that? What does it make heard *before* what is heard is sounded? How can a sound impinge on our sensory experience before the sound exists in sensory form?

The hearing aid for these sounds yet to be is language. For Vogelin, language can neither represent nor describe sound, but it can elicit sound through the power of naming. A name given to a sound while one is hearing it makes that sound available for hearing later. The name "represents no truth but generates its own. [It] cannot be assumed to exist beforehand and it cannot be deduced from a description that matches it."[2] If animals are in question, naming the sounds they make recalls the naming of the animals themselves in the Garden of Eden: "And Adam gave names to all cattle, and to the fowl of the air, and to every beast of the field" (Genesis 2:20). The names Adam gives them makes the animals knowable for what they are—as the name has made them. The name endows the creatures with resonance even if both it and they fail to exist, as John Hollander's poem "Adam's Task" demonstrates by making it happen:

> Thou, verdle; thou, McFleery's pomma;
> Thou; thou; thou—three types of grawl;
> Thou, flisket, thou, kabasch; thou, comma-
> Eared mashawok; thou, all; thou, all.[3]

Naming does its work both as designation and as sound. The intimate "thou" opens the channel of designation; its rhythmic pulse binds each named animal to its fellows as well as to the name-giver. The result is that the particular "thou" metamorphoses into a general thou" that takes in the whole Creation—while also, of course, getting it wrong. Never mind that the names are nonsensical to our ears; they are no more so than the names that have lost their sonorous exuberance to familiarity (not a problem in Eden). Listening in, we might even come to think that we know what McFleery's pomma sounded like. If we can name the inaudible, its name becomes what Vogelin calls the "portal" to its auditory reality: "The inaudible in the soundscape is not literally the sound of the unicorn, but 'the sound of the unicorn' is what engenders its imagination."[4]

But the name is only the beginning. Unlike the proper names in *The Bridge* or "Into the Dusk-Charged Air" (pp. 147–51) but in common with the species names in "Adam's Task," auditory names must create their own charisma; they do not come mantled with it. For those without the privilege of Adam, such names cannot act on their own. "'The sound of the unicorn'" says nothing about how the unicorn would sound if unicorns existed. It is not the name of a sound in the way "rustle" or "whinny" is, nor in the way of seemingly similar phrases built on prior hearing acts, like the Biblical "voice of the turtle" or Sophocles's "voice of the shuttle." If I want to compose or synthesize the sound of the unicorn, I need to imagine the sound in relation to the legend. I need to ask how such a creature as the legendary unicorn would, after all, probably sound. And to answer I need a description. I even need a description twice over, because the legend of the unicorn is preeminently pictorial. My effort to bring its whinny, to call it that, to life requires me to form an understanding that combines my recollection of what I have read about the unicorn with what I have seen of the unicorn in tapestries and paintings. The test of that understanding is that I could, if asked, describe what the unicorn's whinny, or call, or cry should sound like.

That does not mean that my description can convey the sound; it means that the sound rises to the level of concrete potentiality on the basis of the description. If the sound subsequently becomes actual, then the sound conveys the description rather than the reverse, while at the same time it adds to and exceeds the description. What generates the imagination of the unicorn's sound is something like this: "a high, pure monotone like a note sustained on the piccolo but with a strange resonant undertone"; or, just as plausible, or not, like this: "a low warble penetrated by a deep strain of melancholy." Access to the inaudible is granted by the very description that would fail to account for the sound in its audible form.

Literary language is full of such descriptions. Lines like the first two of Crane's "Repose of Rivers"—a random example—give potential sound a description to live up to: "The willows carried a slow sound, / A sarabande the wind mowed on the mead." Music has the same capacity when we know the question to which it forms the answer. When Thomas Adés, in the opera he based on Shakespeare's *The Tempest*, writes the part of Ariel in a range well above the norm even for coloratura sopranos, he not only answers the play's own impossible question—what does Ariel sound like?—but also gives us something new to listen for. Whether musical or verbal, the description of sound is part of the genesis of sound. The world is full of inaudible sounds that do not escape us even if we never hear them.

On Saying "I am"

I. VALERY AND RILKE

The French poet Paul Valéry did not like the sentence "Je suis" (I am). He wrote of Réne Descartes's famous philosophical proof of existence, "Cogito ergo sum" (widely known as "the Cogito": I think therefore I am): "[It] has no meaning because that little word *sum* has no meaning. No one dreams of saying or needs to say 'I am' unless he is taken for dead and wants to protest that he is not. In any case he would say 'I'm alive.' But a cry or the slightest movement would be quite sufficient."[1]

A cry or a movement: either would be enough to demonstrate life because the two are the obverse and reverse of the life that shows itself from one sentient being to another. Sound is motion; motion makes sound. The ancient criterion of life as the self-moving implies the criterion of life as self-sounding. Valéry's remarks are not about this confluence, but they reflect it memorably in part because of their sheer unreflective certainty: no one, no one at all, dreams of saying "I am" because anyone who says anything makes that affirmation in the act. Released from its off-handedness, this claim anticipates Levinas's postulation that there exists a condition of saying that precedes anything said and at the same time acknowledges, as Levinas does not, that this primordial saying is no less auditory than the speech it frames. The saying is the material condition of having life in common to move through and hear.

At times we can discern the sound of transition from the saying to the said, a faint but distinct sound that conforms to Valéry's "cry or slightest movement." The cry too may be of the slightest. The last of Rilke's "Sonnets to Orpheus" seems to be searching for one just like that.

Rilke's poem has the peculiar virtue of proving one part of Valéry's statement wrong while acknowledging a kernel of truth in it. The poem is the last of the sequence. Like most of the sonnets preceding it, this one is concerned with the relationship between loss and poetic utterance, the latter identified with the song of Orpheus, which, chanted, is also poetry. Real sounding music left Rilke feeling mostly suspicious, if not downright hostile. In one passage of his novel *The Notebooks of Malte Laurids Brigge*, he celebrates Beethoven's deafness and, for the scene of ideal music making, imagines the composer playing his "Hammerklavier"—both the instrument and, presumably, the celebrated piano sonata—in the Theban desert, where early Christian ascetics went to renounce the world. No one can hear the music, not even an angel, who flees in fear that the playing might begin.

This distrust of music is important because the "cry" with which the poem ends is a faint sound installed within the music of its language. Although perfectly audible if the poem is read aloud, this slightest cry is probably more at home in silent reading, better half-heard than heard.

The poem addresses an indeterminate "you" in whom the reader and the poet himself become indistinguishable. It consists of a series of injunctions in which "you" is told to transform suffering to meaning, but a meaning that cannot be said, only heard. This is the meaning that becomes audible in the last stanza, which, of course, is the conclusion of the entire sequence. The original language is essential here, though I will try to catch something of the sound in translation:

> Und wenn dich das Irdische vergass,
> Zu der stillen Erde sag: ich rinne.
> Zu dem raschen Wasser sprich: ich bin.

> And if the earthly has forgotten you,
> To the still earth say: I stream.
> To the swift water speak: I am.

One does not, it seems, have to be taken for dead to dream of saying "I am." Being bereft or forlorn is quite sufficient. But it turns out, or so these lines ask us to hear, that to say "I am" requires passage from the saying to the said. The saying comes not in a statement but in the flow, the stream of song, which (in German as well as English) both gives motion to the unmoving (still) earth and gives sound to the silent (still) earth. The two endowments are indistinguishable. The said comes in a speech act to the swift water, that is, to the material waters of the earth and to the stream of song from which the said emerges as the affirmation of being: "I am." In saying that, the speaker in the present of the poem and in the future of what "you" is enjoined to do, also says "I'm alive": I move and sound. This statement, however, does not become fully audible in the words.

For that one needs the rhyme, which my translation could not reproduce but which it aims to echo in the −*m* sound closing "I stream" and "I am." Rilke writes "ich rinne" and "ich bin." The rhyme is a culmination as well as a repetition. By dropping the "-ne" of "rinne," with its vowel sound, and so compressing "rinne" into the form of "bin," that is, the first-person present form of the verb "to be," the poem embodies in sound the movement from the stream of the saying to the solidity of the said. Even the duration of the last word contributes to the audibility of its meaning, since "bin," denoting what endures, cannot compose a rhyme unless it endures here only for an instant. The sense of life sounds in the fleeting break in the stream.

II. BEETHOVEN (1818)

Rilke notwithstanding, music too can pass between the saying and the said. The sonata that the poet would prefer to have been played to no one in the Theban desert can be heard to make that passage, this time in the other direction.

The third movement of the *Hammerklavier* (Beethoven's Piano Sonata no. 29, Op. 106) is a long slow movement of extraordinary intensity, even for Beethoven. The finale is a knuckle-busting fugue marked in the score, with slightly sardonic understatement, as taking "some license." In between there is an extended transition, much of it unmeasured, in which the music seems to be searching for the right kind of ending. Some years later, the finale to the Ninth Symphony would begin by doing the same thing. But why does it have to?

In the sonata's case, the slow movement has gone so far beyond the bounds of ordinary sense and expression that it seems less to have exceeded them than to have made any immediate return to them impossible. Anything normal would seem banal. Too much transcendence risks too much disappointment in the real, and the disappointment may linger much too long. This problem is one that interested Beethoven throughout his career; he sought it out. The danger of being carried away, which Kant made a philosophical issue, was intimately bound up with the contemporaneous aesthetics of the sublime—that which exceeds all measure and comprehension—and with the upheavals in European life during the

Napoleonic era and its aftermath.[2] In his final sonata, no. 32, Op. 111, Beethoven solved the problem by embracing it. The two-movement work ends with its parallel to the Adagio sostenuto of the *Hammerklavier*, in effect saying: if nothing can follow, so be it. In the *Hammerklavier* he went to the opposite extreme, demanding that one sublime excess form the answer to another.

But that does not solve the question of how to get from the one to the other: hence the transition. Here I will single out just a single feature of the latter, one that bears comparison to Rilke's rhyme of "rinne" and "bin."

The Adagio concludes with a series of quiet, widely spaced F-sharp-major chords, four measures of them. The first three measures sound the chords alternately high and low, pianissimo, with the sustaining pedal down but with the soft pedal engaged. The result, as in the "Tempest" Sonata considered earlier, is to build up a lingering, hovering sonority that envelops the chords. The final measure then releases that floating sonority to its own independent existence. The measure begins with a slow arpeggio, rising low to high, now marked *ppp* but with the soft pedal released. When the arpeggio stops, the hovering sonority continues, thanks to the sustaining pedal, and it is on that sound, receding toward the audible, that the movement ends. Everything has now been said, and we can hear the said as it sums itself up and departs.

The transition turns from the said to the saying by forming a mirror image of what has just happened. (Example 1.) Keeping the slow tempo, the transition begins with the rise, an octave at a time, of a single note from the low bass to the high treble. The repetitions of the one sound are again supported by the sustaining pedal, and again they reach a pause at which the pedaled sonority lingers in the air. This time, however, the enveloping sound is the audible form, not of culmination, but of potentiality. What it portends is still inchoate, its sound stripped down to that of a single tone, but it is also definitely engaged and attuned to the future. The identity of the note confirms this reorientation: it is F-natural, a half step away from the preceding F-sharp. Eventually, the F will evolve into the dominant of the key of the fugue, B-flat major, in the process exchanging the height it initially reached as an octave in the high treble for the depth of an octave in the low bass. At that point the sound of the note is inexorable, but the crescendo it supports nonetheless begins pianissimo, as if still

Example 1. Beethoven, Piano Sonata Op. 106, *Hammerklavier,* transition to finale.

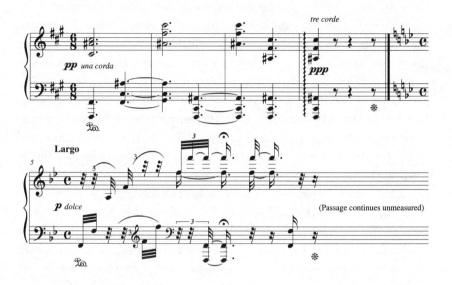

mindful of its slightly skewed rhyme with the end of the Adagio. That rhyme, the musical passage from "rinne" to "bin," is what enables the music, having said what it is, to go on and say what it will become.

III. BEETHOVEN (1821)

A few years later, the same thing happens again in a new form. The last movement of Beethoven's Piano Sonata no. 31, Op. 110, is two movements in one: a "lamenting song" (Arioso Dolente) and a fugue, both of them labeled in the score. The combination is unprecedented; it recalls the Adagio and fugue of the *Hammerklavier* but compresses their separate spheres into one, where each, nonetheless, is heard twice. In Op. 110, the transition between the segments speaks to another of Beethoven's most persistent concerns, and one of the reasons his music continues to enthrall us: the conviction that, whatever form it may take, release from human suffering can come only after an unconditional immersion in that suffering. Height is cut only to the measure of depth. Accordingly, this movement first traces a failure of release. Before its burden can be lifted, the lamenting song must be sung twice, the second time more intensely and forlornly than the first. Before the fugue can soar, it has to hover.

To deepen and intensify these relationships, Beethoven again revisits the "Tempest" Sonata—also a case in which the second utterance is an intensified form of the first—with its continuous use of the sustaining pedal to envelop a quasi-vocal melody with a resonant aura (pp. 59–60). But whereas the "Tempest," concerned with distance, creates its pedal haze around a full melodic line, Op. 110, concerned with intimacy or interiority, deploys the pedal around the repetition, first, of a single note, and then of a single chord. The model shifts to the *Hammerklavier* but in reverse; the music now moves not from fullness to potentiality but from potentiality to fullness, from the saying to the said. Or, more exactly, first from the saying to the said well and then from the saying to the said better.

The failure of the first arioso-fugue pair to bring full release is foreordained by the repeated pitch: a dissonance slowly smothered by its own resonance. The second pair succeeds because the repeated sonority is a consonance, and because its repetitions create a reversal of the relationship between sounding and resounding. Although the resonance arises from the chords, it gradually ceases to behave as their aftermath. Instead, the chords evolve into crystallizations of the resonance. Each chord sounds as the last leg of a triplet that contains no other attacks; the written pattern is rest-rest-chord. At first we hear the chords without the pedal, so that we learn their position within the beat and the measure, hear the silences around them, and grow prepared (as if unawares) for what will follow. Then the pedal is engaged and remains so for nearly three measures. (Example 2.) The resonance accumulates as the sound of the off-beat attacks carries over into the following beats, including the downbeats; meanwhile the chords grow louder and fuller, amplifying the resonance still further. By the midpoint of the passage, the resonance has become full enough to mark the beats and downbeats on its own, in a kind of spectral counterpoint with the chords. Each new off-beat chord captures and solidifies the floating sound and releases it again.

The pattern holds steady, in contrast to the off-beat dissonances of the earlier transitional passage, which are restless and irregular. In the third measure, the sonority of the chord brightens from minor to major, a

Example 2. Beethoven, Piano Sonata Op. 110, second transition from Arioso Dolente to Fugue.

change that becomes progressive as the resonance of the minor third fades into the resonance of the major third. The decisive transition follows in a single additional measure. With the pedal still engaged, the chord ascends from the bass as an arpeggio, countering its rise in pitch with a fall in volume, as if to seek the threshold of audibility. (At least the opportunity exists to perform it that way, so that the fugue can emerge from the "slightest cry" of meaningful sound.) From there, the second fugue emerges, as fugues do, on a single unaccompanied "voice." Beethoven marks it "Little by little coming to life again" (Nach und nach wieder auflebend). The Arioso Dolente could not be consoled but it could be transfigured, and the fugue—its earlier subject inverted to mark the reversal of fortune—achieves its ecstatic climax as an audible efflorescence of the audiable.

Though it is perhaps naïve to ask, it is hard to forbear, especially in light of Rilke's bizarre fantasy of Beethoven playing the Hammerklavier in the Theban desert: could anything be more utopian for a deaf composer? But the movement should be utopian enough for anyone, as long as utopia does not exclude lament. There is a generic difference between the finale's two segments that amplifies the significance of their slow-growing union. An arioso is a distinct type of vocal music that moves between the speech-like inflection of a recitative and the melodic fullness of an aria. If the sonata's instrumental arioso connotes voice, opera, and breath, its keyboard fugue connotes the complement: intellect, abstract form, and hands at work. The result is a kind of transcendental prelude and fugue in which the passage from one genre to another is a transfiguration. The passage between them goes by way of the audiable.

The Shriek

Near the end of Act 2 of Wagner's *Tristan and Isolde*, the lovers are surprised in their mutual ecstasy by the retinue of King Mark, the man whose trust both Tristan and Isolde have betrayed. As the intruders arrive, Isolde's companion Brangäne emits a piercing shriek that tears the opera in two. This shriek is more than just a cry of despair. It marks (and the bilingual pun is worth making) the return of what the opera itself identifies as the world—that world, also identified with the day, that the lovers in their night are seeking to shuck off, and with it all the weight of worldly judgment, obligation, responsibility, rationality, and care. "The world pales," they sing together, "at the blinding radiance [of my bliss] . . . Then I am myself the world."

In seeking to become a world unto themselves, the lovers are artists of a sort. Wallace Stevens would voice the same understanding in "The Idea of Order at Key West," a poem whose speaker responds with bliss to a woman singing by the shore (when Tristan dies Isolde will dissolve both of them into a billowing sea of sound, singing of it as she does it—by singing):

> She was the single artificer of the world
> In which she sang. And when she sang, the sea,
> Whatever self it had, became the self
> That was her song, for she was the maker.[1]

So understood, the relationship of the artist to the real world, the mundane world, is ultimately antagonistic. If the voice cannot make a world, the world will unmake the voice. One way to understand Brangäne's shriek is as the violent antithesis of the audiable: sound at the limit of sound that gives not life but a death blow. (Tristan shortly afterwards receives— invites—the wound of which he will later die.)

The shriek is that and more. In his prose poem "The Artist's Confession," roughly contemporaneous with *Tristan*, Charles Baudelaire hears something just as piercing conducted along his own tightly strung nerves as the sensory world plays on them too heavily:

> The energy in my pleasure creates a malaise and a positive anguish. My nerves, too taut, give out nothing but shrill and painful vibrations.
> And now the depth of the sky disturbs me, its clarity irritates me. The insensibility of the sea, the immutability of its vista, revolts me . . . Ah! Must one suffer eternally or eternally flee beauty? Nature, pitiless enchantress, ever victorious rival, let me be! Stop tempting my desires and my pride! The study of beauty is a duel in which the artist cries out in fright before being vanquished.[2]

Brangäne's shriek is not her own. It does not belong to her as a person. It is the artist's cry of fright before the world breaks in with the audible form of absolute silence.

Metal

The eight-part TV drama *The Night Of* (2016) tracks a New York murder case from the commission and discovery of the crime through the justice system. Part of that process involves travel to and from the city's infamous Riker's Island jail, as well as time spent in the facility awaiting trial. The scenes involved, especially those involving transport, have a soundtrack filled with harsh environmental noise: voices mixing in a highly reverberant space, a distorted undertone that sounds like a combination of a rumbling motor and bass distortion on a loudspeaker, and above all the clang of metal: of doors slamming, grates screeching, and manacles rattling, all at volumes well in excess of what an observer would hear if physically present. This surplus noise, which extends even to seemingly innocuous sounds like pens scratching, is especially prominent in the second episode, which recounts the accused man's introduction to life in captivity.

Sound treated in this way would in most cases represent the sensory experience of the character who hears it; the heightened sound would bring the audience to identify with the character's subjective standpoint. That, however, is precisely what these scenes in *The Night Of* pointedly avoid doing. The visual cues that would normally prompt such identification are largely lacking; such cues as do appear fail to take precedence because they share auditory space with so many others. The camera eye is impassive and objective, depriving the soundtrack of a virtual ear. The viewer hears the sounds as sensory abstractions, in excess of the otherwise perfectly intelligible conditions that produce them.

The symbolic value of this soundscape is obvious—and unimportant. No one could fail to recognize that the metallic cacophony, in association with shackles and prison cells, conveys the experience of imprisonment as one of depersonalization; the grinding mechanism of the prison system reduces those who must endure it from organic life to mechanical existence. The literally more resonant import of all the clangor rests with the sensation it elicits in the audience: the experience of a sound that belongs to no one, answers to no one, and cares about no one—cares about nothing. The sound exposes the insignificance, not of a person caught up in the proverbial wheels of justice, but of the sentient being who cannot refuse to register in the flesh the material weight of his, her, ultimate but also intimate powerlessness.

Worse yet, perhaps, is the sense of betrayal: the sound on which we rely for the feeling of animation deprives us of just that. The clanking metal removed from all subjectivity is an auditory Medusa's head. Inanimate itself, it turns the listener to worse than stone: an echo of inanimate sound.

This attack on hearing depends on the technology of sound and video recording; it would not be possible without the acoustic imbalance by which the sounds become, not alive, but undead. But what the soundtrack reveals is not itself dependent on technology. The hard thing to deal with is neither noise nor mechanism, but inertness. Wallace Stevens captures something of what this loss of animation feels like in "The Man on the Dump," a poem that inexorably becomes the echo of its own leading metaphor:

One sits and beats an old tin can, lard pail.
One beats and beats for that which one believes.
That's what one wants to get near. . . . Is it peace,
Is it a philosopher's honeymoon, one finds
On the dump? Is it to sit among mattresses of the dead,
Bottles, pots, shoes and grass and murmur *aptest eve:*
Is it to hear the blatter of grackles and say
Invisible priest; is it to eject, to pull
The day to pieces and cry *stanza my stone?*[1]

Is *stanza my stone* a claim that one's verse is a stone tablet to mark death or immortality (and in that case, what's the difference?), or a plea or imperative to make of one's empty stone, *tabula rasa*, a stanza, or just a defiant bit of alliterative sputtering, a noisome noise like the blatter of grackles? And what's the difference?

Here Comes That Song Again

Haunting melody—it is not quite done with us. Is that any surprise?

To reprise: Haunting melodies became interesting to Theodor Reik after he was all but persecuted by one (p. 126). It happened after the premature death of his mentor, Karl Abraham, on Christmas Day in 1925. Abraham's peers widely considered him preeminent among the first post-Freudian generation of psychoanalysts. Freud thought so too, and he asked Reik to deliver a eulogy at a meeting of the Vienna Psychoanalytic Society. Reik was happy to oblige, although the eulogy, as he later observed, was notably ambivalent. Meanwhile, as he began writing the eulogy, Reik found himself humming a melody that he did not recognize at first. After a few minutes, he realized it was the chorale theme that begins the final movement of Mahler's Second Symphony, a work commonly known by the name "Resurrection" precisely because of this movement. Then the floodgates opened:

That tune . . . began to haunt me whenever I thought of Dr. Abraham. . . .
But it also interfered with other trains of thought which had nothing to do
with him. It surprisingly occurred to me in the middle of small talk with

some guests of the hotel. It interrupted my writing a letter. It came to mind when I waked up and it was the last thought before I dozed off. It haunted me from that evening [Christmas night] until New Year's Day, and rarely left me for more than an hour. It was as if that melody had thrown a spell over me. I could not get rid of it, however much I tried to shake it off. A melody had followed me before for some hours, but I have never experienced an obsession of such tenacity before or since.[1]

Two things about the chorale especially bothered Reik, apart from the malicious agency it assumes in his description. (The melody seems more obsessed with Reik than he with it; it stalks him.) First, he could not remember the music that follows the chorale in the symphony, no matter how hard he tried—and he tried hard; the haunting melody had split off from its source and would admit no company in Reik's mind. Second, the text of the chorale, with its promise of resurrection, was at odds with Reik's irreligious mentality; he was an atheist, a secular Jew who regarded religion with clinical detachment. "For the life of me," he wrote, "that life whose continuation in the beyond I disbelieved, there was nothing in the chorale to which I could relate myself" (224). Reik understood that his indifference to the melody's consoling religious character disqualified it as a simple response to Abraham's death. What seemed like an appropriate response was actually incongruous. Reik reacted to this quandary as a psychoanalyst was supposed to. He regarded being haunted by the chorale as a symptom and he resolved to find a "solution" to it.

Eventually he did—but it took him twenty-five years. The solution, which I will not describe in detail, involved an analogy between Mahler's reaction to the death of the eminent conductor Hans von Bülow and Reik's to the death of Abraham. In both cases the mentor had left the mentee feeling rejected, discouraged, and resentful. For Mahler, the incitement was von Bülow's reaction to the movement that would begin the Second Symphony: "If what I have heard is music, I understand nothing about music!"

Reik has confidence in his construction and he makes its discovery the payoff of a long and winding narrative. But his solution left him unhappy in one essential respect. It depended on nonmusical associations to the melody, which was consistent with Freudian theory but insufficient to satisfy Reik. Reik also wanted a specifically musical solution, and he could not find one. Although very musically literate, like virtually any educated Viennese of his generation, he believed he did not know enough about music to solve this part of the riddle.

Freud was aware of the problem. In the sixth of his 1916 *Introductory Lectures on Psychoanalysis,* he had claimed that "tunes that come into one's head without warning turn out to be determined by and to belong to a train of thought which has a right to occupy one's mind though without one's being aware of its activity. It is then easy to show that the relation to the melody is tied to its text or origin." In other words, the melody itself doesn't matter; with the right text or origin, any melody will do. But Freud goes on to observe that things might be otherwise for "really musical people"—people unlike himself—for whom "the musical content of the tune is what decides its emergence."[2] He even goes on to remark on the genuine charm of a certain tune by Offenbach that haunted one of his patients. He thus implies that *not* just any melody would do. The unconscious choice would have multiple sources. It would be, as he liked to say, overdetermined. Freud thus also implies, as Reik acknowledges, that the aesthetic character of the music might also be a factor in its power to haunt.

The "charm" in this case is worth thinking about further, because it involves the patient's love life. The tune is from Jacques Offenbach's operetta *La Belle Helene,* a farcical sendup of the romantic triangle that, in myth anyway, sparked the Trojan War. In the familiar story, the Trojan prince Paris, encountering three goddesses on the slopes of Mount Ida, is asked to choose the most beautiful of the three. He chooses Venus, who promises him the hand of the most beautiful woman in the world—namely Helen of Sparta, wife of Menelaus, who becomes Helen of Troy. Freud reports that his patient was "positively persecuted for a time" by Paris's song, "(incidentally a charming one) . . . until his analysis drew his attention to a contemporary competition in his interest between an Ida and a Helen."[3]

The play of names might seem to render any musical explanation unnecessary, but the element of charm does suggest something more. Paris's song recounts the beauty contest among the goddesses. The music is buoyant, carried along on a rapid waltz rhythm under lyrical tenor lines. It reaches a slow, sensuous climax at the choice of the third goddess, Venus, and ends ebulliently with a return to the buoyant tempo. Everything is bright and unambivalent even if, in context, Paris is just a shade too proud of himself. These musical qualities might be said to have been telling Freud's patient that the choice of his own Helen had already been made, that it was really predestined, or else that the music was making the choice for him—and thus sparing him any regret or guilt over the outcome. He could just waltz away with his prize, or so he kept trying to convince himself.

But there is still a problem. Offenbach's melody may have haunted the lovesick patient, but it is not a haunting melody *within* the operetta. It is just a normal melody that comes and goes. The question, then, remains, and it is essentially the same question—call it the haunting question—that Reik could never answer. Is there a *musical* category of the haunting melody: a melody that, *in* the music that presents it, assumes a haunting character for musical reasons?

Mahler has already supplied the answer. In a word: Yes. But that had not been the answer for very long; it is part of the history of hearing, which means—such is my theme song in this book—that it is part of hearing itself. Musically haunting melody, melody represented as haunting within a piece of concert music, is a nineteenth-century invention.

The first clear-cut instance is the melody identified by Hector Berlioz as an idée fixe in his *Symphonie fantastique* of 1830. According to Berlioz's narrative program, the musical protagonist hears in this melody the character of the woman he loves unrequitedly. In one form or another, the melody returns to haunt him in all five movements of the symphony. The result both anticipates Freud's rule about haunting melody and establishes its musical exception. In narrative terms, the melody persists because of its associations with the elusive beloved. In musical terms, the associations exist only because the melody keeps returning. Cause and effect become indistinguishable. The melody we hear hovers ambiguously between signifying an idée fixe and being one.

The term *idée fixe* first appears in the early nineteenth century in the work of the French psychiatrists Etienne Esquirol and Jean-Etienne Georget; the associated concept of an idea or image that recurs involuntarily and obsessively became widely known as the primary symptom of monomania, the signature mental disorder of the period and one that quickly took on associations with artistic genius.[4] It does not seem to have occurred to anyone until Berlioz snapped the concept up that an *idée fixe* could take the form of a melody. The device caught on musically, with important later examples by Schumann and Ravel, among others. Schumann's four "Night Pieces" for piano, composed in 1839, even allude to the *Symphonie fantastique*, and, like Ravel's "Le Gibet" [The Gallows] from *Gaspard de la Nuit,* also for piano, composed in 1908, they connect the experience of haunting melody to gruesome intimations of death and despair. Mahler, in short, has company. But the notion of a musical *idée fixe* largely lay fallow in the era's medical and literary discourse, despite early appearances in Gerard de Nerval's 1831 poem "Fantaisie" and Edgar Allan Poe's 1845 story "The Imp of the Perverse."

Poe's account forms a link between Berlioz and Reik, not because of any direct line of influence—there is no evidence of any—but because of what it intuits about haunting melody. Poe's narrator likes to entertain himself with the thought that he has safely committed a murder. But the thought turns against him, and when it does a musical parallel arises:

> The pleasurable feeling grew, by scarcely perceptible gradations, into a haunting and harassing thought. It harassed because it haunted. I could scarcely get rid of it for an instant. It is quite a common thing to be thus annoyed with the ringing in our ears, or rather in our memories, of the bur-then of some ordinary song, or some unimpressive snatches from an opera. Nor will we be the less tormented if the song in itself be good, or the opera air meritorious.[5]

Berlioz's program for the *Symphonie fantastique* traces the same downward arc from pleasure to persecution, ending with a dream of a witches' Sabbath in which the "noble and shy" *idée fixe* makes its final return in the form of "a vulgar dance tune, trivial and grotesque." Reik's description of being harassed by Mahler's chorale theme follows the same course and turns the theme itself into a perverse imp. He, too, can scarcely get rid of it for an instant. Poe's pithy self-paraphrase captures the principle involved: "It harassed because it haunted." No matter how well it begins, haunting ends badly. And as Berlioz, Poe, and Reik all imply, harassment by a thought takes a general form that is perversely musical: an excess that overtakes the melodic repetition which is otherwise a common feature of music. The sufferer hears too much, too often, even while hearing nothing with the bodily ear.

Some years later, in 1893, an American psychologist, J. Mark Baldwin, could still identify the question of "internal song" as a new one, and ask, "What do we mean, when we say that a 'tune is running in our head'?" Although he is not interested in psychodynamic explanations, Baldwin anticipates where Freud would later look for them, not in the music but in the words: "Many persons find internal tunes generally fuller, more real, and sometimes only tunes at all because they remember the appropriate words, because they have sung the words to the tune, or at least, because they have hummed the refrain aloud."[6]

Apart from word associations, haunting melody has a nonmusical explanation in memory, as Baldwin's statement implies. Reik is also inclined to appeal to memory, though not to the kind of easily accessible practical memory that concerns Baldwin. The psychoanalytic point would not be the memory *of* the music, but the memory concealed *behind* the music. For example, casting around for precedents, Reik mentions an experience with haunting melody described—another bit of haunting here—in the autobiography of none other than Jacques Offenbach. The melody in question is significant precisely because there is nothing mysterious about it. Offenbach does not even particularly like it, but he cannot escape it because the melody reminds him of home and childhood. Just what it brings back to him would be the analytic question. In that respect it is worth noting that Offenbach's memory refers to a scene of love that is now out of reach forever. The strange thing, again from an analytic perspective, is that a waltz melody that gives no pleasure in itself should cause the person it haunts to wax nostalgic over the family circle of his childhood. The surplus that is a haunting melody arises where something has been lost, and accuses the person haunted of having lost it.

Offenbach's haunting waltz echoes, and may even have been influenced by, Nerval's description of an old air in "Fantaisie." The poem shares in the complex of ideas—lost time, lost love, lost peace of mind—that has begun to emerge as typical, and that will culminate in Mahler's scherzo. Nerval's poem is short enough to quote in full; the translation is mine:

There is an air for which I would surrender
All of Rossini, all Mozart, all of Weber,
A very old air, funereal and languid,
Which for me alone has secret charms.

And every single time I come to hear it
My heart grows younger by two hundred years . . .
It's under Louis treize, and I seem to see
A green hill yellowed by the setting sun,

Then a chateau of brick squared off with stone,
With windows tinted amid hues of red,
Circled by ample parks, and with a river,
Bathing its feet, that flows among the flowers;

Then a lady, on high at her window,
Blonde with black eyes, dressed in antique clothes,
Whom in another life, it may be,
I have already seen there . . . and remember![7]

Nerval's speaker is not so much haunted by the old air as he is seeking to be haunted by it. The air commands his memory of another life, yet he cannot seem to remember the air or to hear it in his mind's ear. Its magic works for him only when he comes to hear it, chances to hear it, from without. As to Rossini, Mozart, and Weber, they almost seem to get in the way. Their melodies fail to haunt. Perhaps they are too modern for that, or even too capable of the musical beauty that made them famous. When the old air does reach the speaker, what it gives him is strangely self-negating: a landscape visualized in detail, none of whose details is auditory. This silence takes the place of the audiable. It corresponds to the intimations of loss, of love and pleasure out of reach, that frame the scene: the setting sun, the antique clothes, the lady at her window, high up, apart, unattainable—except in the feeling of memory conveyed by the air, at least on the rare occasions when the air itself is not out of reach, not held back like the tune to which Mahler's dancers are whirling.

But perhaps there is a long-ago feeling in these very observations. Latter-day investigations of brainworms have tended, predictably, to focus literally on brain mechanisms and not to worry much about the meaning of haunting melodies. That approach is credible in the sense that the old

Freudian idea of psychic determinism is a bridge too far. There is no reason not to make room for chaos and chance and admit that many a brainworm really has no wider significance. But there is also no reason to rule out the contrary possibility. The impromptu history I have put together here suggests that the early recognition of haunting melodies depended in part on a link between the musical experience of being haunted and the problem of love at a distance. That, I trust, is worthy of being noted *as* history. But the link, or something like it, may also still apply, both in music and people's heads, and perhaps in the new link between them, namely earphones or earbuds wired into handheld devices. Music, for that matter, has become so ubiquitous in contemporary life that one might even say that many of its uses and forms have come to take haunting melody as a model.

The Mirror of Silence

In August Strindberg's short monodrama, *The Stronger*, a woman walks into a cafe, sits down next to another woman whom she thinks has had, or is still having, an affair with her husband, and starts talking. When she finishes, she declares herself the stronger of the two, claims her husband for herself, and leaves. In the meantime the other woman has uttered not a single word.

In Jean Cocteau's play *La voix humaine* (The Human Voice), and the opera based on it by Francis Poulenc, a woman sprawls on her bed and talks into the telephone, mostly to her lover of five years who is now leaving her. When she finishes, she has nothing but her misery and the now meaningless phrase "je t'aime" to claim for herself, and she dies, or appears to, with the phone cord wrapped around her neck.

The similarities of topic and technique between these two modernist works are obvious, but the difference between them is more resonant. What does the introduction of the telephone, and with it the force of communications technology, tell us about speaking into silence? That is literally what Strindberg's speaker does, followed figuratively by her counterpart in Cocteau, or rather, since my concern will be with the opera, in

Poulenc. The woman on the phone does hear the speech of others, one of whom is her lover, at the other end of the line, but we, the audience, hear only her, so in symbolic terms her situation and that of Strindberg's speaker are identical. But just what is that situation and what can we learn from it?

The silence of the other is the space into which the aggrieved party pours her utterance and from which she receives back an acoustic image of her romantic destiny. The silence is a kind of auditory mirror. In *The Stronger*, the result may be either genuine personal triumph or delusion; the play can be acted either way. And either way, the safeguard of this mirroring silence is the visible presence of the addressee. The silence is something we can hear because we see it. Strindberg could perfectly well, from a technological standpoint, have anticipated *La voix humaine* and channeled his monodrama over the telephone. He could have made the addressee invisible. But if he had, the equivocal ending of the play would have been impossible. The invisible silence would have no limit; no speech would be adequate to meet it. In this respect the telephone in *La voix humaine*, "the apparatus" (*appareil*) as the speaker often calls it, is an instrument of destruction. Picking up the phone is already suicidal.

The silence of the addressee in *La voix humaine* has no safeguard: no frame. The invisibility of the lover renders him as absent as his unheard voice, so that in a symbolic and also an acoustic sense no one is there and the woman's voice pours into a void, which continually empties rather than filling. And then there is the apparatus, which serves less to connect the speakers than to disconnect them. The Parisian telephone system circa 1930 is notoriously subject to human error—dependent on switchboard operators, to whom the woman too often finds herself speaking—and prone to dropped calls. Noise overshadows signal—the risk in all communication systems—so that the line connecting the woman to her lover is repeatedly cut (*coupée*). In the end, the material form of the line strangles her: it takes her life by cutting her off at the source of her voice.[1]

In the opera, the music of the orchestra takes the place of the mirroring silence that the telephone cannot provide. The paradox of sound in the place of silence is not as strange as it may seem; as Strindberg demonstrated, the silence of the addressee is a place-holder for sound, the zero that allows the balance sheet of feeling to be worked out. The orchestra thus echoes the woman's feelings but not her singing; the voice and orchestra run along different lines. But the orchestra too is repeatedly cut off, once again exposing a void and sealing the woman's doom. This happens under two circumstances, which gradually stand revealed as equivalent. First, the orchestra falls silent whenever (or as near as need be) the telephone connection is cut, especially when the singer repeatedly issues a futile "hello, hello?" Second, the orchestra stops essentially at random, for no particular reason, thus confessing that its substitution for the mirror of silence is an illusion, a phantasm called into being by the apparatus. The end of the work confirms the truth of this confession when woman's dying words, "je t'aime . . . t'aime" break off with an expulsion of breath and the orchestra follows suit in a matter of seconds.

The human voice appears in the opera in three distinct modes: singing like speech; singing unlike speech, most often associated with the expressive prolongation of single syllables in key words; and the recurrent sound of the woman crying. In short the full range of human vocalization is symbolically present, but it is nonetheless futile at every point, because the voice—we can hear this very well—has no meaning except within earshot of another voice, even if the latter does not speak. What speech asks from silence is the possibility of speech in return. The one-sided phone conversation translates the woman's emotional condition into the acoustic condition that exposes its fatality: she is not really speaking to anyone, not even to herself, but just emptying her voice into the void at the other end of the line. Unspeaking silence cuts the thread.

Rhythmic Hearing

In an essay on the sense of time, Alan Burdick alludes to William James's effort to show that, as James put it, "We have no sense for empty time."[1] Burdick quotes a passage from James's *The Principles of Psychology* (1890):

> Just as with closed eyes we perceive a dark visual field in which a curdling play of obscurest luminosity is always going on; so, be we never so abstracted from distinct outward impressions, we are always inwardly immersed in

what Wundt has somewhere called the twilight of our general consciousness. Our heart-beats, our breathing, the pulses of our attention, fragments of words or sentences that pass through our imagination, are what people this dim habitat. Now, all these processes are rhythmical, and are apprehended by us, as they occur, in their totality; the breathing and pulses of attention, as coherent successions, each with its rise and fall; the heartbeats similarly, only relatively far more brief; the words not separately, but in connected groups. In short, empty our minds as we may, some form of *changing process* remains for us to feel, and cannot be expelled.[2]

This passage, itself alluringly rhythmical, does not remark on its sensory preference, but the preference marks a discovery of the audiable. The dim background to consciousness appears first as a fading of vision, a twilight, and then as the unseen scene, the dim habitat, of what the twilight embodies, the irreducible minimum of sentience that never deserts us while we live. But the forms that people this habitat are all auditory. Even attention goes forth in pulses, beats sensed in the ear no less than in the veins. The twilight of our general consciousness is not seen but heard. Its rhythms link consciousness to both the elements of life—breath, heartbeat, pulse—and the elements of language. The parallel phrasing in the evocation of these ways of sounding link the two also to each other, so that, in effect, life speaks and language lives.

For James, what matters most about these links is the association between the sense of time and the perception of changing process; he wants to say that time is never empty. (He may or may not be right about that.) But the passage says something beyond that. Or rather it shows, in its language, that our immersion in the ground of sentience consists in an openness to the possibility of rhythmic hearing that cannot be expelled. That possibility has its own auditory form, which we feel and hear in equal measure.

Media All the Way Down

In 1837, the publisher of Giacomo Meyerbeer's opera *Les Huguenots* asked Honoré de Balzac to write a novella that would help publicize the opera.

Balzac obliged, but with a twist. Instead of revisiting the historical tragedy dramatized on a vast scale by the opera—the St. Bartholomew's Day Massacre of Protestants in Paris in 1572—Balzac wrote a treatise on the ontology of music in the form of a narrative about a visionary (and more than slightly mad) composer. Although the results are highly speculative, they are firmly grounded in the science of the era. They suggest the wider emergence of a fantasy or desire to find, through music, an intimation of the elemental medium of sensory experience. As the possibility of religious doubt becomes woven ever more closely into the fabric of culture, music comes to suggest the presence of a material body with spiritual resonance. The degree to which this resonance is metaphorical remains uncertain—which is part of the point.

Balzac's titular composer, Gambara, sweeps aside the traditional opposition of sound and light. The two become the sources of a unified sensory field that translates matter into thought: "Sound is light, perceived under another form; each acts through vibrations to which man is sensitive and which he transforms, in the nervous centers, into ideas." The vibrating substances are constituents of the air, "a vast variety of molecules of various degrees of elasticity, and capable of vibrating in as many different periods as there are tones from all kinds of sonorous bodies." The visual equivalent of this tonal resonance, and also the half-physical, half-mystical sign of its universality, is the Chladny effect (named for its eighteenth-century discoverer):

> Whereas each sound produced by a sonorous body is invariably allied with
> its major third and fifth, whereas it acts on grains of fine sand lying on
> stretched parchment so as to distribute them in geometrical figures that are
> always the same, according to the pitch—quite regular when the combina-
> tion is a true chord, and indefinite when the sounds are dissonant—I say
> that music is an art conceived in the very bowels of nature.

From this claim Gambara takes a leap reminiscent of the one taken by Coleridge (p. 61) in contemplating the action of the Aeolian harp: "What may we not attain to if we can discover . . . an ethereal substance diffused in the atmosphere which is the medium alike of music and of light, of the phenomena of vegetation and of animal life!" This ethereal substance is not the vibratory air but instead the elemental medium through which the air vibrates. The air follows the principle that one elemental medium reveals another, but the still more elemental medium of ethereal substance reveals only itself.

The aspiration to grasp this substance in both sensory and conceptual terms runs like a thread throughout the history of the auditory. The nineteenth century is perhaps its great age, home both to the scientific search for proof of the existence of the ether which, since Newton, had been postulated as the medium of light, to the conjectures of imaginative writers such as Coleridge, Balzac, and, to round this segment off, E. T. A. Hoffmann. Like Balzac, Hoffmann thinks of the search for the ethereal substance of sense as primordially musical, but he conceives (or has one of his characters conceive) of the search as nostalgic rather than progressive. In the "primordial condition" of humanity, nature was audibly filled with "wondrous tones" that later ages can discern only in remnants. But the remnants are still powerful enough that even the "least impressionable persons" are susceptible to their darker reverberations.

Such tones of nature as remain form a continuous ground bass to experience. Like the music of the spheres (to which Hoffmann alludes), these tones are inaudible, more the objects of thought than of sense—except under special circumstances:

> On quiet nights, with a moderate breeze blowing, I used to distinctly hear tones, sometimes resembling the deep, stopped, pedal pipe of an organ, and sometimes like the vibrations from a deep, soft-toned bell. I often distinguished, quite clearly, the low F, and the fifth above it (the C), and often the minor third above (E-flat) . . . and then this tremendous chord of the seventh, so woeful and so solemn, produced on one the effect of the most intense sorrow, and even terror![1]

The autumnal setting and the sublime effect of nature's unresolved dominant-seventh chord point to the condition of exile suffered by latter-day humanity; the organ and the bell counter with ecclesiastical majesty. Misery and misery fuse in elemental sound. Between Hoffmann and Balzac, something like the audiable becomes the medium of the nineteenth century's grand presiding myths of decline from the past and ascent to the future.

The Auditory Window

And what of the century afterward? The thread continues in an episode from Virginia Woolf's *Mrs. Dalloway* and in two from W. G. Sebald's *The Rings of Saturn*. All three center on a threshold of hearing in the form of a window. The placement is a reminder that sight passes through the pane or frame only if one looks out, but sound comes in whether one listens or not.

Woolf's novel begins with Clarissa Dalloway walking hither and thither through the streets of London, something that every other major character will do before the book is over. For Clarissa's daughter Elizabeth the walk brings a series of auditory revelations on a rising scale from the mundane to the metaphysical. The steps on the scale rise from the body's ear to the mind's and from noisy instrumental sound to sublime vocalization. Shock turns to rapture as reality yields to conjecture:

> Suddenly there were trumpets (the unemployed) blaring, rattling about in the uproar; military music; as if people were marching; yet had they been dying—had some woman breathed her last and whoever was watching, opening the window of the room where she had just brought off that act of supreme dignity, looked down on Fleet Street, that uproar, that military music would have come triumphing up to him, consolatory, indifferent.
>
> It was not conscious. There was no recognition in it of one's fortune, or fate, and for that very reason even to those dazed with watching for the last shivers of consciousness on the faces of the dying, consoling. Forgetfulness in people might wound, their ingratitude corrode, but this voice, pouring endlessly, year in year out, would take whatever it might be; this vow; this van; this life; this procession, would wrap them all about and carry them on, as in the rough stream of a glacier the ice holds a splinter of bone, a blue petal, some oak trees, and rolls them on.[1]

The purely imaginary window transforms the real music in Elizabeth's ears from the sound of social protest to what would be, at that window, the sound of consolation. The music would not cease to be noisily militant, but it would be consoling because of its indifference to the presence of a death—of death—within earshot. But this music would also have undergone a further and a larger change, becoming the sound, not of a military band, but of a singing voice. The voice would belong to everyone and no one. It would be the voice of life in general, indifferent to the mortality of life in particular. It would match the year-in, year-out motion that exhausts particular life. By that means the voice would become an inexhaustible gift, "pouring endlessly" in a song that is no less real for remaining inaudible. The voice would acknowledge mortality—like a glacial stream carrying a splinter of bone or a blue petal—but not be halted by it. Or it would, were any of this possible, which nothing in the passage confirms or promises. The life-affirming voice is auditory only in the form of an as-if. But if nothing else, the episode identifies just which as-if the affirmation requires.

Sebald reaches a similar understanding by negative means. Near the start of his novel, his narrator listens at a hospital window and, disappointed by what he hears, finds the stream of life-affirming voice in the two nurses who take his pulse—who, that is, literally reaffirm his continuing life. Near the end of the novel, at another window, this one closed, he will take it all back. But first windows first. The earlier episode is a refusal of silence:

> An ambulance with its light flashing was negotiating a number of turns on its way from the city center. . . . I could not hear its siren; at that height I was cocooned in an almost complete and, as it were, artificial silence. All I could hear was the wind sweeping in from the country and buffeting the window; and in between, when the sound subsided, there was the never entirely ceasing murmur in my own ears.[2]

The murmur is not acousmatic, that is, a sound without a visible source; it literally has no source at all. It is the bare minimum of sound, indistinct and inarticulate, yet incessant. The murmur is what remains when even the wind—the paradigm of what can be heard but not seen—is still. It sounds in the narrator's ears but may or may not be the sounds of his pulse. This murmur is the speech of the audiable, and it is what makes the next act of hearing possible:

> Through the resounding emptiness my ears caught the voices of the two nurses. . . . Of the everyday matters they chatted about I understood very little. All I heard was the rise and fall of their voices, a kind of warbling such as comes from the throats of birds, a perfect, fluting sound, part celestial and part the song of sirens. Of all the things [they said] I remember only one odd

scrap [describing] . . . a holiday in Malta . . . where the Maltese, with a death-defying insouciance quite beyond comprehension, drove neither on the left nor on the right, but always on the shady side of the road (18).

As in Woolf, it is not so much what the narrator hears as what he imagines himself hearing that gives auditory consolation. The sounds persist but their identity changes. More exactly, it compounds: the women's voices do not cease to be audible, but they sound in polyphony with their own tonal contour and with their own metamorphosed forms as the music of the spheres and as siren songs—the first traditionally audible only at moments of special blessedness, the second irresistibly beautiful as long as one does not get too close.

But of course one does get too close, no matter how well the Maltese may defy death by their driving habits. Sebald revokes these invocations of the audiable in the penultimate section of *The Rings*, an account of the deforestation wrought on the east coast of England by the great hurricane of 1987. The scene is apocalyptic, the landscape leveled, but the ultimate form of this secular apocalypse is auditory: "Where a short time ago the dawn chorus had at times reached such a pitch that we had to close the bedroom windows, where larks had risen on the morning air above the fields and where, in the evenings, we occasionally even heard a nightingale in the thicket, its pure and penetrating song punctuated by theatrical silences, there was now not a living sound" (268). The concluding words say it all but explicitly: the world without the hum of the world is dead.

The description that leads to this end reveals what death this is. The conjunction of the lark and the nightingale invokes a grand tradition of poetry that here loses its voice because it loses its auditory basis: from the aubade in *Romeo and Juliet* ("It was the nightingale and not the lark") to the lark in Shakespeare's Sonnet 29 which, "at break of day arising / From sullen earth . . . sings hymns at heaven's gate"; to Shelley's blithe spirit, the lark "that from heaven, or near it, / Pours forth [its] profuse strain / Of unpremeditated art"; and from Milton's nightingale "most musical, most melancholy bird," to Keats's, whose song "oft-times hath / Charm'd magic casements, opening on the foam / Of perilous seas, in faery lands forlorn."

Sebald's text reverberates with many of these images but only to cancel them, in an inclusive palinode. In the dearth of the audiable is the death of the symbol. The silence of the birds opens onto a silence more absolute; it revokes the flutelike warble of the pulse-takers and marks the death of song. In the vacancy that Sebald's narrator describes, the entire symbolic order has collapsed like one of the many ruined buildings—crumbling manors, estates run to seed, stately homes put to the torch—that appear throughout *The Rings of Saturn.*

Cacophony

DISPOSSESSION (BECKETT)

The audiable ties us to life, to sentience, to the horizon of being. But what if one does not want to be so tied?

In his stage monologue "Not I," Samuel Beckett gives the audiable a name that expresses his resentment of it. He calls it "the buzzing," or, more exactly, "the buzzing, so called": "what? . . . the buzzing? . . . yes . . . all the time the buzzing . . . so called . . . in the ears . . . though of course actually . . . not in the ears at all . . . in the skull."[1] The hum of the world thus contracts to the drone of an insect, or of a swarm, perhaps above all of flies. Was Beckett recalling Baudelaire's poem "Le Charogne" [The Carrion], in which flies buzzing around the belly of a corpse inaugurate

> A strange music,
> Like flowing water and wind,
> Or a winnower's grain that he shakes and turns
> With rhythmical grace in his basket.[2]

The speaker in "Not I" appears only as a mouth illuminated in a theater in which all the house lights have been extinguished. The mouth belongs to an old woman who has suffered what seems to be a paralytic stroke. Falling to the ground "on that April morning," "wandering in a field . . . looking aimlessly for cowslips" (all ellipses in original), she enacts a travesty of Proserpina gathering flowers in the fields of Enna, from which she is abducted to the underworld: "herself a fairer flower," wrote John Milton, who "by gloomy Dis / Was gathered" (*Paradise Lost* IV.270–71). The speaker, identified only as Mouth, awakens to find that she is strangely incapable of suffering ("imagine!" she cries, a cry she will often repeat). Her body lacks all feeling except for the sensations associated with the vocal apparatus: lips, tongue, cheek, jaws, lips. She is, as her pseudonym says, all mouth. And from that mouth, from Mouth, pours a rapid, continuous stream of words, emitted in short, repetitious bursts, a few words at a time, linked by quick catches of breath. So, at least, Mouth sounded in Billie Whitelaw's 1973 performance, which was intensively coached by Beckett to make her, precisely, his Mouthpiece.[3]

Mouth does not so much speak as form a conduit for speech. The voice that comes from her is, she says, not her own, nor does she fully hear it, nor does she will or consent to it. The outpouring of this intimate but alien voice meets with obstacles at irregular intervals. The obstacles are what seem to be questions, voiced by an interlocutor whom only Mouth can hear. The questions may represent the thoughts of a cloaked, silent figure posted on the margins of the stage, identified by Beckett as Auditor. Or perhaps they are purely imaginary. Mouth does not know and neither do we.

In any case, the questioner does only two things. He, she, or it (call it "he" for convenience) tries and fails to get Mouth to acknowledge her own identity, which she wards off by what Beckett describes as her "vehement refusal to relinquish third person." The refusal, expressed in the sequence, "what? . . . who? . . . no! . . . she!" forms a refrain that divides the monologue into five quasi-musical movements characterized by the progressive recurrence of fraught words and phrases. The chant-like circling cuts across the vestiges of linear narrative, which appear only in fragments.

Less overtly, but more insistently, the questioner casts doubt on Mouth's perception that, except for the voice she emits, there is nothing but silence. The questioner speaks (and it is telling that we never hear the speech) for the audiable. He draws Mouth back to the sound of the buzzing, so called, and it is that sound that drives Mouth into the quintessential action of the Beckett character: to go on when going on is most impossible. The buzzing accompanies the effort of Mouth, via the voice, to say the one thing that needs to be said, the one essential thing that always, just because it is essential, hovers just out of reach—out of earshot: : "yes . . . all the time the buzzing . . . dull roar . . . in the skull . . . ferreting around . . . painless . . . so far . . . ha! . . . so far . . . then thinking . . . oh long after . . . sudden flash . . . perhaps something she had to . . . tell . . . could that be it? . . .

something she had to . . . tell . . ." (221). It is impossible to say whether the sought-for word, or Word, would be one of vindication, reconciliation, acceptance, defiance, among many other possibilities. Whatever it is, the compulsion of the voice is to make the buzzing speak.

Or to make it sing. In Whitelaw's performance, which Beckett called "miraculous," the words themselves sing in being uttered. Each of the recurrent words and phrases—"so far," "the brain," "imagine," "spared that," "no love," "the buzzing," "what? . . . who? . . . no! . . . she!" among others— receives its own distinctive dynamics and intonation, so that the melodizing of speech becomes completely literal. Beckett, who loved the music of Beethoven and Schubert, bends this musicalized voice, which at various moments babbles, shouts, screams, laughs, burbles, whispers, and utters, into an inverse form of the Schubert song that he earlier used as a framing motif in the radio play "All that Fall": Undeath and the Maiden.

Euphony

REPOSSESSION (BECKETT)

And yet, speaking of Schubert: Beckett's television play "Nacht und Träume" (1982) forms something like a palinode on "Not I" (1972). The later play contemplates the one force that seems able to mitigate the denial of life and self which Mouth pursues so relentlessly in the earlier. That force is music. More particularly it is song, and more particularly still it is song by Schubert. For Beckett the mitigation may be as much cause for regret as for relief, but he acknowledges that when sound is alluring, its song, half celestial and half siren, may be just too hard to resist. "Nacht und Träume" replies in advance to the death of sound in Sebald's *The Rings of Saturn*. It is as if Beckett, unwilling to believe in absolute silence even if he might want to, were seeking to make his audience hear that sound is inherent in what we mistakenly call silence, and even to make audible the understanding that to break the silence is to embrace the world. (His play "Breath" contemplates this equation with a minimum of means and a maximum of ambivalence. The play lasts less than a minute; the stage is empty except for litter. The action consists of an inhalation followed by a cry and a cry followed by an exhalation. "Important," Beckett notes, "that [the] two cries be identical.") Song, exemplified by the unguardedly beautiful Schubert Lied, is a call to affirmation even, or especially, when there seems nothing left to affirm.

The site of affirmation is the transitional state between waking and sleeping in which the half-heard becomes audible, at least for the audience. We see an elderly figure, his head bowed and hands resting on a table in a twilit room; we hear a male voice humming "last 7 bars of Schubert's Lied 'Nacht und Träume,'" and then, as the light fades, the voice singing "last 3 bars of Lied, beginning 'holde Träume.'" The figure then lowers his head to his hand and dreams. We witness the dream hovering over the dreamer from the middle distance. It shows, in silence, a pair of hands caressing the hands of the dreamer, giving him a cup of water, and wiping his brow. The dreamer then awakens, or half awakens, and we hear the music as before; then the dreamer bows his head and the dream is repeated, "in close up and slower motion," before it fades out, followed by the dreamer.

The music is strangely disembodied. Beckett's first stage direction for it, "Softly hummed, male voice," suggests that the singing voice does not come from the figure we see, but rather comes to him, in the form of memory. In the original television production, the sound does seems to be coming from the figure, but he is so shrouded by dimness, distance, and his shaggy hair that we cannot see his lips move; the sound is disembodied before our ears. For the audience it is music in the air.

In any case, the link of the music to memory is paramount. The turn from humming to singing suggests a progression from recalling the melody to recalling the words. One retrieves as much as one can. But memory cannot restore presence; both melody and words return only as fragments. Still, they return, and their return does more than one might expect. The music returns not only to make but also to fulfill, or half fulfill, the plea voiced in the only words we are given to hear: "Holde Träume, kehret wieder!"—Lovely dreams, come back again! One dream, at least, does just that, and does it twice. The song is a remnant, but it is also summons to which the dream pays heed.

The play's acts of remembered hearing, that is, the hearing of unheard music, unheard voice, form the prologue to the dream. The remembered song even composes the dream, as the answered plea and the repetition of the whole sequence suggest. The dream in turn translates the music into the memory of touch, or the identity of sound and touch, realized, however tentatively and fleetingly, in the acts of kindness shown by the hands to the dreamt self. The kindness has clear religious overtones, but its auditory aspect is no less important. The kindness of the hands extends the touch that makes music at the piano. The absence of that music from the Lied we hear hummed and sung is itself audible. In the same way, the prevailing silence consummated in the dream becomes the medium in which the breaking of silence becomes audible in its own right. "What," the play asks, "can one hear in this music, or the remnant of it?" The dream is the answer.

Worldly Dissonance

Kaja Silverman argues that the world "intends" us to see it, and in particular to see its beauty.[1] Like some speculative realist philosophers who take seriously the idea of panpsychism—the idea that all things animate and inanimate possess mind-like qualities, even if not mind—Silverman sees (precisely that: sees) the world not merely as a surrounding but also as an agency, and in particular as an agency of seeing, in every sense of *see*.

The argument is compelling, especially in its critical transformation of the privilege of the visual. Vision is no longer the correlative to a fixed perspective or commanding view identified with truth, power, or reason. Instead, an ever unfinished, collective act of constructive seeing freely does the world's bidding. Drawn by the beauty, moved by desire, vision simultaneously witnesses and symbolizes. But this view entails the omission of something painfully obvious—literally so.

Horror, ugliness, and pain also "intend" us to see them. They dare us to see them with either compassion or indifference and their address cannot be overlooked. They must be tended, mitigated where mitigation is possible, and witnessed no matter what. Silverman's "mistake" in not reckoning with this is traceable to the character of the visual itself: one part of the power of the image is that it can make virtually anything "beautiful," iconic, open to contemplation. The visual aestheticizes despite itself, and despite the contrary demands of a certain ethics (worship no images) and a certain logic of the sublime (see to it that no image can be seen).

It is for this reason that the visual requires its supplement in the audible: not so much in the word, which Silverman, like Mitchell and Deleuze, subsumes under the rule of the visual, as if all speech were latent writing, but in the speech act and in the production of tone, things that can be audiable without even being audible, as in signing. The sphere of tone is wider than we often suppose. Think of operatic voice, the voiceover in old-fashioned newsreels, the voice we adopt for young children, the role of voice in romance and erotic love. Unlike the visual, the auditory (comprising both the audible and the audiable) is not pan-aestheticizing. Not everything can be heard with equanimity; some sounds are like caressing splinters or walking on shards of glass. Some are worse.

The notorious fact that one cannot avert one's ears as one can one's gaze makes sound an index of vulnerability. Perhaps Edvard Munch's painting *The Scream* is so popular precisely because, even without meaning to, it compensates for that failure. The painted figure hears the scream despite covering his (her? its?) ears, or the place where the ears would be, but the spectator *sees* the scream in the undulating lines of the background and thus reduces the intolerable sound to silence. Music sometimes flirts with the limits of sound as wound, for example when operas call for screams, but sonorous wounds are too hard to take for many listeners. One index of their excess, though a crude one, is the relative failure of "dissonant" sounds in concert music to win auditors during the twentieth century as compared to the success of the equally "dissonant" visual arts at winning spectators: Jackson Pollock yes, Elliott Carter no.

Sounds of Battle

THE CIVIL WAR

The Civil War Battle of Fredericksburg, Virginia, fought between December 11 and 15, 1862, was a calamitous defeat for the Union army, famously described by a Pennsylvania infantryman, John L. Smith, as "simply murder." One of those who fought in the battle was Joshua Lawrence Chamberlain, who before joining the army had been a professor of languages and rhetoric at Bowdoin College. Chamberlain played a heroic role in the Battle of Gettysburg, was wounded six times, rose to the rank of major general, and accepted the formal surrender of the Confederate army at Appomattox.

Chamberlain wrote about his war experiences. A memoir of the aftermath of the first day of fighting at Fredericksburg lays particular emphasis on sound:

> We lay [that night] on the trampled and bloody field. . . . Little sleep was to
> be had there, I assure you. Our eyes and ears were open. We could hear the
> voices of the rebels in their lines, so near were they, and could see many of
> their movements. I did sleep, though, strange though you may think it, in
> the very midst of a heap of dead close beside one dead man—touching him
> possibly—the living and dead were alike to me. I slept, though my ears were
> filled with the cries and groans of the wounded, and the ghastly faces of the
> dead almost made a wall around me.[1]

Sight and hearing divide here, just as touch goes awry. In this sensory phantasmagoria, sound alone remains meaningful. The faces of the dead form a barrier, a wall of noncommunication, a blank stare multiplied without limit. But the voices of the rebels carry, and the sighs and groans of the wounded convey the terrible cost of the battle, which Chamberlain earlier records in strongly auditory terms as culminating in a "hellish din" amid which "it seemed as if . . . the very sky were crashing down on us; the bullets hissed like a seething sea" (40).

The most remarkable detail is the sound of the cries and groans. Chamberlain is a careful writer, and what he says about these sounds strongly intimates that they not only failed to keep him from sleeping but, on the contrary, that he slept *on* them rather than *through* them: he heard them in his sleep. The cries and groans, a mixture of verbal and visceral sounds, become the tie to life in a field full of the dead. Otherwise "the living and the dead were alike." Chamberlain and his companions were themselves thought to be dead by men scavenging the same field for cloaks against the cold—until the scavengers saw the eyes of the men whose sleep they had disturbed without a sound. (Chamberlain and a friend had earlier done exactly the same thing, though in vain. The night was cold.)

The role of sound as the thread that links the traumatized sufferer to life appears by negation in a tableau glimpsed after the battle by another Union officer, General John W. Ames. Coming upon a "low brick house," Ames observed six dead bodies, two on the doorstep and four inside. Further within sat a woman, "gaunt and hard-faced," with "crazy hair," staring by candlelight "with wild eyes" into the darkness outside "with the look of one who heard and saw not, to whom all sounds were a terror" (41). For this woman, the thread had broken. Chamberlain, also coming upon a brick house, perhaps the same one, heard a sound that underscored the fragility of the acoustic link. A loose window shade flapped between the sash and the wall. To Chamberlain's ear it seemed to be chanting rhythmically, like the cries and groans suspended between calling and wailing: "Never—forever; forever—never!"

Sounds of Battle

WORLD WAR I

In the distance the front thunders. The walls of the hut rattle.

—Erich Maria Remarque, *All Quiet on the Western Front*

What passing bells for these who die as cattle?
Only the monstrous anger of the guns.
Only the stuttering rifle's rapid rattle
Can patter out their hasty orisons.

Wilfred Owen, "Anthem for Doomed Youth"

War should detain us longer.

The audiable reveals itself through historical events, but is also embedded within history. Events may change it, either in passing or permanently. One of the turning points in its history was the Great War, World War I, if the recorded memory of the war is any guide.

Benjamin Britten's *War Requiem* was composed in 1961–62 to mark the reconstruction of Coventry Cathedral, which had been destroyed during the Blitz in World War II. But Britten's focal point is World War I, the century's original baptism by fire. The *War Requiem* combines a setting of the Requiem Mass with settings of nine war poems by Wilfred Owen, who was killed in France just a week before the war ended. The first of Owen's poems in the sequence is "Anthem for Doomed Youth." Britten answered Owen's opening question with the sound of tubular chimes hammering out a dissonant interval that will resonate throughout the eighty-five-minute composition. Owen had written that his poetry was concerned with the pity of war: "The poetry is in the pity." Britten responds in kind, as if to say: the mourning is in the clamor. For the pealing of the bells goes two ways, and its divergence from itself is at the heart of the music. The chimes are like church bells, solemn passing bells; but the chimes are dissonant, and their metallic clang lingers in the air, material, harsh, implacable. We hear them throughout the opening "Requiem aeternam" and as a frame for the setting of Owen's "Anthem," which comes next. Britten gives Owen's ironic metaphor a realization in sound, as if to say: not the guns only, but these bells, these bells, these. The anger is still there.

The mass and the poetry in the *War Requiem* sound in different voices. There is a liturgical voice composed of a choir, a solo soprano, and a boys' choir, in varied combinations, and a war voice composed of just two solo singers, a tenor and a baritone, who speak on behalf of the dead. It is never quite clear whether these voices communicate with each other. At times they are plainly at odds, especially during the *Offertorium*, the part of the *Requiem* that pleads for deliverance.

The poem for this section recounts the story of Abraham and Isaac, but with a sting in its tail. When the angel appears telling Abraham to sacrifice a ram instead of his son, Owen reverses the Biblical outcome: "But the old man would not so, and slew his son, / And half the seed of Europe, one by one." As the boys in their high treble sing (in Latin) the *Hostias,*

> Lord, in praise we offer to Thee
> sacrifices and prayers, do Thou receive them
> for the souls of those whom we remember
> this day: Lord, make them pass
> from death to life,

the tenor and baritone, singing together for the first time, repeatedly interpolate the phrases of Owen's bitter final line in the registers of grown men—grown enough, at least, to be sacrificed.

The men's voices first alternate, then combine; they retain their singularity but share their doom, voicing their words differently except for the last, the doubled "one" in "one by one." That tally becomes the dominant utterance in the passage. On each repetition it shows how the separate voices of each one unite in death to become the voice of every one. (Ironically, the men's voices have sung in rhythmic unison shortly before to voice the command of God that the "old man" disobeys.) Meanwhile the boys' choir sings on unperturbed. The contrary voices of the men and the boys unite in the audience's perception of their overlap, but in relation to each other they turn the litany of the one and the parable of the other into a cycle of call and nonresponse. It is a cycle that reaches deeply into the cultural memory of the war.

It also reaches into the history of the audiable. When a voice calls repeatedly without response, the voice may become the absence its call reveals. This absence often becomes manifest as an absence of place or person, the two coordinates any voice depends on to be recognized. Virginia Woolf's *Jacob's Room*, the story of a young man whose largely inconsequential life comes to matter when he loses it in the Great War, begins with an unanswered call from Jacob's brother, aptly named Archer, the arrow of whose voice cannot find its mark. Archer's syllables, "Ja-cob! Ja-cob," not quite rising to the level of the name, resound in the text three times. But the voice that emits the syllables is no longer his, and it goes everywhere and nowhere: "The voice had an extraordinary sadness. Pure from all body, pure from all passion, going out into the world, solitary, unanswered, breaking against rocks—so it sounded."[1] This voice is its own echo. It recedes from itself; it becomes its own death knell: "so it sounded." Instead of breaking silence, this voice is broken by it, split into pieces: "Ja-cob! Ja-cob." The faint resonance between the syllables shows the audiable in its tragic mode as the edge—the limit, the blade—of silence.

Woolf does not try to imagine the trenches; she kills Jacob offstage, offhandedly. But her passage resonates in an uncanny way with an episode in the World War I novel by Erich Maria Remarque that we know in English as *All Quiet on the Western Front*. Here the narrator and his comrades hear the voice of a wounded man whom they cannot locate, and in the end fail to find, as if his voice were all that was left of him. As they listen, the voice passes through the stages of its dying, becoming its lament for itself. Here, too, voice without place or person becomes a medium in which the audiable resonates as tragedy. The fortunes of this voice, like those of the call in Woolf, condense the entire narrative into a single arc of utterance:

> He grows gradually hoarser. The voice is so strangely pitched that it seems to be everywhere. . . . At first he only called for help—the second night he must have had some delirium, he talked to his wife and his children, we often detected the name Elise. Today he merely weeps. By evening the voice dwindles to a croaking. But it persists still through the whole night. We hear it so distinctly because the wind blows toward our line. In the morning when we suppose he must already have long gone to his rest, there comes across to us one last gurgling rattle.[2]

Like the hyphen in *Jacob's Room*, the wind in *All Quiet* becomes both a threshold and a medium, the minimum of the audible through which the promise or, here, the threat of sound becomes perceptible. On the front, this minimum takes the specific form of a lack of respite. It is a leftover from a continuous barrage of sound: "At the front there is no quiet. . . . Even in the remote depots and rest areas the droning and the muffled sound of shelling is always in our ears. We are never so far off that it is not to be heard."[3]

No quiet: the English title of the book is memorable but misleading. In German the title is *Im Westen nich Neues*—Nothing New in the West. The Great War was noisy. Remarque's narrative is full of its noise.

The noise is so domineering that it becomes the principal source of orientation for hardened soldiers in a world in visual chaos. New recruits who do not quickly learn to read sound are quickly killed. But the war disorients sound itself, splintering it into strange phenomena like that wind-borne voice of a dying soldier who could be, and is, anyone. On the front, the thrum of nonsilence nullifies the "soundless apparitions" that compose the memories of peacetime. The memories, and the desires that go with them, become lost objects, discernible but forever out of reach. Their loss feels like a fatal wound: "We are dead and they stand remote on the horizon, a mysterious reflection, an apparition, that haunts us, that we fear and love without hope."[4]

The haunting continues far beyond the front. When Paul, the doomed narrator, returns home on leave, he takes no note of sound. When he is temporarily posted to a training camp, he regains his ability to take pleasure in things seen. But the misery of Russian prisoners held within the camp reawakens his sensitivity to sound as uncanny, sound as wounded. When the prisoners sing a chorale for one of their dead, the voices separate and abolish themselves, receding into a drone, an apparition on the horizon: "They sing in parts, and it sounds almost as if there were no voices, but an organ far away on the moor."[5] When the prisoners hum along with a violin, the sound of the instrument leaves them behind and thins to a whisper: "The voices cease and the violin continues alone. In the night it is so thin it sounds frozen; one must stand close up" (ibid.). The frozen sound is barely sound at all. It is the residue of all the layers of sound that have been stripped away to expose the audible, and that reveal it, again, not as the promise of something to come but as the terrible inversion of that promise, the dim intonation of what the narrator elsewhere calls a "vast inapprehensible melancholy."[6]

Owen's auditory experience during the war years touched on both this apparition and its contrary: obverse and reverse. Thinking of Alfred Tennyson's late poem "Crossing the Bar," which seeks to anticipate death with equanimity ("Sunset and evening star / And one clear call for me / . . . And let there be no moaning of the Bar / When I put out to sea"), Owen grew outraged: "Did he hear the moaning of the Bar, not at twilight and evening bell only, but at dawn, noon, and night, eating and sleeping, walking and working, always the close moaning of the Bar; the thunder, the hissing, and the whining of the Bar?"[7] Where Remarque, also a soldier in the war, heard the spectral resonance of lost life, Owen heard a distillation of sheer suffering.

Yet he also heard the contrary. Unlike Remarque's narrator, Owen on convalescent leave could still hear, not frozen and nullified voices, but the continuity of shared life in a streak of sound. Writing of "conviviality" and glossing it for good measure—"(L. *vivere:* to live)"—he restores the audible to its dimension of promise, even if only in recollection:

Some day I must tell how we sang, shouted, whistled and danced through the dark lanes through Colinton; and how we laughed till the meteors showered around us, and we felt calm under the winter stars. And some of us saw the pathway of the spirits for the first time. And seeing it so far above us, and feeling the good road so safe beneath us, we praised God with louder whistling; and knew we loved one another as no men love for long.[8]

The path from sound to spirit also opens in the *Sanctus* of the *War Requiem,* which follows the *Offertorium.* But the path is a hard one. The *Sanctus* begins with an alternation between pitched percussion and solo soprano. Led by the chimes, the percussion executes a crescendo with a tremolo on a single note, concluding with a single, separate stroke. As the sound of that stroke lingers and fades, the soprano intones the word "Sanctus." The two forces then combine as the soprano draws out "Sanctus" on a long undulating melody and the percussion executes a decrescendo on evenly spaced single strokes. A repetition of this pattern follows for the soprano's second phrase, "Dominus Deus Saboath," but with a different note for the percussion—dissonant in relation to the first—and with an undulating "Sanctus" returning for the decrescendo.

The percussion is all metal; its sound cuts into the voice's sacred utterance with the vibration of profane matter. The soprano begins her undulations in tune with the repercussions around her but dissonances creep in as she continues. Her "Sanctus" suggests an effort to keep the bell cohort from falling out of its anointed place. The earlier ambiguity surrounding "Anthem for Doomed Youth" returns: where Owen had forged weapons into passing bells, Britten here almost forges bells into weapons. Almost: but not quite. The "Sanctus" passage ends with a sudden fortissimo on the percussion that overpowers the voice (abruptly wrested onto the right note) and, after the voice falls silent, continues, with its long decay, to linger in the air. When the sound has faded to pianissimo, another stroke at that level recapitulates the fall from *ff* to *pp* as a fall from *pp* to nothing. But as the sound fades, it becomes less harsh. It even becomes strangely reassuring, even soothing in its near intangibility. The music resumes just as the fading resonance approaches the threshold of its disappearance.

Rising to pianissimo, the double basses and bass voices begin a free chant on "Pleni sunt coeli et terra gloria tui" that rises gradually through the ranks of choral voices. Dying, the music brushes the audiable and revives.

Ulysses in Auschwitz

In Canto XXVI of the *Inferno*, Dante encounters the shade of Ulysses. Condemned as a false counselor, Ulysses cannot be seen; he is wrapped in a cloak of flame that embodies his tormented self-consciousness. Called on to speak, he tells of his final voyage: his departure, with a small group of shipmates, from the Ithaca he had previously so long sought. Moved by a restless desire for "knowledge and excellence," he sets sail for the unknown and finds it in the form of a fatal shipwreck.

Dante's account is remarkable for the heroic allure it invests in a voyage it is bound to condemn. It is remarkable no less for its collapsing of the visible into the auditory. When Ulysses speaks, the flame that enwraps him appears as the source of his voice: "its point waved to and fro as if it were / A tongue that spoke."[1] Both features have a long echo; they will come together again in Primo Levi's account of an afternoon's walk through a later inferno. The story of the walk occupies a chapter of the book known in English as *Survival in Auschwitz*. The title of the chapter is "The Canto of Ulysses."[2]

Levi and a companion go to retrieve the day's rations of soup. They take the long way to the kitchens to prolong this respite from the oppressive order of the day. As they walk, the journey recounted in the Canto of Ulysses fuses with their own. Levi precipitates the fusion by recalling Dante's verses. He pushes through unavoidable gaps and omissions to recite the verses from memory and translate them to his companion. The latter is a kind of trusty responsible for overseeing Levi's work brigade, and Levi becomes increasingly intent on making this man understand the poetic force and human meaning of Dante's verses—a force and meaning that condemn the camp and everything it stands for. Unlike Dante, Levi takes the words of Ulysses to his shipmates as the expression of an ideal, not of moral blindness:

THE HUM OF THE WORLD

> Think of your breed; for brutish ignorance
> Your mettle was not made; you were made men,
> To follow after knowledge and excellence. (113)

The effort to convey this message turns the walk to the soup line into a version of the voyage that the verses narrate. Like its model, the voyage ends badly. Time runs out before minds can meet; soup intervenes. So pressing is the feeling of unfinished business that the language of Levi's chapter changes mode from narration to apostrophe. As if he were still speaking, Levi as authorial voice addresses the other man across the gap of years as if the affirmation he, Levi, had sought in the Canto of Ulysses were still possible. It is not. The chapter ends, accordingly, with a quotation of the verse describing the end of Ulysses's voyage: "'And over our heads the hollow seas closed up'" (115).

The closing of the waters takes the form of a failure of language, a failure of speech melody, a failure of music. Losses of meaning multiply as the walk proceeds. Levi's memory leaves gaps in the verses which he only widens by trying to fill them. Wracking his brain does not help; neither does "rushed commentary." Because his companion does not know Italian, Levi must translate the truncated verses and find himself wanting; he judges his translations "wan." Dante's original words and phrases progressively isolate him, almost imprison him, in his understanding of their nuance and sonority. Even though the other man tries to listen, he cannot really hear what Levi finds it "vitally necessary and urgent" to convey to him. The time is too short; the language is too rich.

The result is that Ulysses's expression of what is proper to human life— the search for knowledge and excellence—rebounds on Levi as a chastisement. As he intones Dante's verse, it no longer carries the sound of his own voice nor even the imprint of Dante's, but instead falls on his ear with the sound of an apocalypse that will not happen: "As if I also was hearing it for the first time: like the blast of a trumpet, like the voice of God. For a moment I forget who I am and where I am" (113).

The moment makes Levi's desperation worse, not better. The more strongly he feels the need to communicate the Canto of Ulysses, no longer merely to translate it, for his companion, the less communicative he becomes. Each step in the direction of the kitchens takes him further from his goal. So far, indeed, that his arrival at the line for rations sinks the fading ideal of knowledge and excellence under the watery soup of sheer bathos. Even the prospect of the ultimate bad ending—"He or I might be dead tomorrow"—becomes inert. Levi must stop intoning Dante to hear the *soup du jour* announced: "*Kraut und Rüben? Kraut und Rüben*": cabbage and turnips, cabbage and turnips (115).

The repetition of that banal German phrase means more than it says. Its singsong overtakes the text and the reader as if from behind their backs. *Kraut und Rüben* is the refrain of an old German folk song in which the speaker complains that if his mother had been a better cook he would have stayed home longer. The journey for nourishment of mind and spirit as well as of body is thus grafted onto the text in the form of its ironic negation. (*Grafted* is a borrowed word; the source will come soon.) But this old folk song carries another sound as well. It is one of two such songs on which J. S. Bach based the last of his *Goldberg Variations*. The other, suggestively, is a call for someone to come back after a long absence: *Ich bin so lang bei dir gewest. / Ruck her, ruck her, ruck her* (I've been apart from you so long. C'mon back, c'mon back, c'mon back). The variation has nothing like the gravity of Levi's thwarted canto, but it is an anticlimax, with a touch of plaintiveness. Celebrated for their combination of formal rigor and expressive force, the thirty variations—the stuff of another long voyage—find that what awaits them at their destination is lost companionship and bad soup.

Levi may or may not have known this, or known or remembered it consciously, but he certainly knew Paul Celan's poem "Death Fugue," which, he said, "I carry inside me like a graft."[3] "Death Fugue," too, is a text about bad maternal nourishment, superlatively bad, nourishment turned to poison:

> Black milk of daybreak we drink it at nightfall
> we drink it at noon in the morning we drink it at night
> we drink it and drink it[4]

The poem also merges the bad mother whose breasts yield black milk with the bad father, Death, who is her spouse: "He shouts play sweeter death's music death comes as a master from Germany." The metaphor of the fugue and the hinge between death's music and the coming of a master from Germany declares all but explicitly that the master is in part a travesty of Bach. The poem turns its rage against this iconic figure to suggest that the aesthetic of pure order familiarly credited to the Bach fugue may become, all too easily, an aesthetic of pure death. The mentality that reveres the one may find itself devoted to the other. The result for the victims is to be delivered over to a mechanism of annihilation that resembles a fatal music.[5]

Celan's verbal fugue systematically inverts the quest for knowledge and excellence that Levi's auditory memory, the sound of Dante's Italian words, tries to uphold. The same inversion echoes in Levi's text in the German singsong, *"Kraut und Rüben, Kraut und Rüben."* No less than Celan's, Levi's text is one that cannot be read silently. It can be read at all only in the thrumming space of the half-heard. But the reader of either text will find that space invaded, contaminated, turned sour, like black milk.

Intermezzo

What, then, does it mean to listen, in the sense borne by the phrase "really listen"? For one thing it means to understand that the auditory exceeds the acoustic. We continue to hear beyond the ear. What sounds also resounds: re-sounds in new media. To listen is to participate in this resonance. To participate makes possible a relay that extends the resonance further. To listen, really listen, thus also means to understand there is resonance everywhere, and that without resonance there is no knowledge. Knowledge is intoned. There is a music inherent to it that must be heard if the knowledge is to thrive: to come to life. Its resonance is not an adjunct but a necessity. This is the resonance we discern when we listen to the continuous passage of sound from the acoustic to the auditory, from sound received to sound apprehended. It is this passage that at times we can apprehend in its own right as a vibrancy, the hum of the world, the audiable.

This auditory plenitude is what makes life a matter of sense. "Sense" in two senses that cannot be divided: what one feels and what one understands, or, more exactly, what one feels in understanding and what one understands in feeling. Music is one exemplary realization of this reciprocity, but there is also another. I have said it here before in various ways, but the point cannot be overstated. To apprehend sense in its vibrancy requires that the auditory pass through language. For human beings, the destiny of sound is speech, be it heard or half-heard.

But this destiny is not the end—not the terminus, not the aim. The role of language is not conclusion but continuation. Language makes good on the futurity latent in all sound. In its full auditory dimension, heard and half-heard, intoned, accented, voiced, rhythmically impelled, language well used gives back in new forms what it receives from the heard world. To listen, really listen, thus also means to make our saying responsible to our hearing, so that utterance may hope both to crystallize for a moment the resonance of sense and to foster receptivity to everything that language itself shows it cannot convey.

Sounding Bodies

Does the history of modern listening begin with the noise of industrialized cities? With the sounds of the railways? With the invention of the phonograph? Or does it begin with something less obviously transformational—say the invention of the stethoscope?

This now iconic device was invented in 1816 by the French physician René Laennec, who was seeking a substitute for the diagnostic practice of "immediate auscultation," that is, the application of the physician's ear to a patient's chest. The stethoscope made possible what Laennec called "mediate auscultation" by introducing a technological device, a prosthetic ear canal, between doctor and patient. The instrument thus engendered, perhaps for the first time, what we now recognize as a cyborg, though only for as long as the diagnostic session lasted.

Laennec's account of his *eureka!* moment is famous:

> In 1816, I was consulted by a young woman presenting general symptoms of a heart disease, and with whom percussion and the application of the hand gave minimal results because of [her] corpulence. The age and sex of the patient making [immediate auscultation] inadmissible, I happened to recall a well-known acoustic phenomenon: if one applies the ear to one end of a beam, one hears very distinctly the stroke of a pin made at the other end. I imagined that in this case one might be able to take advantage of this property of bodies. I took a quire of paper [four sheets folded into eight leaves], I rolled it into a tight cylinder and applied one end to the pericardial region, and, placing my ear at the other end, I was equally surprised and pleased to

hear the beating of the heart much more finely and distinctly than I ever could by the immediate application of the ear.

Thenceforth I presumed that this device might furnish a useful method, and one applicable not only to heartbeats but also to all the movements that can produce sounds within the chest cavity, and consequently to the exploration of respiration, the voice, the rattle, and perhaps even the fluctuation of liquid spilled within the pleura or pericardium.[1]

The stethoscope plays a pivotal role in Michel Foucault's study *The Birth of the Clinic*, which traces the eighteenth-century development of medical knowledge based on the examination of particular living bodies rather than on a generic human image. For Foucault, the clinic links perception to rationality for the first time. The primary source of this link is, unsurprisingly, visual; the stethoscope, arriving at a relatively late date, merely allows auditory perception to add itself as a supplement, a role in which it is joined by touch wherever touch is "admissible." The result is a triangle with a very clear apex:

One must not lose sight of the essential. The tactile and auditory dimensions were not simply added to the domain of vision. The sensorial triangulation indispensable to anatomo-clinical perception remains under the dominant sign of the visual: first, because this multi-sensorial perception is nothing but a way of anticipating that triumph of the gaze that is represented by the autopsy; the hand and the ear are nothing but temporary, substitute organs until such time as death brings to truth the luminous presence of the visible.[2]

Laennec would not have agreed, and neither, in the end, did Foucault himself. As Lauri Siisiäinen has observed, Laennec's treatise on mediate auscultation grants privileged knowledge of the dead body to vision but reserves equivalent knowledge of the living body for hearing.[3] Only auditory knowledge is true to life, the presence of which is more sonorous than luminous. Foucault would never go that far, but a few years after writing *The Birth of the Clinic* he published an essay, "Message or Noise," which suggests that the health or sickness of the living body announces itself primarily by making noise. As Siisiäinen notes, this noise is purely corporeal; for Foucault, clinical knowledge is concerned only with the individual body, not with the person or subject.[4] But Foucault says perhaps more than he knows when he posits that clinical knowledge should start with the living body's "primordial noise," which he glosses as "the non-silence of the organs." Take an imaginary stethoscope to the hyphenated compound, and the sound that comes forth is worth heeding. To be alive, the organs must be non-silent; they must therefore harbor the potentiality of resonance independent of any actual resonance. The hyphen holds the place of that potentiality; the organs resound from the place of the audible.

Laennec would say they speak. His treatise consistently represents the body as a speaker, no less a speaking subject than the person for whom it speaks. His clinical vocabulary—*pectoriloquism, bronchophonism, egophonism*—testifies to the volubility of the living body. The stethoscope gives a language to the noises dimly perceived through immediate auscultation. It enables the body's utterances not only to be heard but also to be recorded. Laennec specifies that the stethoscope is to be held "in the manner of a pen"; the physician who wields it becomes the amanuensis of the patient's speaking body. But the auditory pen transcribes only what it has itself made audible. The instrument allows, or shall we say that it coaxes, the body to speak in the body's own voice, which is not the speaking voice. (The speaking voice assumes new guises when heard from the listening post of the chest cavity.) In using the stethoscope the physician becomes not only a stenographer but also a kind of ventriloquist through whom the body's secrets are revealed. The diagnostician acts "in the manner" of the oracles of ancient Greece, whose prophecies were delivered by a kind of ventriloquism, literally "belly speaking."

The form of hearing enabled by the stethoscope, which prefigures the close attention that would soon be demanded for music, aligns itself not only with rationality and observation, as Foucault maintains, but also with a degree of sensory discrimination that rivals that of vision, as both Siisiäinen and Jonathan Sterne observe. This fine discrimination must be mediated in more than one way. It begins with the device, but, as Laennec's metaphor of the pen suggests, it does not end there. The fine discrimination can be made manifest only in language. It requires both the quasi-language of the body that speaks through the stethoscope and the descriptive language of the physician who, as writer, employs a vocabulary rich in auditory terms and free with metaphor. Contrary to Siisiäinen, this reliance on metaphor is not an eccentricity in Laennec's scientific discourse, but a necessity. It is not a lapse. Laennec makes the point himself: "Simple sensations cannot be depicted except by comparisons, and although those that I use may seem very just to me, one should not expect a perfect similitude. I hope nonetheless that the description I will give of these sounds (*bruits*) will suffice for each of them to be recognized by a moderately attentive observer, because they are much less difficult to distinguish than to describe" (44).

Here as elsewhere (that is, everywhere), metaphor acts not to designate but to orient, and at the same time to remain open to further metaphor. Laennec makes good on his point immediately. Here he is comparing two of the five kinds of rattle in the chest: "Most of the time [the mucous rattle] offers the image of bubbles analogous to those one makes in blowing through a pipe or reed (*chalumeau*) in soapy water. . . . [Whereas with] the crepitous rattle . . . it seems as if a multitude of tiny bubbles of the same size emerge all at once and quiver rather than boil on the surface of a liquid" (45).

Laennec never hesitates to elaborate his comparisons in detail. A little earlier, he describes egophonism (egophony; excess vocal resonance heard during auscultation) as "a particular resonance of the voice that accompanies or follows the articulation of words: it seems a voice more sharp, more shrill, than the patient's, and silvery in some way, trembling on the surface of the lungs; it appears more as an echo of the patient's voice than the voice itself" (33). Not content with that, Laennec adds that this secondary voice has a constant character from which he derives its name: "It is trembling and bleating like the voice of a goat, and its timbre also approaches the voice of the same animal" (ibid.; αἴξ, aix, is the classical Greek word for a goat). The silvery bleating, moreover, is as much surmised as it is heard; "it rarely enters the tube and almost never traverses it fully" (ibid.). The ear and the instrument have to coax it into audibility.

This kind of mediated listening, such as one might also bring to music, integrated auditory perception not only with rationality but also with the full spectrum of experience and enunciation. Sound thus becomes, in this sector of history, the sensory medium in which the interior of the body becomes directly knowable, beyond mere repercussion, much as the exterior becomes fully exposed to the clinical gaze. Focused listening accomplishes this penetration not by eliminating noise, but by sensing polyphony as an intrinsic element of sound and auditory knowledge—not just bubbles, but a chorus of bubbles in reciprocal vibration, and as if blown through a kind of impromptu wind instrument.

This polyphony, both within and between metaphorically mediated perceptions, can, if we let it, diffuse itself through the visibility of the world as well as the invisibility (or former invisibility; technology has since intervened) of the body cavity. Such auditory perception potentially resonates beyond the clinic, with multiple consequences. For Sterne, it is exemplary in producing an individual auditory space around the listener and thus in preparing the way for listening to become a commodity.[5] But, more agreeably, such listening integrates not only vision but also the touch that Laennec wishes to replace by it. Directed listening, explicitly mediated listening, is virtually prehensile, as Laennec's footnote suggests. It grasps its objects and distributes them in polyphonic space while exercising the power of what Ernst Mach, later in the nineteenth century, would identify as the "accommodation phenomenon" in listening: the use of auditory attention to bring out certain strains in the mesh of sounds,[6] much as a listener, scarcely less than a performer, "brings out" certain contrapuntal lines in music, most often changeably, as the music takes its course.

Pandemonium?

But some sounds cannot be accommodated. Noise does not simply bother us; at its worst it seems to pursue us, which is why we are so acutely vulnerable to it. We can even hear it in our sleep. Unwanted sound feels like an attack; it strikes like blows. Screams pierce, cries shatter, blasts deafen. When sound intensifies to a high level of violence, as it did for Chamberlain at Fredericksburg, for Owen and Remarque on the Western Front, and even for Britten in the *War Requiem* (pp. 189–94), it strips away the listener's defenses and drums in an especially keen feeling of helplessness. I would like to say that such violence drowns out the audiable. It replaces the hum of the world with a roar. It exchanges the promise of the expressive for the threat of the unbearable. But I would also like to say that this is a violence directed against sound itself.

Pascal Quignard, in his *The Hatred of Music*, indicts sound for its power to pass through walls—and bodies: "What is heard knows neither eyelids, nor partitions, neither curtains, nor walls. . . . Sound rushes in. It violates."[1] Not to put too fine a point on it, but this is nonsense. It is like saying that touch is treachery because it is the medium of pain. That sound can be abused does not mean that sound is abusive. The senses go wrong when we do.

The power of sound over solids takes innumerable forms, from diffusion to penetration, from ethereal caresses to savage blows. In a famous passage from *Song of Myself*, Walt Whitman thinks about collecting and incorporating as many auditory inroads as he can:

I think I will do nothing for a long time but listen,
And accrue what I hear into myself. . . . and let sounds contribute toward me.

I hear the bravuras of birds. . . . the bustle of growing wheat. . . . gossip of flames. . . . clack of sticks cooking my meals.

I hear the sound of the human voice. . . . a sound I love,
I hear all sounds as they are tuned to their uses. . . .
    (1855, ll. 584–88)[2]

The self accumulates as a polyphony without end as the listener takes in each sound and transforms it. Natural sounds become music and talk (bravura of birds, gossip of flames); the cosmos of sound is tuned by use to form an everyday version of the harmony of the spheres. (A later line alludes to that ancient figure in the "orbic flex" of a tenor's mouth.) Whitman does not shy away from acoustic violence ("The ring of alarm bells . . . the cry of fire"; l. 593). The climax of the passage describes being sexually penetrated by music. The tenor's song is a pouring and filling; the soprano's "convulses me like the climax of my love-grip." The explosive orgasm that follows is both agonizing and ecstatic:

I am exposed. . . . cut by bitter and poisoned hail,
Steeped amid honeyed morphine. . . . my windpipe squeezed in the fakes of death,

Let up again to feel the puzzle of puzzles,
And that we call Being. (1855, ll. 607–10)

The "fakes" that throttle the listener are coils of nautical rope. To be overwhelmed by music is to be rendered speechless and therefore annihilated, only to be released and resurrected with the power of speech restored: hence these verses. Speechlessness is retuned as eloquence. The listener learns to sing by suffering song.

This release brings an unexpected gift in its wake. It sets the listener free for a direct encounter with the mystery of sentience (the subject of the following section) and with Being itself. The moment completes a gradual transformation in which hearing and feeling, always mingled, reverse priority. The music over, its mysterious remainder registers the mysteries as feeling. In other words, mine, not Whitman's, the moment reverberates, and in the reverberation, Being becomes the audiable.

Songs of Entropy

The first mechanical recordings of the human voice are well over a century old. The passage of time has lent them a spectral aura, not only because so many years have gone by, but also, perhaps more so, because the audibility of the recording mechanism is so much a part of their sound. The signal-to-noise ratio, enhanced by decay, is too nearly even, so that the sound of the apparatus becomes an expression of the voices' remoteness in time. The noise assumes aesthetic resonance. These recordings come to us less as harbingers of a world in which, at long last, the voice is no longer ephemeral, than as relics of a world in which the ephemerality of voice was inherent in voice itself. Recorded voices were the exceptions that proved the rule before they became the rule. The predestined erasure of voice was audibly present in the very recordings that promised to prevent it. That recordings allow the dead to speak is no longer remarkable. But in listening to words uttered in the 1880s, or '70s, or '60s, we are still hearing death doing the talking.

Or the singing. The earliest known recordings of a human voice preserve both speech and song, with pride of place going to song. In the first one of all, made in Paris in April 1860, the inventor, Edouard-Leon Scott de Martinville, sings a phrase from the folk song "Au clair de la lune." But there's a catch: these recordings were inaudible by design. It has only become possible to hear them thanks to present-day technology. Martinville's recording device, the phonautograph, was meant to produce a visual, not an auditory, record of sound. The machine, as its name announces, would permit sound to write itself down. The writing would be readable and therefore reproducible in the manner of a musical score, but of a score recalling an actual performance rather than projecting a potential one. The result, Martinville wrote, would be "an imperishable trace of those fugitive melodies which the memory no longer finds when it seeks them."[1]

Oblivion will have met its match. The snippet that Martinville sings says as much. The first verse of the folk songs begins: "Au clair de la lune, / Mon ami Pierrot, / Prête-moi ta plume / Pour écrire un mot" (By the light of the moon, / My friend Pierrot, / Lend me your pen / To write a word." Martinville has just enough time to reach "Prête-moi," but the allusion is clear: the phonautograph will supply the pen, which the sad clown Pierrot, in the next stanza, proves unwilling or unable to do.[2] The subtext of the song suggests that the lovelorn Pierrot lacks more than just a pen. The inventor's device will supply what is missing; it will allow his voice to inseminate sound.

The earliest known recording of singing voices that allowed for audio playback is an Edison cylinder of an extract from "Moses and the Children of Israel," a section of Handel's oratorio *Israel in Egypt*. The recording was made on June 29, 1888, at London's Crystal Palace. The voices numbered four thousand, backed by a five-hundred-piece orchestra performing for more than twenty-three thousand spectators. The number of singers is astounding today, but voices in the thousands were a normal feature of Victorian Handel festivals.[3] The grandiosity of the ensemble finds its musical expression in the tempo of the performance, which is much slower than the twenty-first-century norm. These festivals were regarded as religious occasions, and the recording offers proof, if any were needed, that the Victorians liked them solemn.

The cylinder is badly degraded. Most of the time the music barely floats over the noise of the recording. Here and there the voices become more distinct before sinking back toward the threshold of audibility and, in one passage near the end, sinking below it as the noise blots them out. The decay affects the quality of the sound as well as its clarity. Only the higher voices are generally audible; there are a few scattered traces of the lower voices; the orchestra goes unheard. The recording is less compelling for what it preserves than for what its poor condition could not destroy. Listening to what remains gives a pleasure and a knowledge of its own.

What pleasure and what knowledge may be clarified by an analogy to watching a film on decaying celluloid stock. Bill Morrison's film *Decasia: The State of Decay* (completed 2002) makes an aesthetic of that apparently anti-aesthetic experience. The film is an extended collage of damaged footage from silent films; the blots, blotches, and erasures, carefully preserved, become part of the images they supposedly degrade. Morrison frames the film with a shot of a whirling dervish, whose motion becomes a self-reflective image of cinematic projection in the celluloid era. The dancer, Morrison says, "is the projector, the feed reel holding the future and the take up reel spooling up the past."[4] True to historical practice, the dance goes along with music, but the soundtrack, by Michael Gordon, is, of necessity, so detached from the imagery that the film at times reproduces the effect of uncanny separation of seeing and hearing that Mahler made audible in the Scherzo of his Second Symphony (p. 126). Morrison's expressive aim, however, was exactly the contrary of Mahler's. "I chose . . . shots," he explains, "that fit my narrative and also looked strikingly beautiful. I was interested in images that interacted with the decay, so that figure and ground were always interrelated. . . . I wanted people to feel an aching sense that time was passing and that it was too beautiful to hold on to."[5]

The 1888 Handel recording inadvertently works to the same end. Like the counterparts in the images of *Decasia*, the sonorous blotches on the voices are not merely cancellations, nor are the vocal sounds that remain merely attenuation. Their combination, the counterpart of signal and noise, has a positive form. What we hear on this recording is less a reduced form of the music and the voices than it is the full form of the music and the voices in the act of their disappearance. As the music and singing flicker in and out of discernibility, as the thin, lightly shrill sound of the higher voices persists through the auditory mist, what we hear is the lingering and the persistence. The recording discloses—half discloses, half imparts—the impetus in the sound to go on resonating. In this sound from the otherwise inaudible past, the recording detects sound seeking a future for itself. The recording is a rare one indeed. It is not just a recording of lost and winnowed voices. It is a recording of the audiable.

By Hand

In 1897, Henry James discovered that his writing hand had, as he put it later, "gone smash." He accordingly bought a Remington typewriter, hired an amanuensis, and began dictating both his correspondence and his fiction. Shorthand was not involved; James's words were typed as he spoke them. But he was not happy about this expedient, as he explained in an apologetic letter to his friend Morton Fullerman:

> 25th February 1897
> Forgive a communication, very shabby and superficial. It has come to this that I can address you only through an embroidered veil of sound. The sound is that of the admirable and expensive machine that I have just purchased for the purpose of bridging our silences. The hand that works it, however, is not the lame patte which, after inflicting on you for years its aberrations, I have now definitely relegated to the shelf, or at least to the hospital—that is to permanent, bandaged, baffled, rheumatic, incompetent obscurity.[1]

James presumably knows that the apparatus of pen, ink, and paper is just that, an apparatus, but his knowledge is conceptual, not sensory. It is also inactive, not acknowledged in what he writes, nor in what he dictates. The novelty of the typewriting machine obscures the perception that the older equipment is no less mechanical. The older technology has long since become second nature; the new technology is a surrogate, an artifice. James feels that writing by hand, or so he says in writing, is an act of direct communication. So too is its reception by the reader of the written hand. The bond thus created may even outdo anything available from face-to-face conversation—always, for James, a medium of indirection and deception. Handwritten messages are a kind of refuge from insincerity. James treats inscription by hand as the ideal form of writing. It is presumably the source of authenticity of works in print. James trusts his handwriting without a second thought to convey his thought directly.

Directly—and silently. Writing is as soundless as the thought it imparts. Read in silence it transfers thought from mind to mind. But again, there is a sensory knowledge that says otherwise. There is no silence in either writing, with the scratch of the pen, the rustle of paper, or reading, with the unfolding and turning of pages, and even, in both, in the quietest of spaces, the subtle sound of respiration that moves in time with the words. Writing keeps mum on a cushion of sound. It too needs the audiable.

Writing as James felt it was a way to bypass voice, with voice understood as more mediation than expression. Dictating to a typewriter (person and machine alike, in James's day) is awkward, embarrassing, like a bodily indiscretion, because it doubles the mediation of voice with the mediation of noise, the clatter of the machine, which somehow echoes off the typewritten page. On the same day he wrote to Fullerton, James also wrote to James McNeill Whistler that it must be "an outrage to a man with your touch to address him in accents condemned to click into his ear—thanks to interposing machinery—a positive negation of every delicacy." The irrepressible clicking weaves the embroidered veil of sound: the hand of the sender discerned but not touched, because the veil, as veils do, gets in the way. The image of embroidery adds a second veil atop the first: the embroidery, like the clarity of the typewritten page, is perhaps beautiful in its own way, but merely decorative at worst, merely distinct at best ("May its distinctness make up for its indirectness!" James wrote to another correspondent). The embroidery keeps the reader from noticing that its very perfection obscures the idiosyncrasy of the hand—the character of the written characters. But James will not allow the loss of the hand (both the personal calligraphy and the body part) to be forgotten, and so, in that first letter to Fullerton, he issues a self-rebuke in the image of his hand as a "lame patte"—a worn-out strap for fastening the halves of a coat.

Past and Present

Friedrich Kittler dates the modern revolution in media technology to the invention of cinema and sound recording, which for the first time were capable of capturing the movement of time.[1] Only these continuous media could record and thus preserve the elapsing of a real event, and by that means extend the past into the indefinite present. This possibility changed the very nature of the past. It gave the past a sensuously apprehensible form, the very thing that, by its lack, had defined the past as past. Previous recording media, including writing, drawing, and painting, were incapable of animating the information they preserved. They made the past comprehensible but not apprehensible. Continuous media could, on the contrary, make the irretrievable retrievable.

But that they could does not mean that they must, or that they did. Documentary sound and video recording quickly gave way to edited forms, most obviously in cinema but also in the phonograph recordings built of many takes much as films were built of many shots. The audible and visible events recorded in continuous media are for the most part fictitious. They never actually happened, though bits and pieces of them did. The result is a paradox, and an essential one, not subject to solution or rationalization. Continuous media retrieve the past, not as it was, but as it might have been. That, rather than documentary fidelity, is the norm; the fidelity is the exception and its own kind of fiction. But although the past made perceptible by continuous media is a fiction, the perception of it is real. Continuous media realize an inherent possibility in the relationship of past and present, a possibility gestured at imperfectly by earlier recording media such as playtexts and musical scores. We can neither see nor hear the past, but we can both see and hear its presence.

Of the two, hearing is the more fraught. Continuous media need sound, as their history attests: recorded sound has historically flourished independent of visual association, whereas recorded motion was no sooner invented than it began searching for an auditory wrapping. One reason why may be the persistence in vision of material forms that do not seem to change. Vision is the receptacle in which the present expands beyond the instant. Events unfold before the eyes against a background of objects and places that elapse far more slowly than the events, anchors of stability that form the sensory link between past, present, and future. To put it crudely: my crossing of the street elapses in a matter of seconds, but the street persists for years, decades, even centuries, its own elapsing rendered invisible by its rate of change. When changes do occur perceptibly in this slower time stream, they are likely to be felt as disconcerting or traumatic, as Baudelaire observes in his poem "The Swan":

> Old Paris is no more (a city's form, alas!
> Changes more quickly than a mortal's heart).
>
> I see in spirit alone this camp of barracks,
> These piles of barrels and squared capitals,
> The grass, the big rocks greened by puddled water,
> And, shining in the panes, mixed bric-a-brac.[2]

Sounds, on the other hand, elapse once and for all. Once heard, they are abolished. Unlike landscapes, soundscapes are continuously destroyed in the act of being created. The capacity to record sound, to arrest its disappearance and assure its reappearance on demand, changes the nature of transience. It is not only that, as the earliest uses of phonographs attested, sound recording allows the dead to speak, but also that the past in general becomes what Henry James (on the threshold of the real possibility) called visitable. The past acquires a virtual life through, so to speak, the hearing aid of continuous media.

One way to understand the audiable is as the immanent possibility of that virtual life. The audiable has perhaps the slowest time scale of all, which is why perhaps it is more easily or at least more often imagined than heard. Because it is auditory, it belongs to passing time, but it does not seem to pass. It is always intercepted, never bounded. It cannot be recorded on its own, but it does not need to be. The audiable may even be the sensory form of elapsing itself.

Consciousness

I. ALTERNATIVES OF SENTIENCE: THE ZONE

Modern thinkers looking for a plane of transcendence within the world rather than beyond it, whether they believe in the latter or not, have sometimes posited a form of experience that is intelligible but not conscious. This "contemplation without cognizance," as Gilles Deleuze calls it, resembles N. Katherine Hayles's "cognitive non-consciousness" (p. 77) but it bears more ontological weight.[1] Deleuze intimates that weight with the term "contemplation," which normally applies only to conscious awareness, and higher awareness at that. Everything about this state is strange. It can be lived but not known, yet we cannot live it without knowing it from afar in our descriptions. For Deleuze it occurs in two quite different venues, sensation and habitual action. In sensing without willing and acting without thinking, we inhabit (I'm not sure one can say "feel") a sense of sheer being. Giorgio Agamben elaborates on this idea by dwelling, so to speak, on sheer sheerness: "The zone of non-consciousness . . . is not something like a mystical fog . . . but the habitual dwelling in which the living being . . . is perfectly at ease." But this is an ease that has work to do: precisely the work of separating awareness from consciousness. It requires "the quiet cancellation of every attribute and every property: *vivere sine proprio* [to live without the 'own']."[2]

What sensory form does this non-conscious sense of being take? The language used by Deleuze and Agamben is visual ("contemplation," "not something like a mystical fog"), but in the zone they seek there is no need for looking. And because what happens in this zone involves the cancellation of every positive attribute, the happening does not separate itself into discrete events and the experience cannot be inventoried or sorted into categories. So if we really do have access to some such zone, how do we sense it?

To answer, we might think about which sensory forms can be cancelled while still leaving the living being at perfect ease. Vision is the first to go. We close our eyes and remain at ease for a multitude of reasons. Touch goes next. One can be at ease without active touching and without registering passive touch. Proprioception—the sense of position—goes in turn. A feeling of floating freely may be perfectly easeful. But sound remains. It remains inclusive of what we call silence. The cancellation of sound draws the living being out of the zone of living. It yields perfect unease. The sensory form of what we might call affirmative non-consciousness is hearing, and in particular the hearing of sound as continuation, sound to come, to keep coming.

At least two conclusions follow. The first is that such records as we have of living without the "own" need to be understood in auditory terms, however else we may come to understand them. Henry James meets that need when, in *The Wings of the Dove* (discussed above, pp. 69–70), he has one character grasp another's vulnerable being as "like something sentient and throbbing, something that, for the spiritual ear, might have been audible as a faint, far wail." But the book in your hands is full of examples.

The second conclusion is that non-conscious awareness is not what Agamben would have it be. It is not something severed from conscious life. The omnipresence of sound, building itself up in waves and layers from the audiable, forms a discernible, material link between the conscious and non-conscious sentience of the living being. This does not mean that the products of this link are easy to locate, describe, or evoke—again, this book is full of examples. But it does mean that there is no impermeable barrier separating meaning from being. The sound of each carries, and carries us, between them.

II. ALTERNATIVES OF SENTIENCE: THE BREAK

But consciousness can no longer rest secure, if it ever could. The digital era has fostered an epochal change in the way we process knowledge. Priority has shifted increasingly from close attention (absorbed, prolonged, text-based) to diffuse attention (detached, fleeting, screen-based). In *Interpreting Music*, I proposed that classical music—the music I care about, write about, and compose—could provide a home for close attention in a diffuse world, an occasion for absorption and reflection in a regime of dispersion and intuition. This extension of the music's traditional role as an artwork would primarily be a function of live performance, with all the openness and uncertainty that go with it: the elements of music that recording cannot preserve.

Nearing the end of my text, I will take the liberty of giving conjecture a free hand and going much further. I want to entertain the thought that consciousness itself is a function of the possibility of close attention. The mode of sentience associated with diffuse attention is accordingly not consciousness at all but something else, a post-consciousness for which as yet no name has been found. Consciousness remains an immanent property of the human, but the human turns out to be a historical condition—not in the familiar sense that human life is historical by definition, but in the much stronger sense that the human is a bounded and transient condition within the history of the species.

Music of any kind might seem to play a small role against such a cosmic background, but since virtually all human cultures have some form of music, its role might be larger than first appears. It is at least worth asking what its place has been and may be within this frame of reference. The question, it turns out, also concerns the character of auditory knowledge and the relationship of awareness to the audiable.

III. THE POSTHUMAN

N. Katherine Hayles has linked the shift in priority from "deep" to "hyper" attention, as she terms them, to a larger shift away from consciousness as a central point of reference for human knowledge.[3] The higher-order shift belongs to the emergence of a so-called posthuman condition marked by the accelerated naturalization of machine-human interfaces, by the digital storage and display of information, and by a preference for randomness over pattern.

But Hayles's version of an alternative to consciousness is very different from the one I have in mind. She draws on cognitive-science models that hypothesize consciousness as an epiphenomenon supporting the illusion of control and choice in order to rationalize unconsciously determined actions decided prior to any consciousness. As recent advocates of this model make a point of not knowing or acknowledging, its basic contours were established somewhat less crudely by Nietzsche and Freud, in their different ways, a long time ago. Neither would have made the mistake of concluding that brain activity preceding conscious awareness by a half second or so indicates simple unconscious determination, as if one had never been conscious *before*. (Furthermore, as Ruth Leys has shown, the evidence for this notorious half second is more than a little equivocal.[4]) Whatever its origin or status, consciousness cannot be dismissed once it has been formed, any more than its unconscious counterparts can be. But there may be situations in which consciousness, and the sense of self that goes with it, is not formed at all.

Likewise the claim that modern thought has destroyed "the illusion of a bounded, impenetrable, and autonomous ego" is anything but new;

indeed, the wording I have just used was framed by a French psychologist, Alfred Fouillée, in 1891. But Fouillée had been preceded in 1886 by Ernst Mach, whose *The Analysis of Sensation* reduces the "I" to an "unsaveable" (*unrettbar*) fiction whose only justification is its occasional practical usefulness.[5] Consciousness and the ego probably started falling apart on the day they were first recognized, which, needless to say, has not kept them from having a long and eventful career. What I am seeking to describe here is not a diminution in the role or credibility of consciousness but an emergent post-conscious formation of sentience. This posthuman sentience inevitably brings with it ways of being in the world that differ dramatically from those that familiarly still structure our experience, or at least our language about it.

IV. SEVEN THESES ON CONSCIOUSNESS TODAY

1. The essential ingredient of consciousness is continuity. If diffuse attention disperses continuity to the point where it is neither available nor missed—and better, if the loss is not even observed—then what emerges is a new form of knowing that is *not* given in consciousness but in some alternative to it. *Consciousness* has always seemed to be an absolute term; the suggestion here is that it is becoming, even has already become, a conditional one.

2. Along with this dispersion of consciousness goes the dispersion of the self both in the traditional sense of an integrated, defined personality projected into both past and future *and* in the modernist-postmodernist sense of a decentered construction disseminated through a tangled chain of signifiers. The new self is vacant but not void, null without being opaque. It is a functional node or locus for a mass of inconsistent, competing energies or percepts, a realization of David Hume's eighteenth-century reduction of subjectivity to "nothing but a bundle or collection of different perceptions, which succeed each other with an inconceivable rapidity, and are in a perpetual flux and movement."[6] One cannot even speak of "images" here since the nature of an image is to connect, remind, and integrate. The post-conscious self becomes entirely empirical, without foundation in anything but the immediate present.

3. This subjective dispersion of the self, among those not born into its regime and perhaps even for many of those who are, does not cancel out

the need for the sense of self, illusory as it may be. Perhaps because our bodies are bounded and linear—and mortal—whether we like it or not, no matter how powerful their technological prostheses may become; perhaps because, historically speaking, historical forms of subjectivity tend to persist, after they disappear, as imaginative or imaginary rather than everyday forms; perhaps because we have simply not yet discovered a way to "have" or live experience without attaching it to a recipient—whatever the reasons, the fiction of an "I" has not proven expendable. But getting the fiction right is notoriously difficult. The need for a substantial, not a merely grammatical, "I" is often filled, as contemporary events show all too clearly, by drastically simplified ideologies, fundamentalisms of all sorts that only begin with the religious variety and may reproduce the latter's reductionism while firmly convinced they are doing something else. The defining characteristic of these –isms is that they are rigidly univalent. They contain no questions, only answers; they cannot problematize; they do not serve, challenge, or interact with the self but substitute for it; they enforce a uniformity of thought and conduct that is taken as an embodiment of truth. Those who share in these systems attain a deceptive sense of community; in the meantime, an empty exchange of signifiers replaces genuine social bonding. This overspecified mode of cognition is the destructive form of post-conscious cognition.

4. The traditional structures of meaning and selfhood associated with close attention become inaccessible when the mode shifts to diffuse attention, at least as long as the new mode is switched on. The three-dimensional tangles of thought and feeling contract to the tracery of a one-dimensional grid, a pure surface without limit. Interpretation fades into noticing and tabulating; succession and superimposition, no longer distinguished from each other, take the place of connection and antagonism. The symptomatic becomes the purely phenomenal.

5. Under this dispensation the affective pattern of intensification and cathartic release becomes impossible because it depends on meaningful tensions disclosed by close attention. For a vacant subject who does not experience relationships of transferred meaning—the province of metaphor and the cognate modes of displacement, substitution, surrogacy, reconfiguration, and so on, which are the fundamentals of knowledge under conditions of close attention—there is no source from which

meaning can proceed to irradiate experience. Whatever happens is always unsatisfying, but not in the sense of the Romantic prolongation of desire; one simply takes satisfaction in the rewards of the moment because there is nothing else and, therefore, no point in desiring anything else.

6. The character of experience thus undergoes a fundamental change. Instead of an organized if ever-changing body of meanings, there is only an anarchic plurality of events. Because the event is regarded as purely ephemeral and disposable, without any remainder, the number of events must constantly be replenished and multiplied. The grid has to expand like a late-capitalist economy or its geographical projection, the urban sprawl pushing edge cities ever further away from a center that has long since ceased to be one. At its worst, the replenishment becomes a form of studied emptiness: the sphere of twitter storms, alternative facts, and the willful debasement of language.

7. But the story does not and cannot end simply with a eulogy of close attention and a dystopian characterization of diffuse attention. The latter will not go away; the former will never regain its former preeminence. Not everything about close attention is rewarding and not everything about diffuse attention is troubling. The question that remains is how to address their mutual engagements. Close attention is no longer a norm that structures the vicissitudes of observation and to which all observation must ultimately defer. Instead, close attention is an alternative in continual interaction with diffuse attention. It represents a cluster of values concerning reflection, absorption, and a certain disposition of the body, that many will wish to preserve as those values too encounter new alternatives and the human body becomes less a norm than an alternative in a world of body-machine interfaces.

V. MUSICAL HABITS

To what features of everyday posthuman life does this theoretical scenario correspond?

Part of the answer may be found on your phone or other device, or rather in the business end of its delivery system. The headset of any sort is a portable soundproof room. It banishes ambient sound, silencing the audiable, muffling the background hum of audibility as such that grounds the sense of living being. The headset is thus a primary posthuman interface, although there is no "face" about it. Headsets protect others from the noise of the listener's privacy, but to do so they must shade that privacy into a state of isolation. The effect is almost comically obvious in, say, a crowded commuter train in which the headset links people by wires to their mobile phones. But it does no good to decry this situation overmuch; it has become just another facet of everyday life.

Indeed, the ubiquitous use of earbuds and headsets to transmit recorded sound has normalized a prosthetic effect to the point of second nature. But the music changes accordingly. By emitting music within the dome of the ear, cupping it into the body cavity, headsets abolish all but the most minimal sense of distance between the music and the listener. For popular song that may well represent a sort of ideal. But classical music is meant to be heard at a distance, which corresponds to its wish to be contemplated, not just heard. In a sense it is simply not possible to listen to classical music through a headset, and (as we now realize) it never has been. Something similar is true of mp3 playback through speakers, although in that case the effect of abrogated distance becomes figurative rather than physical. This was not so much of a problem with analog phonographic systems, which had a certain romance about them; even CDs retained some trace of distance by their mere materiality. But when one simply summons music as if out of nowhere, distance dissipates. For classical music to "work," to do the cultural work it was designed for, it must resist the ease of manipulation made so abundantly available by digital technology.

But that is not necessarily bad news. For it opens the possibility of restoring classical music to the place it held at the time of its greatest cultural impact, which was also the time before it could be mechanically reproduced, at least not with any degree of duration or fidelity. The flip side—to borrow a metaphor from an older form of recording technology— to the prosthetic reduction of classical music in digital media is the possibility of its singular, irreproducible enactment, its fulfilled embodiment, in live concert performance. The enactment is distinctive because it is also a *re*enactment of music inscribed as its own potentiality in a detailed score, and because it is addressed to a listening body momentarily detached from machine interfaces. Please silence your cell phones.

VI. CLASSICAL MUSIC AND POST-CONSCIOUS LIFE

So far, so good; but I promised to go farther. What if classical music, which historically was modeled on the vicissitudes of consciousness, especially after the Enlightenment, instead became a model *of* consciousness? What if, as consciousness grows less familiar because we use it less, inhabit it less, the very character of consciousness were to change in relation to the limited forms that preserve it, including this music? What if even the flattening and fragmentation that go with the digital distribution of classical pieces, usually broken *into* pieces—scraps and fragments—were to import into post-conscious sentience an impulse, call it an unconscious impulse, to become conscious?

Could any of this happen? Surely not as an effective social reality; the aesthetic, to which classical music belongs, is always weaker than the society that (in every sense) consumes it. The aesthetic always exaggerates its own importance and cannot do otherwise. But perhaps this singing school of consciousness could happen conjecturally, symptomatically, as part of a conceptual and critical project. The question would then be what such a project would have to offer in the way of knowledge.

VII. APPREHENSION NOW

One way to answer would be to take the shift from close to diffuse attention, together with the felt need to keep both, as carrying with it a historical change in the relationship between sight and sound, looking and listening. The changed relationship would be predicated on a sustained fluctuation between consciousness and post-conscious sentience. Looking would become, as it already has become, the primary medium of diffuse attention, at home in a world dominated increasingly by, indeed coming almost to consist of, images in motion. Listening would enhance its capacity for close attention, and so help limit the progressive attenuation of close attention in a world that needs and discards it in equal measure. These usages are obviously not exclusive; they are tendencies, availabilities, not rules. But it is worth observing, for example, that a news broadcast with multiple split screens, captions, and a crawl still has only one layer of sound except at moments of transition that add background music.

The affinity of vision with diffuse attention begins with the simple fact that vision cannot be fixed for very long. To sustain itself, visual attention needs to slide, to slip without friction across the visual field. Contemplation has a built-in time limit. Virtually no one stares at a painting, for example, for as long as one typically listens to a piece of concert music or absorbs oneself in the virtual voice of a novel. Vision can know things all at once but it has trouble holding on to what it sees. For that very reason, however, vision is quite amenable to diffuse attention. The eye has to move, and with a little practice it can as easily move across multiple fields of vision as it can across one. Vision is inherently spread out on a split screen.

But there is only one soundscape at a time. Sound is inherently polyphonic; its field is a multivoiced counterpoint that constantly expands and never stops. When Thomas Tallis composed his forty-part motet (p. 110), he was making listening audible to itself. Janet Cardiff's installation version (p. 110) extends the reflection to bodies in motion among the disembodied voices in song. As visitors wander among the world-like oval of the speakers, the silences interspersed with the music's own oval orbit let in the faint but transfixing hum of the audible.

Listening is not simply amenable to close attention. It is a *form* of close attention—perhaps *the* form. We see in scenes but we hear in layers. We split the soundscape into melody, countermelody, and accompaniment. If we aim to preserve a space of consciousness, reflection, absorption, and so on in a posthuman world where sentience tends to outpace consciousness, the best means to that end is a new conceptualization and a new cultivation of listening. That should lead in turn to the thought of the audiable and the logics to which we have heard it give rise: of sound as promise, of auditory knowledge, of reflective hearing. Music would certainly have a significant role in this scheme of things, especially classical music, or so I would hope. Melody, with its innate demand for repetition—its "Sing me again! Play me again!"—would provide a model for the transformation of auditory sensation into auditory sense. But the scheme far exceeds any of its media, including the music that occasionally illustrates it. It tells how (*this* time) to intone the sentence with which we began: *The world is alive with sound!*

All right, then: Alive how? Ultimately, the audiable is not only the promise of speech, the promise of voice, but also the promise of sentience.

It is the assurance that the world is there to be sensed, that the presence of the world in the sense and senses of transient creatures such as ourselves is inherent in the world itself and will continue, if not forever, then the next best thing. The knowledge of this promise may be hard to come by. We have to learn to hearken for the audible in all its indirectness. We have to be content with the fleetingness of our access to it. But from another perspective the audible is as common as air. Our knowledge of it does not depend on extraordinary moments or acoustic epiphanies, valuable though those may be. The audible is an everyday affair. Its assurance would not much matter otherwise.

This assurance carries a primary moral as well as a primary ontological force. It is, in its own way, the material form of Kant's categorical imperative in the first of its formulations: "Act only according to that maxim whereby you can at the same time will that it should become a universal law."[7] The audible is nothing if it is not shared. Its universality consists in making audible, however faintly, however briefly, the power of the world to exist in being sensed, known, felt, seen, heard. Like us, says the audible, the world is nothing in itself alone. The world needs voice. It comes to being in a call.

Acknowledgments

Portions of "Music in the Air" were previously published in my "Caliban's Ear: A Short History of Ambient Music," in *Ubiquitous Musics: The Everyday Sounds That We Don't Always Notice*, ed. Anahid Kassabian, Elena Boschi, and Marta Garcia Quiñones (Aldershot: Ashgate, 2013), 15–30. My thanks to the publisher for permission to reprint this material.

Notes

PRELUDE

1. Much of the impetus for these debates has come from Bruno Latour, especially from his book *We Have Never Been Modern,* trans. Catherine Porter (Cambridge, MA: Harvard University Press, 1993). Latour rejects the characteristic modern separation of culture from nature in favor of recognizing a wide variety of phenomena that do not fit easily into either compartment. So far, so good. But he veers too much into hyperbole, polemic, and, at worst, a kind of veiled dogmatism, the latter a tendency also noted by Barbara Herrnstein Smith, "Anthropotheology," *New Literary History* 47 (2016): 331–52 at 343–44.

THE AUDIBLE: AN INTRODUCTION

1. Annie Dillard, *Teaching a Stone to Talk: Expeditions and Encounters, Revised Edition* (New York: Harper Perennial, 2013), 89–90.

SOME LEITMOTIFS

1. *Interpreting Music* (2010), *Expression and Truth: On the Music of Knowledge* (2012), and *The Thought of Music* (2016), all published by University of California Press.

THE STANDARD OF VISION

1. Joseph Conrad, preface to *The Nigger of the "Narcissus,"* www.gutenberg
.org/files/17731/17731-h/17731-h.htm.
2. Aristotle, *Metaphysics*, Book I, Part 1, trans. W. B. Ross, http://classics.mit
.edu/Aristotle/metaphysics.1.i.html.

A PHILOSOPHY OF LISTENING?

1. Alexandra Ivanoff, "'Porgy and Bess' with a White Cast Stirs Controversy,"
New York Times, January 18, 2018, www.nytimes.com/2018/01/30/arts/music
/progy-and-bess-white-cast-budapest.html.
2. Bruno Latour, "Why Has Critique Run Out of Steam," *Critical Inquiry* 30
(2004): 227. The "hard-won evidence" refers to climate change.
3. See Sharon Marcus and Stephen Best, "Surface Reading: An Introduction,"
Representations 108 (2009): 1–21.
4. For a full account, see *Expression and Truth*.

CONSTRUCTIVE DESCRIPTION

1. *Interpreting Music*, 52–60.

SIGHT, SOUND, AND LANGUAGE

1. See in particular Martin Jay, *Downcast Eyes: The Denigration of Vision in
Twentieth-Century French Thought* (Berkeley and London: University of California Press, 1994).
2. Immanuel Kant, *Critique of the Power of Judgment*, ed. Paul Guyer, trans.
Paul Guyer and Eric Matthews (Cambridge and New York: Cambridge University Press, 2000), sec. 53, pp. 203–7.
3. Jonathan Sterne, *The Audible Past: Cultural Origins of Sound Reproduction* (Durham, NC: Duke University Press, 2003), 15–18.
4. G. W. F. Hegel, *Aesthetics: Lectures on Fine Arts*, vol. 1, trans. T. M. Knox
(Oxford: Clarendon Press, 1975), 39.
5. G. W. F. Hegel, *Aesthetics: Lectures on Fine Arts*, vol. 2, trans. T. M. Knox
(Oxford: Clarendon Press, 1975), 622.
6. John P. Cater, *Electronically Speaking: Computer Speech Generation* (Indianapolis: Howard M. Sams, 1983), 72–74.

7. Richard Leppert, *Aesthetic Technologies of Modernity, Subjectivity, and Nature: Opera, Orchestra, Phonograph, Film* (Berkeley and London: University of California Press, 2015), 119. Subsequent references are given in text.

8. Jürgen Habermas, "Modernity—An Incomplete Project," trans. Seyla Ben-Habib, in *The Anti-Aesthetic: Essays on Postmodern Culture*, ed. Hal Foster (New York: New Press, 1983), 3-15.

9. Michel Chion, *Sound: An Acoulogical Treatise*, a translation by James Steintrager of *Le Son: Traite d'acoulogie*, 2nd ed., 2010 (Durham, NC: Duke University Press, 2016).

10. Nina Sun Eidsheim, *Sensing Sound: Singing and Listening as Vibrational Practice* (Durham, NC: Duke University Press, 2015).

SEEING, SAYING, AND HEARING

1. Gilles Deleuze, *Foucault*, ed. and trans. Sean Hand (London and New York: Continuum, 1999), 41-51. The terms refer not to natural properties but to the products of the way that knowledge is organized; Deleuze credits the idea to Foucault.

2. W. J. T. Mitchell, *Picture Theory: Essays on Verbal and Visual Representation* (Chicago: University of Chicago Press, 1994).

THE AUDIABLE: VARIATIONS ON A THEME

1. Wallace Stevens, *"Esthetique du Mal* XV," in *Collected Poems* (New York: Alfred A. Knopf, 1954), 326.

2. Jessica A. Holmes, "Expert Listening beyond the Limits of Hearing: Music and Deafness," *Journal of the American Musicological Society* 70 (2017): 171-220, esp. 175-82.

3. Martin Heidegger, *The Question Concerning Technology and Other Essays*, trans. William Lovitt (New York: Garland, 1977), 136.

4. Emanuel Levinas, *Otherwise than Being or Beyond Essence*, trans. Alphonso Lingis (Dordrecht and Boston: Kluwer Academic, 1991), 45-68 and throughout.

5. Walter Benjamin, "On Language as Such and on the Language of Man," in *Reflections: Essays, Aphorisms, Autobiographical Writings*, ed. Peter Demetz, trans. Edmund Jephcott (New York: Schocken, 1978), 314-22.

6. Timothy Morton, "An Object-Oriented Defense of Poetry," *New Literary History* 43 (2102): 205-24 at 206. Morton's title alludes both to Percy Shelley's 1821 essay "A Defence of Poetry" (which compares the mind to a wind harp) and

to the philosophical movement known as object-oriented ontology originated primarily by Graham Harman.

7. Raymond Williams, *Politics and Letters* (London: New Left Books, 1979), 168.

8. Friedrich Schleiermacher, "The Hermeneutics: Outline of the 1819 Lectures," trans. Jan Wojcik and Roland Haas, *New Literary History* 10 (1978): 1–16.

9. Holmes, "Expert Listening," 191–94.

10. Jane Bennett, *Vibrant Matter: A Political Ecology of Things* (Durham, NC: Duke University Press, 2010), xvi. See also Latour, *Reassembling the Social: An Introduction to Actor-Network Theory* (Oxford: Oxford University Press, 2005), 70–82.

MUSIC IN THE AIR

1. For a brief account, with references to the extensive literature on this subject, see Herve Vanel, "John Cage's Muzak-Plus: The Fu(rni)ture of Music," *Representations* 103 (2008): 94–128, at 96–106 and associated footnotes. For more extensive surveys, see Joseph Lanza, *Elevator Music: A Surreal History of Muzak, Easy-Listening, and Other Moodsong* (New York: St. Martin's Press, 1994) and David Toop, *Ocean of Sound: Aether Talk, Ambient Sound and Imaginary Worlds* (London: Serpent's Tail, 1995). For further interpretation, see Ronald H. Radano, "Interpreting Muzak: Speculations on Musical Experience in Everyday Life," *American Music* 7 (1989): 448–60. On the department store, see Linda L. Tyler, " 'Commerce and Poetry Hand in Hand': Music in American Department Stores, 1880–1930," *Journal of the American Musicological Society* 45 (1992): 75–120.

2. Thomas Hardy, *Far from the Madding Crowd* (New York: New American Library, 1971), 19–20.

3. See Wendell Clausen, *A Commentary on Virgil, Eclogues* (Oxford: Oxford University Press, 1994), 36.

4. Lines 18–19, 21–25. My translation.

5. Text from William Shakespeare: *The Complete Works*, ed. Alfred Harbage et al. (Baltimore: Pelican, 1969). The Folio gives Prospero's speech here to his daughter Miranda, but the attribution is probably (I would say surely) an error or misprint.

6. Percy Bysshe Shelley, "With a Guitar: To Jane," *Shelley's Poetry and Prose*, ed. Donald H. Reiman and Sharon Powers (New York: W. W. Norton, 1977); W. H. Auden, "Caliban to the Audience" from *The Sea and the Mirror*, in Auden, *Collected Poems*, ed. Edward Mendelssohn (New York: Random House, 1991), 422–44.

7. *The Shorter Poems of Robert Browning*, ed. William Clyde Devane (New York: Appleton-Century-Crofts, 1934), 238–44. The text is easily

accessible online. Note that Caliban speaks of himself in the third person; the start of the first quoted line "'Hath'" (for "He hath") thus refers to Caliban himself. The imaginary speaking or singing pipe, cast as a little Caliban, stands to the big Caliban exactly as the big Caliban stands to the imaginary god Setebos.

8. This transformation occurs almost literally in the final scene with the participation of unseen choirs. For more see my "The Talking Wound and the Foolish Question: Symbolization in *Parsifal*," *Opera Quarterly* 22 (2006): 208–29 and David Lewin, "Amfortas's Prayer to Titurel and the Role of D in *Parsifal*: The Tonal Spaces of the Drama and the Enharmonic C-flat / B," *19th-Century Music* 7 (1984): 336–49.

9. James Agee and Walker Evans, *Let Us Now Praise Famous Men* (Boston: Houghton Mifflin, 1969), 467–68.

10. Richard Middleton, *Voicing the Popular: On the Subjects of Popular Music* (New York: Routledge, 2006), 175.

"NO SOUND WITHOUT MUSIC"

1. X.xxxiii.49. My translation from James J. O'Donnell, *The Confessions of Augustine: An Electronic Edition*, http://faculty.georgetown.edu/jod/conf/.

LANGUAGE AND THE HUMAN

1. I.viii.13. My translation.

LORD BACON'S ECHOES

1. Sir Francis Bacon, *The Wisdom of the Ancients, and New Atlantis*, trans. Sir Arthur Gorges (London: Cassell, 1900), 185; via Google Books.

2. From *Sylva Sylvarum*, in *The Works of Francis Bacon, Volume IV*, ed. Basil Montagu (London: William Pickering, 1826), 106; via Google Books. Translation (by W. Rawley) slightly modified.

3. From *Sylva Sylvarum*, in *The Works of Francis Bacon, Volume IX* (London: M. Jones, 1815), 129; via Google Books. Translation slightly modified.

4. Ibid., 145.

5. *Vocalis* means tuneful as well as vocal. *Syrinx*—the name of Pan's other love interest, mentioned earlier in Bacon's text—means a reed, used in the ancient world as a writing implement.

6. Sir Francis Bacon, *De Augmentis Scientiarum* [The Advancement of Learning], in *The Works of Francis Bacon: Philosophical Works, Volume I*, ed.

James Spedding, Robert Leslie Ellis, and Duncan Denon Heath (London: Longmans, 1879), 529–30; via Google Books. My translation.

RIPPLE EFFECTS: DISTANT VOICES

1. *Goethe's Travels in Italy*, trans. George Nisbet (London: George Bell, 1883), 53; via Google Books. Goethe's account exists in several versions; the one discussed here is the fullest.
2. *Travels*, 56, 57; translation slightly modified.
3. Here and below, my translations from *Goethes Sämtliche Werke: Italien* (Stuttgart: J.C. Cotta, 1895), 227–29.
4. The unusual pedaling is clearly marked in the first edition (1802), available online at imslp.org (item 51116). Several nineteenth-century editors subsequently "normalized" the passage by inserting releases.
5. *Italien*, 229. For more on this passage, see my "Primitive Encounters: Beethoven's 'Tempest' Sonata, Musical Meaning, and Enlightenment Anthropology," *Beethoven Forum* 6, ed. Glenn Stanley (Lincoln: University of Nebraska Press, 1998), 31–66, and Janet Schmalfeldt, *In the Process of Becoming: Analytic and Philosophical Perspectives on Form in Early Nineteenth-Century Music* (New York: Oxford University Press, 2017), 41–50.

THE INFINITE BROADCAST

1. Charles Babbage, *The Ninth Bridgewater Treatise: A Fragment* (London: John Murray, 1838), 112; via Google Books.
2. Samuel Taylor Coleridge, "The Aeolian Harp," www.poetryfoundation.org /poems/52301/the-eolian-harp.
3. Henry David Thoreau, *Walden and Other Writings* (New York: Random House, 2004), 206–7.
4. Journal, July 21, 1851; Bradford Torrey and Franklin Benjamin Sanborn, eds., *The Writings of Henry David Thoreau: Journal* (Boston and New York: Houghton Mifflin, 1906), 330; via Google Books.
5. Ibid., 222. On Thoreau's attitude toward sound, with emphasis on bodies and materiality, see Laura Zebuhr, "Sound Enchantment: The Case of Henry David Thoreau," *New Literary History* 48 (2017): 581–603.

IMMANENCE

1. Latour, *We Have Never Been Modern*, 1–12, 51–59.

READING TRANSFIGURED: ST. AUGUSTINE

1. For a review of these debates, see William A. Johnson, "Toward a Sociology of Reading in Classical Antiquity," *American Journal of Philology* 121 (2000): 593–627.
2. VI.iii.3. My translation.
3. VIII.xii.29. My translation.
4. Friedrich Nietzsche, *On the Genealogy of Morals* and *Ecce Homo*, trans. Walter Kaufmann (New York: Random House, 1969), 242.

TO THE LIFE: THE IMAGE

1. Henry James, *The Wings of the Dove* in *Novels 1901–1902* (New York: Library of America, 2006), 359.
2. Ibid.

MOVING PICTURES

1. Ludwig Wittgenstein, *Philosophical Grammar, Part One: The Proposition, and Its Sense*, ed. Rush Rhees, trans. Anthony Kenny (Berkeley and London: University of California Press, 1974), 146.

MODERN TIMES: THE CARTOON

1. Walter Benjamin, *Illuminations*, trans. Harry Zohn (New York: Schocken, 1968), 83–110.
2. Quoted in Leonard Maltin, *Of Mice and Magic: A History of American Animated Cartoons*, rev. ed. (New York: New American Library, 1987), 85.
3. Richmond Lattimore, *The Iliad of Homer* (Chicago: University of Chicago Press, 1951), 386.

THE SOUND OF MEANING

1. N. Katherine Hayles, "Cognition Everywhere: The Rise of the Cognitive Nonconscious and the Costs of Consciousness," *New Literary History* 45 (2014): 199–220.

MUSIC AND THE AUDIABLE: A SUITE IN THREE MOVEMENTS

1. Note to Peters Edition of 4' 33", www.editionpeters.com/product/433 /ep6777.

PLATO'S SINGING SCHOOL

1. Julia Kristeva, *Revolution in Poetic Language*, trans. Margaret Waller (New York: Columbia University Press, 1984); Jacques Derrida, "Khora," in idem, *On the Name*, ed. Thomas Dutoit, trans. David Wood, John P. Leavey, Jr., and Ian McLeod (Stanford: Stanford University Press, 1999), 89–127.
2. William Wordsworth, *The Prelude: 1799, 1805, 1850*, ed. Jonathan Wordsworth (New York: Norton, 1979). Subsequent references given in text.

THE MUSIC OF LANGUAGE

1. Giorgio Agamben, *Potentialities: Collected Essays in Philosophy*, trans. Daniela Heller-Roazen (Stanford: Stanford University Press, 1999), 42; *Language and Death: The Place of Negativity*, trans. Karen E. Pinkus and Michael Hardt (Minneapolis: University of Minnesota Press, 2006), 34–35.

THE SOUNDSCAPE

1. R. Murray Schafer, *The Soundscape: Our Sonic Environment and the Tuning of the World* (Rochester, VT: Destiny Books, 1977).

SONG

1. John Durham Peters, *The Marvelous Clouds: Towards a Theory of Elemental Media* (Chicago: University of Chicago Press, 2015).

NOISE AND SILENCE

1. http://nautil.us/issue/38/noise/noise-is-a-drug-and-new-york-is-full-of-addicts.

FISH, FLESH, OR FOWL

1. The word acquired its reference to language as early as 1652, according to the OED. (The market is much older.) As language, Billingsgate is not only foul but loud, even on the page.

2. E. C. Womack, "Walking as Labor in Henry Mayhew's London," in *Walking Histories, 1800–1914*, ed. Chad Bryant, Arthur Burns, and Paul Readman (London: Palgrave Macmillan, 2016), 131; quotation from Mayhew, 132.

3. From Volume 1, 1861 edition: Billingsgate, http://dl.tufts.edu/catalog/tei /tufts:MS004.002.052.001.00001/chapter/c5s3.

4. From Volume 2, 1861 edition: "Of the Street Sellers of Live Birds," http:// dl.tufts.edu/catalog/tei/tufts:UA069.005.DO.00078/chapter/c2s6.

5. Ibid. Mayhew is quoting the conclusion of Wordsworth's poem "Hart-Leap Well."

6. Ibid.

SENSORY HYBRIDS

1. www.bertoiastudio.com/sound-sculptures/. According to Bertoia's son Val, who has continued his father's practice: "[The] sculptures become abstractions of sound as they sway and knock against one another. The sounds are organic and mysterious, as tones resonate and flow into each other."

2. www.smithsonianmag.com/arts-culture/how-do-you-make-a-painting-out-of-sounds-38014594/. Jones has also sought to restore the role of African Americans like herself in the history of modernism by combining expressionist visual forms with sound collages drawn from bebop and free jazz.

3. George Sand, *Consuelo*, https://ia800209.us.archive.org/7/items /cu31924027303274/cu31924027303274_djvu.txt. Translation modified.

4. Sand, *Consuelo*, https://ia600806.us.archive.org/30/items/afe0976.0004.001 .umich.edu/afe0976.0004.001.umich.edu.pdf. Translation modified.

5. "Italian Music in Dakota," from the 1891 edition of *Leaves of Grass*, http:// etcweb.princeton.edu/batke/logr/log_222.html.

6. All quotations from Richard Powers, *Prisoner's Dilemma* (New York: Harper Perennial, 1988), 147.

7. T. S. Eliot, *Collected Poems, 1909–1962* (New York: Harcourt Brace & World, 1963), 177.

"WAITING TO BE THE MUSIC"

1. Sidney Bechet, *Treat It Gentle: An Autobiography* (New York: Hill and Wang, 1960), 4.

2. Nicolas Abraham, "Notes on the Phantom: A Complement to Freud's Meta-psychology," *Critical Inquiry* 13 (1987): 287–92.

3. James Baldwin, "Sonny's Blues," in *The Jazz Fiction Anthology*, ed. Sasha Feinstein and David Rife (Bloomington: Indiana University Press, 2009), 46.

4. On "speaking melody," see my *Expression and Truth*, 32–56.

CIRCLE SONGS

1. www.youtube.com/watch?v=eitUBS0UxXY.

THE ETHER

1. Quoted in Lydia H. Liu, "iSpace: Printed English after Joyce, Shannon, and Derrida," *Critical Inquiry* 32 (2006): 516–50 at 528n26.

ELEMENTAL MEDIA

1. The concept of the ether has never entirely disappeared, even in physics, though it has mutated to ever-more-rarefied forms. See Robert B. Laughlin, *A Different Universe: Reinventing Physics from the Bottom Down* (New York: Basic Books, 2005), 120–21.

2. *In Vibrant Matter*, Jane Bennett challenges the distinction between "dull matter (it, things) and vibrant life (us, beings)" (vii). She calls for the recognition of "vital materiality" and for "intelligent and sustainable engagement with vibrant matter and lively things" (viii). For Bennett, following Latour, things become vibrant by exercising agency, much as we do. The vibrancy that concerns me in this book is complementary. If Bennett is right, auditory vibrancy is the medium of the inherent liveliness of things. If she is wrong (and for now I am taking no position), auditory vibrancy is the source that endows things with ani-mation. Either way, the matter of life is a matter of sound.

ELEMENTAL FLUIDS

1. Ironically, given the calamity that is Donald Trump's America, the poem anoints the nation as a home for refugees and immigrants. Not that the attitude was widely shared in Lazarus's day, and Lazarus, who was Jewish, was acutely aware that she, like Chopin, was part of a diaspora, even though her family had lived in America for centuries. Lazarus's refuge was imperfect, just as Chopin's was. (Whether she knew of Chopin's anti-Semitism is another question.)

2. Text from Emma Lazarus, *Selected Poems and Other Writings*, ed. Gregory Eiselein (Peterborough, Ontario: Broadview Press, 2002), 81–82.

3. Kate Chopin, *The Awakening*, ed. Margaret Culley (New York: Norton, 1976); quotations from 26, 27, 64.

4. George Sand, *Histoire de mon vie* (Paris, 1902–04), 439–40, trans. Thomas Higgins, in *Chopin: Preludes, Op. 28*, ed. Thomas Higgins (New York: Norton, 1973), 94–95.

5. Quotations from *Selected Poems* (Boston and New York: Houghton Mifflin, 1927), 97–99, via https://archive.org/stream/selectedpoemsofa00lowe/selected-poemsofa00lowe_djvu.txt.

WRITING THE SOUNDSCAPE

1. John Dos Passos, *The 42nd Parallel* (New York: Houghton Mifflin, 2000), xiv.

2. Brom Weber, ed., *The Complete Poems and Selected Letters and Prose of Hart Crane* (Garden City, NY: Anchor Books, 1966), 16.

3. Brian Reed, "Hart Crane's Victrola," *Modernism/Modernity* 7 (2000): 99; quoted by Liu, "iSpace," 531n35.

4. *Complete Poems*, 231 (letter to Waldo Frank, June 20, 1926). In full: "The very idea of a bridge, of course, is a form peculiarly dependent [on] spiritual convictions. It is an act of faith besides being a communication."

HAUNTING MELODIES

1. This paragraph is adapted from my *Expression and Truth: On the Music of Knowledge* (Berkeley and London: University of California Press, 2012), 158.

2. Jacques Lacan, Seminar 23: *The Sinthome*, ed. Jacques-Alain Miller (London: Polity, 2016), 3–7 and throughout.

3. My translations from the text at www.la-belle-epoque.de/mahler/sinf02_d.htm.

4. Phillipe Lacoue-Labarthe takes Mahler's scenario (but not his music) to suggest that rhythm establishes "the break between the visible and the audible." *Typography: Mimesis, Philosophy, Politics*, trans. Christopher Fynsk (Stanford: Stanford University, 1998), 198.

5. www.lucianoberio.org/node/1494?1683069894 = 1.

THE LIFELIKE. THE UNDEAD.

1. Quoted by Caroline von Eck, "Works of Art That Refuse to Behave: Agency, Excess, and Material Presence in Canova and Manet," *New Literary History* 46 (2015): 409–43 at 416.

2. On undeadness see Eric Santner, *On the Psychotheology of Everyday Life* (Chicago: University of Chicago Press, 2007), 18, 22, 36.

3. Von Eck, "Works of Art That Refuse to Behave."

BEYOND WORDS?

1. Ernst Robert Curtius, *European Literature and the Latin Middle Ages*, trans. Willard R. Trask (1953; Princeton and Oxford: Princeton University Press, 2013), 159–62.

2. Wallace Stevens, *Notes towards a Supreme Fiction*, "It Must Give Pleasure," I, in *Collected Poems* (New York: Alfred A. Knopf, 1954), 399.

3. http://nautil.us/issue/47/consciousness/the-kekul-problem.

4. Friedrich Nietzsche, *The Gay Science*, trans. Walter Kaufmann (New York: Random House, 1974), 297 (sec. 354).

5. Sigmund Freud, "The Unconscious," trans. Cecil M. Baines, in Freud, *General Psychological Theory*, ed. Philip Rieff (New York: Collier Books, 1963), 146–48.

6. Cormac McCarthy, *The Crossing* (New York: Vintage, 1995), 407.

7. Thomas De Quincey, *Confessions of an English Opium-Eater: And Suspiria de Profundis* (Boston: Ticknor, Read, and Fields, 1876), 175–75; via Google Books.

THE AUDIABLE AND THE AUDIBLE

1. "The Figure of the Youth as Virile Poet," in Wallace Stevens, *The Necessary Angel: Essays on Reality and the Imagination* (New York: Vintage, 1951), 61.

INTO SILENCE

1. Fifth Walk, from *Selections from the Works of Jean-Jacques Rousseau*, ed. Christian Gauss (Princeton: Princeton University Press, 1920), 218; via Google Books. My translation.

2. Fifth Walk, 219.

3. Quoted in Tom Griffiths, *Slicing the Silence: Voyaging to Antarctica* (Cambridge, MA: Harvard University Press, 2007), 171.

4. www.boosey.com/cr/music/Peter-Maxwell-Davies-Antarctic-Symphony-Symphony-No-8/15134.

ENCHANTMENTS OF THE NAME

1. Crane, *Complete Poems*, 164.

2. *Hart Crane's* The Bridge: *An Annotated Edition,* ed. Lawrence Kramer (New York: Fordham University Press, 2011), 127, 130. On *poiesis* see Susan Stewart, *Poetry and the Fate of the Senses* (Chicago: University of Chicago Press, 2002), 1–3.

3. Stewart, *Poetry and the Fate,* 82–83.

4. John Ashbery, *Rivers and Mountains* (New York: Holt Rinehart and Winston, 1967), 18.

THE INAUDIBLE

1. Salome Vogelin, *Sonic Possible Worlds: Hearing the Continuum of Sound* (New York and London: Bloomsbury, 2014), 157–75.

2. *Sonic Possible Worlds,* 164.

3. The speaker is not Adam himself but a modern person who speaks as if possessed by Adam's utterance. This state of affairs derives from Plato's *Ion* and recurs throughout the history of Western poetry; see Susan Stewart, "Lyric Possession," *Critical Inquiry* 22 (1995): 34–63. Elsewhere in "Adam's Task" the speaker uses his own, more conventionally intelligible language to reflect on the power he exercises vicariously in Adam's voice.

4. *Sonic Possible Worlds,* 165.

ON SAYING "I AM"

1. Paul Valéry, *Collected Works,* vol. 9 (New York: Bollingen Press, 1973), 54.

2. See my "Saving the Ordinary: Beethoven's 'Ghost' Trio and the Wheel of History," *Beethoven Forum* 12 (2005): 50–81.

THE SHRIEK

1. Stevens, *Collected Poems,* 129.

2. My translation from Baudelaire, *Le Spleen de Paris,* www.poetes.com /textes/baud_spl.pdf.

METAL

1. Stevens, *Collected Poems,* 203.

HERE COMES THAT SONG AGAIN

1. Theodor Reik, *The Haunting Melody: Psychoanalytic Experiences in Life and Music* (New York: Grove Press, 1953), 222. All subsequent references given in text.

236 NOTES TO PAGES 167-179

2. Sigmund Freud, *Introductory Lectures on Psychoanalysis*, ed. and trans. James Strachey (New York: Norton, 1966), 108.

3. Ibid. Freud actually uses this example to exclude a musical explanation but his parenthetical remark betrays him. His claim to be "unmusical" is famous but a little disingenuous. Freud knew more about music, and liked it more, than he chose to let on.

4. See Francesca Brittan, "Berlioz and the Pathological Fantastic: Melancholy, Monomania, and Romantic Autobiography," *19th-Century Music* 29 (2006): 211–39.

5. Edgar Allan Poe, "The Imp of the Perverse," *The Works of Edgar Allan Poe*, www.eapoe.org/works/mabbott/tom3t026.htm.

6. J. Mark Baldwin, "Internal Speech and Song," *Philosophical Review* 2 (1893): 385–406 at 397.

7. French text at *Les grands classiques*, www.poesie.webnet.fr/lesgrands classiques/poemes/gerard_de_nerval/fantaisie.html.

THE MIRROR OF SILENCE

1. Many modern stagings of the opera update the telephonic apparatus to avoid anachronisms such as operator assistance and party lines. The impulse is understandable but it erases the emphasis of both the opera and the play on the uneasy fusion of technology and human agency.

RHYTHMIC HEARING

1. Alan Burdick, "Present Tense," *New Yorker*, December 19, 2016, 71–72.

2. William James, *The Principles of Psychology*, vol. 1 (New York: Henry Holt, 1890), 620.

MEDIA ALL THE WAY DOWN

1. From "Automata," in *The Best Tales of Hoffmann*, ed. E. F. Bleiler (New York: Dover, 1967), 97–98.

THE AUDITORY WINDOW

1. Virginia Woolf, *Mrs. Dalloway* (New York: Harcourt, 1981), 138.

2. W. G. Sebald, *The Rings of Saturn*, trans. Michael Hulse (New York: New Directions, 1999), 5. Subsequent references are given in text.

CACOPHONY: DISPOSSESSION (BECKETT)

1. Samuel Beckett, *The Collected Shorter Plays* (New York: Grove Press, 1984), 217.
2. Trans. Geoffrey Wagner, http://fleursdumal.org/poem/126.
3. www.youtube.com/watch?v=M4LDwfKxr-M. In her commentary on the YouTube clip of "Not I," Whitelaw adds apropos the lighting that at the premiere the lightbulbs were stripped from the theater's Exit signs and from the "ladies' loo," so that basically there was "no escape." Sight was reduced to the disembodied appearance of the organ of sound.

WORLDLY DISSONANCE

1. Kaja Silverman, *World Spectators* (Stanford: Stanford University Press, 2000), 145–46.

SOUNDS OF BATTLE: THE CIVIL WAR

1. Mark Nesbitt, ed., *Through Blood and Fire: Selected Civil War Papers of Major General Joshua Lawrence Chamberlain* (Mechanicsburg, PA: Stackpole Books, 1996), 42. Subsequent references are given in text.

SOUNDS OF BATTLE: WORLD WAR I

1. Virginia Woolf, *Jacob's Room* (1992; Oxford: Oxford World Classics, 1992), 5.
2. Erich Maria Remarque, *All Quiet on the Western Front*, trans. A. W. Wheen (1928; New York: Ballantine Books, 1982), 124–25.
3. *All Quiet*, 121, translation slightly modified.
4. Ibid.
5. Ibid., 195.
6. Ibid., 121.
7. C. Day Lewis, ed., *The Collected Poems of Wilfred Owen*, with a memoir by Edmund Blunden (New York: New Directions, 1964), 168.
8. *Collected Poems*, 172.

ULYSSES IN AUSCHWITZ

1. *Inferno* XXVI, l.01–102; Dante, *The Divine Comedy*, trans. Clive James (New York: Norton, 2013), 117.

2. Primo Levi, *Survival in Auschwitz*, trans. Stuart Wolf (New York: Simon and Shuster, 1996). The Italian title is *Se questo è un uomo* [If this is a man]. Subsequent page references given in text.

3. Quoted by John Felstiner, "Translating the Untranslatable: The Wounded Readings of Paul Celan," http://articles.latimes.com/2000/oct/15/books/bk-36804/2.

4. Trans. Christopher Middleton, www.poets.org/poetsorg/poem/fuguedeath.

5. "Death Fugue" has sometimes been criticized for participating in the aesthetic it condemns. For discussion of the issue, and of the poem's relationship to music, see Axel Englund, *Still Songs: Music in and around the Poetry of Paul Celan* (Farnham, Surrey, and Burlington, VT: Ashgate, 2012), 21–54.

SOUNDING BODIES

1. René Laennec, *Traité de l'auscultation médiate et des maladies des poumons* (Brussels: Librairie médicale et scientifique, 1828), 4, my translation; text accessed at http://gallica.bnf.fr/ark:/12148/bpt6k829237/f77.item.r = rate.zoom.

2. Michel Foucault, *The Birth of the Clinic*, trans. Alan Sheridan (New York: Routledge 2012), 203.

3. Lauri Siisiäinen, *Foucault and the Politics of Hearing* (New York: Routledge, 2013), 28–29.

4. *Foucault / Hearing*, 32.

5. Sterne, *Audible Past*, esp. 110, 154.

6. Alexandra Hui, *The Psychophysical Ear: Musical Experiments, Experimental Sounds, 1840–1910* (Cambridge, MA: MIT Press, 2013), 90–91.

PANDEMONIUM?

1. Pascal Quignard, *The Hatred of Music*, trans. Matthew Amos and Fredrik Rönnbäck (New Haven, CT: Yale University Press, 2016), 71.

2. Text from the Whitman Archive, https://whitmanarchive.org/published /LG/1855/whole.html.

SONGS OF ENTROPY

1. Alec Wilkinson, "A Voice from the Past," *New Yorker*, May 19, 2014, www .newyorker.com/magazine/2014/05/19/a-voice-from-the-past.

2. See "The Phonautograms of Édouard-Léon Scott de Martinville," *First Sounds*, www.firstsounds.org/sounds/scott.php.

3. Howard E. Smither, *A History of the Oratorio*, vol. 4, *The Oratorio in the Nineteenth and Twentieth Centuries* (Chapel Hill and London: UNC Press Books, 2000), 265.

4. "Portrait of Decay: Bill Morrison on *Decasia*," *Erasing Clouds*, www .erasingclouds.com/02april.html.

5. Ibid.

BY HAND

1. Henry James, *Selected Letters*, ed. Leon Edel (Cambridge, MA: Harvard University Press, 1987), 302.

PAST AND PRESENT

1. Friedrich Kittler, *Gramophone Film Typewriter*, trans. Geoffrey Winthrop-Young and Michael Wutz (Stanford: Stanford University Press, 1999), 3, 118.

2. My translation from "Le Cygne," http://fleursdumal.org/poem/220.

CONSCIOUSNESS

1. Gilles Deleuze and Felix Guattari, *Q'est ce que la Philosphie?* (Paris: Minuit, 1991), 59.

2. Giorgio Agamben, *The Use of Bodies*, trans. Adam Kotsco (Stanford: Stanford University Press, 2016), 63–64.

3. N. Katherine Hayles, "Deep and Hyper Attention: The Generational Divide in Cognitive Modes," *Profession 2007* (New York: Modern Language Association), 187–99.

4. Ruth Leys, "The Turn to Affect: A Critique," *Critical Inquiry* 37 (2011): 434–72.

5. Ernst Mach, *Die Analyse der Empfindungen*, 9th ed. (Jena: Fischer Verlag, 1922; rpt. Darmstadt: Wissenschaftliche Buchgesellschaft, 1987), 8–9.

6. David Hume, *A Treatise of Human Nature* (Oxford: Clarendon Press, 1888), 252; via Google Books.

7. Immanuel Kant, *Grounding for the Metaphysics of Morals*, trans. James E. Ellington (Indianapolis: Hackett, 1993), 30.

Index

Abraham, Karl, 165–66
Abraham, Nicolas, 106
Adés, Thomas, *The Tempest*, 154
Adorno, Theodor W., 2
Aeolian harp, 60, 61, 92, 96, 176
Agamben, Giorgio, 85–86, 211–212
Agee, James, *Let Us Now Praise Famous Men*, 46–48
Aristotle, 10, 18, 88
Ashbery, John, "Into the Dusk-Charged Air," 151–52, 153
Audiable, the, 4–7, 29–40, 78–81, 143–44
Auscultation, 32, 62, 91, 198–202
Automata, speaking, 21, 72, 75

Babbage, Charles, 60–61, 64
Bach, Johann Sebastian, 46, 196
Bacon, Francis, 20, 53–56
Baldwin, J. Mark, 170
Baldwin, James, "Sonny's Blues," 106–109
Balzac, Honoré de, on music, 175–77
Barnum, P. T., 21
Barthes, Roland, 2, 70
Bartok, Bela, String Quartet no. 6, 104
Baudelaire, Charles, "The Artist's Confession," 163; "The Carrion," 181; "The Swan," 210; "Voyage to Cythera," 130
Bechet, Sidney, 106–107

Beckett, Samuel, "Not I," 181–83, 237n.; "Nacht und Träume," 183–85
Beethoven, Ludwig van, 63, 100, 183; Overture to *Coriolan*, 145; Piano Sonata no. 14, "Moonlight," 102; Piano Sonata no. 17, "Tempest," 59–60; Piano Sonata no. 29, *Hammerklavier*, 156–59; Piano Sonata no. 31, 159–62; Piano Sonata no. 32, 158; String Quartet no. 13, 80–81; Symphony no. 3, *Eroica*, 78
Benjamin, Walter, 2, 36, 73, 104
Bennett, Jane, 39, 232n
Bentham, Jeremy, 93
Berio, Luciano, *Sinfonia*, 130
Berlioz, Hector, *Symphonie fantastique*, 45, 168–69
Bertoia, Harry, 96
Billingsgate market, 93–95
Brainworm, 124–25, 171
Britten, Benjamin, *War Requiem*, 189–90, 193, 202
Browning, Robert, 41; "My Last Duchess," 69; "Caliban upon Setebos," 43–44, 45
Burdick, Allen, 174

Cage, John, *4'33'*, 79–80
Caliban, 41–43, 44, 45, 46, 47, 50
Cardiff, Janet, "Forty-Part Motet," 110–111

241

Caruso, Enrico, 22
Celan, Paul, "Death Fugue," 196–97, 238n
Chamberlain, Joshua Lawrence, 187–88
Chion, Michel, 24
Chladny effect, 176
Chopin, Frédéric, 116–120; Prelude in D-flat
(Raindrop"), 104–105; Prelude in F
Minor, 79–80
Chopin, Kate, *The Awakening*, 116, 117–118
Chora, Plato, 82
Cocteau, Jean, *La voix humaine*,172–74
Coleridge, Samuel Taylor, 63, 64, 176, 177;
"The Aeolian Harp," 61–62
Conrad, Joseph, on making one see, 9, 11, 17,
130–31
Continuous Media, 208–210
Constructive description, 14–16, 30, 31
Crane, Hart, 120–21, 154; *The Bridge*, 122,
147–51
Cross-sensory perception, 96–99

Dante, Ulysses episode from *Inferno*, 194–95
Deafness, 31, 38, 52, 59, 156, 161
De Quincey, Thomas, 141–42
Deleuze, Gilles, 27, 65, 186, 211
Derrida, Jacques, 2, 23, 28, 65; and
khora, 82
Descartes, René, 155
Dickinson, Emily, "Because I Could Not Stop
for Death," 15–16
Dillard, Annie, 4–5
Divination, 37
Dos Passos, John, *The Forty-Second Parallel*,
120–121
Dubois, W.E.B., 48
Dukas, Paul, 76

Echo, and Pan, 55–56
Eidsheim, Nina Sun, 24
Elemental media, 90, 115
Eliot, T.S., 37, 120; "Burnt Norton," 103
Enargeia, 131–32
Esquirol, Etienne, 168
Ether, the, 113–15, 177

Faber Joseph, Euphonia, 21
Fantasia, 76
Five senses, 34, 84
Fleischer, Max, "Bedtime," 74–75; "In the
Good Old Summer Time," 75
Fludd, Robert, 60, 64
Foucault, Michel, 41, 67, 199–200
Fouillée, Alfred, 214

Freud, Sigmund, 19, 33, 65, 136–37, 165–68,
170, 172, 213, 236n
Fullerman, Morton, 207

Gaze, auditory, 10, 32, 102
Georget, Jean-Etienne, 168
Goethe, Johann Wolfgang, 60, 63, 69, 76,
100, 139; singing in Venice (gondoliers
and fishwives), 56–59, 101, 144
Gordon, Michael, 206

Half-heard, the, 58, 63, 68–69, 101, 102, 122,
132, 152, 156, 184, 197–98
Handel, George Frideric, *Israel in Egypt*, 205,
206–207
Hardy, Thomas, *Far from the Madding
Crowd*, 40–41
Hayles, N. Katherine, deep and hyper-atten-
tion, 213; non-conscious cognition, 77, 211
Heard world, 6, 24, 51–52, 86, 152, 198
Hearkening, 6 19, 22–23, 29, 31–34, 65, 81, 220
Hegel, G.W.F., 20, 22, 30, 33, 86, 133
Heidegger, Martin, 35, 65
Hermeneutics, 37
Hinton, Charles H., 113–15
Hoffmann, E.T.A., 75; "Automata," 177
Hölderlin, Friedrich, 35
Holiday, Billie, 108
Hollander, John, "Adam's Task," 153–54, 235n
Homer, automata in *Iliad*, 75
Hume, David, 214

idée fixe, 168
imagetext, 27, 39

James, Henry, 210; on handwriting and typewriting, 207–208; *The Wings of the Dove*,
69–70, 132, 212
James, William, 174–75
Jones, Jennie C., 96–97, 231n

Kant, Immanuel, 18, 23, 133, 135, 157, 220
Keats, John, 180
Kempelen, Wolfgang von, 21
Khora, Derrida, 82
Kiss Me Deadly (film), 22
Kittler, Friedrich, continuous media,
208–209
Koko the Clown, 74–76
Kristeva, Julia, *chora*, 82

Lacan, Jaques, *sinthome*, 125
Laennec, René, 198–202

Latour, Bruno, 12, 39, 64
Lazarus, Emma, "Chopin," 116–17, 232n
Levi, Primo, *Survival in Auschwitz*, 194–97
Leys, Ruth, 213
Levinas, Emanuel, 35–36, 65, 155
Life, auditory perception of, 1, 5, 7, 20, 21–22, 39, 51, 53, 65, 70, 73–75, 85, 88, 103, 116, 127, 129–130, 155, 176–77, 179, 181, 199
Lovelace, Ada, 60
Lowell, Amy, "Chopin," 116, 118–20

Mach, Ernst, 202
Mahler, Gustav, 166; Symphony no. 2, "Resurrection," 126–130, 165, 168, 169, 170–71, 206; Symphony no. 8, 139–141
Manet, Eduard, 133
Martinville, Edouard-Leon Scott de, 204–05
Matisse, Henri, 65
Maxwell-Davies, Peter, 146
Mayhew, Henry, *London Labour and the London Poor*, 92–96; description of Billingsgate, 93–95; trade in songbirds, 95–96
McCarthy, Cormac, on language, 136–38
McFerrin, Bobby, 109–110
Media, 2, 3, 5, 11–12, 21, 28, 32, 34, 60, 73, 76, 81, 84, 99, 115, 123, 125, 175, 197, 208–210, 217, 219
Memnon, 141–42
Meyerbeer, Giacomo, *Les Huguenots*, 175–75
Middleton, Richard, 50
Mill, John Stuart, 93
Milton, John, 180, 181
Mitchell, J. W. T., 27, 70, 186
Montaigne, Michel de, 2
Morrison, Bill, *Decasia*, 206
Morrison, Toni, *Song of Solomon*, 41, 48–50
Morton, Timothy, 36
Mozart, Wolfgang Amadeus, 47, 48, 171
Müller, Wilhelm, 16

Nancy, Jean-Luc, 90
Nerval, Gerard de, "Fantaisie," 169, 170–72
Nietzsche, Friedrich, 2, 65, 69, 137, 213
The Night Of (television series), 163–65

Offenbach, Jacques, 76 170; *La Belle Helene*, 167–68,
Owen, Wilfred, 188, 189–90, 192–93, 202

Peters, John Durham, 90, 115
Phonautograph, 205
Phonograph, 21–22, 113–14, 121–22, 123, 198, 205, 209, 210, 217

Plato, 149; *Timaeus* (chora), 81–83
Poe, Edgar Allan, "The Imp of the Perverse,"169' "The Oval Portrait," 70
Porgy and Bess, 12
Poulenc, Francis, *La voix humaine*, 173–74, 236n.
Powers, Richard, *Prisoner's Dilemma*, 101–103
Psychoanalysis, 33
Proust, Marcel, 13

Quignard, Pascal, 201
Quintilian, 131

Ravel, "Le Gibet," 169
Reciprocal listening, 108, 110
Reik, Theodore, and haunting melody,
Remarque, Erich Maria, *All Quiet on the Western Front*, 188, 191–92, 202
Rembrandt, "The Philosopher in Meditation," 97–99
Ricoeur, Paul, 37
Rilke, Rainer Maria, on Beethoven, 155–56, 161; *Sonnets to Orpheus*, 155–57, 158
Rossetti, Christina, "Up-Hill," 15
Rossini, Giacomo, 171
Rousseau, Jean-Jacques, *Reveries of a Solitary Walker*, 144–45

Sacks, Oliver, 124
St. Ambrose, and silent reading, 66–67, 68–69
St. Augustine, 17, 51; and language learning, 52–53; silent reading, 66–69; *tolle lege*, 67–68
Sand, George, 96–97, 99, 118–19
Schafer, R. Murray, 186
Schleiermacher, Friedrich, 37
Schubert, Franz, 16; "Nacht und Träume," 183–84
Schumann, Robert, "Night Pieces," 169
Scott, Robert Falcon, 145–46
Sebald, W. G., *The Rings of Saturn*, 178, 179–81, 183
Sensory crossing, 96–99
Shakespeare, William, *Pericles*, 112–13; *Romeo and Juliet*, 180; *The Tempest*, 41–43, 45, 46, 129
Shelley, Percy Bysshe, 43, 180
Silent reading, 26, 66–69, 156
Silverman, Kaja, 185–86
Sing-along cartoons, 73–74
Sinthome (Lacan), 125

Siisiäinen, Lauri, 199, 200
Snow, C. P., 11
Sophocles, 154
Sound recording, 7, 21–22, 60, 69, 89–90,
    114, 123, 164, 204–207, 208–210, 212, 217
Sound studies, 1, 3, 9, 24, 129
Soundscape, 2, 3, 21, 22, 30, 36, 76, 86–88,
    92, 95, 100, 120, 129, 153, 164, 210, 219
Speaking melody, 78–79, 108
Speech, inner, 26, 34, 69, 138
Speech synthesis, 21–22
Sterne, Jonathan, 19, 200, 202
Stethoscope, 198–202
Stevens, Wallace, 30, 65, 134, 143, 162, 164
Stokowski, Leopold, 75
Stravinsky, Igor, 76
Strindberg, August, *A Dream Play*, 142–43;
    "The Stronger," 172–74
Synesthesia, 83–85, 96, 128

Talking machines, 21, 72, 75
Tallis, Thomas, "Forty-Part Motet," 110–113
Tennyson, Alfred, 192
Thoreau, Henry David, 63–64
Tolstoy, Leo, "Family Happiness," 102
Tone tests, 21, 22

Valéry, Paul, 155
Vaughan Williams, Ralph, *Sinfonia
    Antartica*, 145–46

Velazquez, Diego, *Rokeby Venus*, 132–33
Vibration, 20, 35–36, 38, 63, 64, 66, 84, 117,
    163, 176–77, 193, 202
Victor dog (Nipper), 123
Virgil, 41, 96
Vogelin, Salome, 152–53
Von Eck, Caroline, 132–33

Wagner, Richard, *Siegfried* 41, 44–46;
    Tristan und Isolde, 46, 118, 162
Waters, Ethel, 108
Weber, Carl Maria von, 171
Whitelaw, Billie, 182, 183, 237n.
Whitman, Walt, 65; *Drum-Taps*,
    148–49; "Italian Music in Dakota,"
    99–101, 103; *Song of Myself*, 147,
    203–204
Wilde, Oscar, 70
Williams, Raymond, 36
Wittgenstein, Ludwig, 2, 13, 19, 37, 71–72, 73;
    and St. Augustine, 52–53
Woolf, Virginia, *Jacob's Room*, 190–92;
    Mrs. Dalloway, 178–80
Wordsworth, William, 95–96; *The Prelude*
    (1805), Book V, 82–83; Book VII, 17, 87;
    Book VII, 87–88

Yeats, W. B., 92

Žižek, Slavoj, 65